PATRIOTISM: RED, WHITE, BLUE & SOMETIMES BLACK

BY
ROBERT M. WADE

Harrison House Publishing

San Antonio, Texas

This is a work of fiction. The events and characters described herein are imaginary and are not intended to refer to specific places or living persons. The opinions expressed in this manuscript are solely the opinions of the author and do not represent the opinions or thoughts of the publisher. The author has represented and warranted full ownership and/or legal right to publish all the materials in this book.

Patriotism: Red, White, Blue & Sometime Black
All Rights Reserved. Copyright © 2011 Robert M. Wade

Editing by Ronda Anderson

Cover art design & layout by J. Alexander, Genesis Productions©

This book may not be reproduced, transmitted, or stored in whole or in part by any means, including graphic, electronic or mechanical without the expressed written consent of the publisher except in the case of brief quotations embodied in critical articles and reviews.

Published by Harrison House Publishing, San Antonio, Texas
HarrisonHousepublishing@hotmail.com
Harrison House Publishing and the "HH" logo are trademarks belonging to Harrison House Publishing.

Paperback ISBN: 978-1-4507-5154-4

Library of Congress Control Number: 2011939033

PRINTED IN THE UNITED STATES OF AMERICA

ACKNOWLEDGEMENTS

My Father in heaven, without Your love and guidance I would not have been able to reach this dream, for I am nothing without You.

My wife, Sun, of thirty plus years, without your love, support and caring heart this book could not have been possible. You are the wind beneath my wings that keeps me aloft, and looking forward to the future.

My daughter/editor, Ronda Anderson, who worked tirelessly editing the manuscript on several different occasions to ensure it is a quality piece of literature.

PREFACE

Sergeant Bobby L. Wood, a Military Policeman in the United States Army, bolted upright in his seat as the plane he was on hit several air pockets making it do a crazy jig. As Sergeant Wood looked around the dancing plane it took him several moments to gather his thoughts and remember where he was. He had been in a deep, dreamless sleep. Now that he was fully awake, and had gotten his bearings, a smile crossed his face. He was on his way back to Korea to marry the woman he loved, Miss Kwak Sun Hui. To him, she was the most beautiful of all women God had ever put on the earth. He pictured her slender 5" 6" frame, dressed in her traditional Korean clothing looking like a fragile china doll labeled "handle with care." He hadn't fully realized how much he missed her until his Military Airlift Command flight took off from Fort Lewis, Washington. He was thinking what a thrill it was going to be for him as he took her into his arms and kissed her. He smiled to himself as the image of her beauty floated around in his head. Sergeant Wood could hardly wait to be with the woman of his dream again, but wait he must. They still had several hours of flying time left before he touched down in Korea, "The Land of The Morning Calm."

Sergeant Wood's happy thoughts faded and were replaced with skepticism as his mind reflected over everything which had occurred since he had gotten his draft notice from good old Uncle Sam, and the two years he had already served prior to his re-enlistment. The smile was replaced with a look of determination as frame after frame of his recent past reeled through his mind. He felt as if he was watching a movie titled, "This is Your Life, Sergeant Bob Wood."

Chapter 1
DRAFTED

It all began on a Wednesday, May 13, 1970, in Helena, Arkansas; a peaceful little country community with a scattered population of 16,000. On that fateful day, Bob stepped off the school bus not knowing that his momma had been to the mailbox and picked up the daily mail. The only piece of mail this day was his draft notice, informing him that the next two years of his life belonged to Uncle Sam. He was in a really good mood that day as he and his good friend, Johnny Tongas, walked the quarter mile from the bus stop to his home. It was a beautiful spring afternoon. The sun was shining brightly, warming everything its rays touched. The grass along the road was now awake after its long winter nap. Everything was green and getting greener with each passing day. The air was filled with the scents of budding apple blossoms and honeysuckle vines. Being surrounded by the beauty of nature made Bob thankful to be young and full of life. He could feel Aphrodite, the goddess of love, touching his yearning, young heart as he sought that special young lady to share his dreams and desires. It seemed spring had that effect on everyone, the young and old alike. To top off this loving and carefree mood, Bob had a date lined up with the most sought-after girl in Lakeview High School, possibly the whole state of Arkansas. He had known her most of his life and they played around at school but, he had been afraid to ask her out because she always said she wouldn't go out with him even if he asked her. What Bob didn't know was she was just playing with his mind. She liked him but wanted to make sure he liked her for who she was, not because of her well proportioned body as his basketball teammates were quick to point out to her. He didn't find this out until he built up enough nerve to ask her for a date.

"Hey, Bob, where are you taking Gina Samson tonight? Up on Lover's Levee?" Johnny asked.

Lover's Levee was a long dike built to keep the Mississippi River from flooding a long string of communities along its bank. The portion of the levee, Johnny mentioned was where most of the high school kids on dates could be found petting, making out, or just admiring the view. On clear nights when the moon was shining brightly, its light would shimmer and sparkle on the water, creating an illusion that the muddy Mississippi was as clear as the community swimming pool. On other occasions, the lovers would call a time out from their heavy petting to watch a riverboat pass by all lit up like a small floating city.

"I don't know. I have a couple of dollars, so I thought I would take her to a movie or something. I think I'll play Mr. Good Guy tonight," Bob answered.

"I get your drift. You can't keep her out too late tonight because you both have school tomorrow and have to get up early."

"Besides, she probably won't put out on the first date anyway," Bob, added.

"Well, whether she puts out on the first date or not is unknown because the guys who have dated her, which is only two, say the bitch wears steel underpants reinforced with a lock and chain. So far as I know, no one has even come close to getting the key from her old lady," Johnny said, showing his investigative skills.

"I get your drift, but you have to play your cards right. Why do you think I've been playing up to Mrs. Samson and Gina's old man? I'm setting the little girl up and once I get her where I want her, it's fun time," Bob beamed, feeling confident his plans would work.

As they walked on, their conversation turned to Vietnam. Several months earlier, Larry James, Bob's former high school basketball teammate and a friend of the Wood family who graduated the previous year, had stepped on a land mine in the jungle of Vietnam. His body had been so torn up that his family had to give him a closed casket funeral. Bob had sworn on that heart wrenching day with tears running down his face, when he was drafted, he would volunteer for duty in Vietnam. He'd help his fellow soldiers show all those little yellow sons-of-bitches they couldn't kill American soldiers and get away with it. He'd help show them that America is the most powerful nation in the world, and if they knew what was good for them, they would give up the fight before they got all their people killed. This he had sworn as Larry's remains were being lowered into the ground. It was the only time the people in his community ever saw him so emotionally upset.

What they didn't know was Bob was supposed to have dropped out of school and enlist at the time Larry had been drafted, so they could serve their time together as brothers in arms. However, when he started dropping hints that he and Larry would make good soldiers, his momma had begged him to wait until he had finished high school before going into the military, to which he had agreed to satisfy her request. Bob felt that if he had gone ahead and enlisted with Larry, he could have somehow prevented him from stepping on that mine. Bob knew it was just foolish thinking, but he couldn't control how he felt.

Bob's Momma's reason for getting him to make the promise to wait until he graduated high school before going into the military was in hope that college basketball scouts would come to watch him play basketball and offer him a scholarship. This way his draft would be pushed back four years, and hopefully the war would be over by the time he graduated. Bob was considered by most coaches in the state to be the best basketball player in the whole state of Arkansas. As Bob was still reflecting over that sad day Larry was buried, Johnny broke into his thoughts, rescuing him from any more mental anguish.

"You know something, Bob," he was saying, "if I get drafted and they send me to Vietnam, I'm going to kill so many of those black pajama wearing bastards, I'll be more decorated than Audie Murphy was during World War II."

"Don't forget, John, we have to get killed and shit before they give us medals. And medals to a dead man ain't shit," Bob responded, remembering the purple heart they had given Mrs. James on Larry's behalf.

"Hey, Bob, I know it was a bad scene for you with Larry and all, but you have to realize he was only over there for two months. He never got a chance to show them what he could do. At least we know Sir Charles couldn't take him out in a gun fight," Johnny assured him.

"You're right. If they sent you and me over there at the same time, they would call us the Two Black Death Machines. The Viet Cong would be so scared of us, they would shit their pants every time they heard our names," Bob declared, showing his

PATRIOTISM

friend that they were on the same wave length.

"Right on, brother," Johnny agreed. "In a year's time they would have to stop the war because there wouldn't be enough of them left to continue the fight." Johnny was beside himself.

"Yeah," Bob agreed half-heartedly. "Well, this is where I get off, good buddy. See you in the morning, or up on Lover's Levee, if I happen to be up that way with old iron pants," Bob laughed. As he walked down the path to his house, he sensed a note of dread in the air. But he couldn't figure out why he felt that way until he saw his momma's face. He knew whatever news she had received it had to do with him. "Hi, Momma. What's wrong with you? Did something happen to Harvey or Ronda?" The look on his momma's face caused him concern.

"You got a letter from Uncle Sam today. You've been drafted." The tone of his momma's voice sounded as if he had been sentenced to the gallows to die instead of being drafted by the U.S. Government.

"You're kidding! Where's the letter? When do I have to report to basic training?" Bob asked, not giving his mother a chance to answer his questions separately, also forgetting he hadn't finished high school.

"Hold it, young man. Calm down. I'll get the letter for you. You know there's a good chance they're going to send you to Vietnam. I'd hate to lose you the way Mrs. James lost Larry. At least they could have waited until after you graduated before sending the letter," she complained.

"Aw, don't talk like that, Momma. I'm not going to leave this old world until my number is called, which I would say is about two, maybe three hundred years from now," he joked.

His mother didn't share his sense of humor. After seeing she wasn't going to laugh at his joke, he asked, "So where's the letter?"

"Don't be so impatient," she scolded. "And I don't see anything to joke about. You know they send all the colored boys to Vietnam to fight the war and the white boys to office jobs, counting how many of you are getting killed," she further complained.

It always amazed Bob to hear his mother and father refer to him as a colored boy, especially with that title being debunked during all the riots of the fifties and sixties. Even with the emergence of Dr. King, Malcolm X, and the Black Panthers on television almost every day telling black people to be black and proud had no affect on their belief system. It didn't mean they were not aware of the times and what changes could occur once the dust settled. They just weren't sure if they were being led down the right road to achieve the equality they were demanding. They actually believed integration was a bad thing.

Bob's momma and daddy believed if the black leaders of the Civil Rights Movement accomplished their goals in getting Negroes to integrate with white people, they were only setting black people up to eventually lose their identity as a people, along with their businesses. His Daddy said White folk weren't going to allow black folks to be economically equal with them because black business owners would eventually want to move their businesses into white neighborhoods, and white folks would not allow that to happen. So there would be a big push to buy, destroy, or force closure of black owned businesses throughout America. And knowing how black people believed in quick money, get what you can today and worry about the

PATRIOTISM

future later, they would sell if the money were right. Of course no one believed what his parents were saying at the time. After all, what did a couple of dirt farmers know about business, or what true freedom for black people in America would bring? They were advised to leave the prophesying to the black leaders leading the charge to a new and brighter day.

"Does Daddy know I've been drafted?" Bob asked, forgetting in his excitement that his daddy didn't get off work for another few hours.

"No, not yet. He's still at work. I'll tell him tonight after supper," his momma said apprehensively.

Bob's momma was a very religious and warm-hearted woman, and very protective of her three children. He was the oldest. She would not hesitate to voice her opinion to the neighbors, or anyone else for that matter, if they happened to mistreat one of her *"babies."* She was also one of the most loved women of the community. Mrs. Wood thought nothing of giving her last dime to anyone who needed it more than she did. On one occasion, Bob saw his Momma loan the blouse off her back to one of his classmates who said she had nothing to wear to school that day.

As Bob read the draft notice, he couldn't help but think of Larry. But he felt no fear. His reporting date was one month from the date of the notice. The only thing he felt was the urge to run to the recruiting office in town and enlist right away. He wasn't looking forward to the month of waiting, or so he thought. He also knew if he went ahead and enlisted, it would break his momma's heart. After all, he had promised to wait until he graduated high school. Bob didn't know it at the time, but his momma had already made out a thirty-day calendar of events on his behalf. He wished she would not worry about him so much, because she was worrying for nothing. He was positive of that. There was no doubt in his mind that he had a long life ahead of him.

Bob's daddy was a man of the earth, straightforward and tough as nails. He took all news, good and bad, with a grain of salt; so it was rare to see him emotional about anything. Bob could already hear what his daddy was going to say when he found out that Bob had been drafted.

"Well, son, I knew it'd only be a matter of time before they called on you to serve your country. I tried to enlist myself in World War II, but they said my feet were flatter than the earth itself, which would cause me serious problems in training and combat situations. I know I don't have to worry about no Viet Cong killing you. No siree. If all these girls you've been messing around with haven't gotten you, no one will."

It was always a big lift for Bob, knowing he had an old man he could talk to and depend on, regardless of what the situation or problem was. Not that they always agreed. It was just great being able to talk to each other. Their biggest disagreement was the role of women in America's society. Bob felt that women were treated as second-class citizens in America and that was wrong. He felt no man should be able to treat his wife or daughter anyway they chose to, because when all was said and done, it was the woman who kept the family intact and the home running smoothly. Therefore, he felt women should be treated equally to men. On the other hand, Joe Wood was a true believer that a woman's place was in the kitchen; barefoot, pregnant, and ready to serve her man whenever he called. But even with that caveman mentality, no one loved women more than his daddy did.

That evening at supper, Bob fidgeted in his seat at the table waiting for his momma to tell his daddy he had been drafted. As the meal progressed and no one said anything about it, little Harvey could stand the suspense no longer. He blurted it out as if it was something he had to get off his chest or he would die. Everyone remained silent, waiting for his daddy's reaction.

Joe Wood turned to his wife and asked, "What the hell's that kid talking about?"

"I was going to wait until we finished supper to tell you, but I guess it doesn't matter now. It's true. Bob's been drafted and has to report to Fort Bragg, North Carolina on the thirteenth of next month for basic training," she explained.

Joe Wood turned to his son with pride in his voice and asked, "Well, boy, how does it feel to be an Army man?" He continued before giving Bob an opportunity to answer. "How about that! The first Army man in the history of the Wood family. Hot damn! Be proud boy. I wish I could go with you," he blurted out in one breath.

"But aren't you afraid they're going to send him to Vietnam, where he may end up as Larry did?" his momma asked.

"Hell, woman, if these ornery niggers around here haven't got him yet, those little Viet Cong bastards will be wasting their time. No sir. The only thing that boy has to worry about is the women over there. I was talking to old Jake Hawkins today about his boy who caught that bad disease over there and can't come home. Old Doc Hilliard told Jake he could cure that boy in two months if they let him doctor on him," Bob's daddy said.

"What can Old Doc Hilliard do that them army doctors haven't already done?" Bob's momma asked.

"I don't know. But whatever it is, it couldn't hurt. They ain't helping the boy none," Bob's daddy answered.

"What kind of zease Mr. Hawkins' boy got, Daddy?" little five-year-old Harvey asked.

"None of your business, you nosey little rat. Now shut up and finish your supper," he said.

"Can I join the Army after I finish school?" Bob's fourteen-year old sister Ronda asked.

"Girl, your place is in the kitchen, running around barefoot and pregnant. Everyone knows most of the girls who join the Army are too ugly to get a man in their hometown to marry them. It's common knowledge that a soldier, especially during wartime, will marry anything that wears a skirt; so joining the army improves their chances of finding a man," he answered.

"Daddy, that's no longer true," Ronda protested. "Besides, you ain't never been in the Army, how do you know so much about what they join the Army for?" Ronda was bold enough to ask.

"Don't get sassy with me girl. You ain't too old for me to go up side your head," her daddy warned her.

"Now Joe," Bob's momma intervened, "You're as bad as the kids. I'm afraid for Bob. He doesn't know anything about those people. Why does he have to go way over there where he may get killed, just to be treated like dirt when he gets back to his sweet America?"

"Dammit woman, it's every man's duty to serve his country in time of war. They should take all these goddamned no good draft dodgers, draft resisters, and communist sympathizers and ship them all off to Russia or some damn place," Bob's daddy spat in disgust.

"What unit did you serve with, dear?" Bob's Momma asked, her voice filled with sarcasm.

"Don't be a wiseass, Zelma. You know damn well why I never served. At least when the Japanese bombed Pearl Harbor, I was one of the first to offer my services. I couldn't help if I had flat feet. Enough about me, are you ready to take that big step from high school boy to being a man of the world?" Bob's Daddy asked him.

Bob was finally given a chance to answer his father's question. "I guess so. You all act as if I'm leaving tomorrow or something."

"Just showing concern for your welfare, dear, that's all," his momma interjected. And on and on the conversation went throughout the remainder of the meal.

After finishing his supper and the excitement of his being drafted died down, Bob went to his room to get ready for steel-pants Gina. As he was soaking in the bathtub, he planned his method of attack. Surely she had heard he'd been drafted by now because the phone had not stopped ringing since right after supper. His momma must've told one of her gossipy old friends, because his classmates were calling non-stop asking him if it was true he had been drafted. He would run down a sad line about how young men go off to war and get killed before they get a chance to experience the joys of sex or love. He knew he had to fit into one of these categories of young men, all he had to do was convince Gina what he was saying was true. He hoped she would anyway. And he would tell her how important it is going to be for him to have someone waiting for him back home. Someone to write him letters to lift his spirits and keep him going when things looked impossible and he wanted to give up. Bob figured she would tell him to fuck off, and stop watching so many of those shitty old war movies on television. But what the hell, it was worth a try. He could only strike out, which would be nothing new. After finishing his bath and getting dressed he made one final check in the mirror, and he was off and running.

Upon reaching Gina's house, Bob didn't know what to expect as he knocked on her door. He had heard Mrs. Samson say time and time again she would never allow Gina to date a service man, whether he had been in the Army for twenty years or had just gotten drafted. *"Because everyone knows soldiers are after only one thing. And it's not marriage,"* she would say. *" I'll soon find out if she meant what she says,"* Bob thought.

He was about to knock again when Gina answered the door. "Hello, Bob. Come on in and have a seat. I'm not quite ready yet, but it'll only take a second," Gina said as she bounded up the stairs.

"Hey, take your time. We have plenty of time before the movie starts," he said after her disappearing frame. Bob could have sworn Gina not being ready had been planned by her parents to give them time to interrogate him, because as soon as the formalities were over, the interrogation began. Bob didn't mind Mr. Samson asking him questions, but Mrs. Samson could have auditioned for the starring German guard role in the WWII prisoner of war movie Stalag 13.

"I fought in World War II," Mr. Samson began, "and let me tell you, son, war is pure hell. It's so important that you are supported by your loved ones back home. And God knows no one supports the servicemen in Vietnam. Well, what are you planning on being in the military? An infantryman or what?"

PATRIOTISM

"I don't really know yet, but if I have a choice, I think I would like to be an artilleryman," Bob answered.

"That's a good field to get into. They really came through for us when I was in France. We were pinned down and surrounded by the Germans. Our commo man got a call through to the artillery battery and gave them our coordinates. After the artillery got through with them, all we had to do was clean up with a dust pan and broom," Mr. Samson laughed.

"Now, Jim," Mrs. Samson barged her way into the conversation, "don't go telling Bob all those old war stories. You may scare the boy. After all, you know the young men of today are not as brave and courageous as you all were."

"Horse shit," Bob said under his breath.

She continued, "Lawd knows you can't tell the men from the women these days. What with all that long hair the young men are wearing today. And all they do is lie and steal. Maybe they all need to go in the Army and learn how to be men." Mrs. Samson was at her best tonight. She knew it pissed Bob off to hear anyone say that the young men of his generation were nothing but liars, sissies, cowards and thieves.

Bob couldn't help but defend his generation of young men. "You're partly right, Mrs. Samson. It's just the young men of today ain't like the young, black men back then who didn't care about being sent overseas to fight and die to help keep white America strong. We're fighting for a piece of mom's apple pie, namely a say-so in the running of the government and our lives." As soon as he finished, Bob knew he had fallen for her baited trap.

Mrs. Samson smiled and said, "Correct me if I'm wrong, Bob. I do believe all of the young men of Jim's time were fighting for the same thing. If not for those old Uncle Tom's, as you kids call them today, you young people would not have the political freedom you have today."

"You're totally right, Mrs. Samson, and I apologize for shooting off my mouth without thinking," Bob said, trying to put an end to the conversation.

Mrs. Samson was not quite finished. An irritating smile crossed her lips before asking, "You're not planning to run off to Canada are you, Bob?"

He could tell Mrs. Samson was enjoying watching him squirm. "No, ma'am, I personally feel it's my duty as a loyal American to serve my country regardless of my personal beliefs," Bob said hoping his answer would get her off his case, but it didn't work.

To make sure he never forgot their conversation, Mrs. Samson said, "I hope you mean that, because so many of you people dodge the draft these days you can't be trusted. Then again, it may be best if you did run off to Canada because you'll probably end up just like that James boy."

Bob was about to blow his top when Gina came bounding down the stairs. *Whew, not a moment too soon,* he breathed a sigh of relief.

"Where you kids going, Gina?"

"We're going to the movies, Momma."

"What time will you be back home? You know you have to get up early for school in the morning," Mrs. Samson reminded Gina.

"I won't be too late, Momma," Gina assured her mother as they were going out the door.

Before leaving, he apologized to Mr. Samson for being such

an idiot to say such a dumb thing about the motive of black soldiers who fought in wars past while serving America. Over the past few months, Mr. Samson had told him of so many heroic deeds accomplished by black American patriots throughout America's military history. Mr. Samson laughed and told him to forget it and have a good time, because he was not the first young feller Mrs. Samson had goaded into saying something stupid. He then turned serious and told Bob not to keep his daughter out too late. Bob assured him he wouldn't.

On their way to the theater, Gina surprised him by suggesting they go park on Lover's Levee after the movie. Throughout the movie, he rehearsed the bull crap story he made up while taking his bath. Bob had his sob story down pat, but after the movie was over, he started feeling a little uncertain about what he was about to attempt. What if his line of bullshit worked and she ended up pregnant? And here he was about to go off to the war. Bob knew his momma wouldn't hesitate to make him marry her when he got back home. And if he didn't, she would never forgive him for bringing a bastard Wood into the world.

Hell, she'll probably turn me down anyway, he thought to himself. *I'm sure other boys have tried and failed. Besides, even if she did end up pregnant, I would be in Vietnam messing up Charlie. She would have to blame it on someone else to protect her family's name.*

On their way to Lover's Levee, Gina kept asking him if anything was wrong with him. He hadn't said a word since they left the theater. He offered a half-assed excuse about having mixed emotions about being drafted, but he was sure she didn't believe him because she knew he wanted to go into the army after graduating from high school. At least that was what he had told all his friends. After parking in the most secluded spot he could find, he rehearsed his lines one final time. When he turned toward her to launch his attack, she began to speak.

"I heard what you said to Momma about feeling it is your duty to serve your country regardless of your personal feelings. I thought it was the most beautiful thing I've heard a boy in Helena, Arkansas say in a long time. I know all you boys in our class call me steel pants," she held up her hand to stop him from protesting, "but I don't really mind. The truth of the matter is, I've been waiting for a long time for you to ask me for a date. Well this afternoon, you finally asked me and made me very happy. When I heard you had been drafted, I wanted so much to be the girl waiting for you to come home to from the war. I even planned to seduce you tonight. You know how it goes. The young man is sent off to war, but just before he leaves, he convinces his girl to have sex with him because he may never return. Only this time the girl would be playing the starring role. I guess I watch too many of those shitty old war movies on television. But I'm serious, do you want me to be that girl waiting for you when you return?" she asked.

Bob was completely lost for words. He sat there momentarily unable to respond. However, during this moment of silence he couldn't help but watch the rise and fall of her perfectly rounded breasts, pulsating under her blouse--breasts he knew the guys in his circle of friends would give almost anything to see or touch. He also noticed her beautiful, golden tan skin that looked as smooth as silk. Her sensuous virgin-looking lips, which he longed to kiss, were quivering slightly. Her beautiful, brown, tear-moistened eyes made him feel guilty for what he had planned. And her perfume was so faint, yet so strong it sent his desire for her to a height he never knew existed within himself. She just sat there quietly waiting for his reply. But what was he to say? She had run down the rap he intended to use on her. So he figured the only thing to do was to come clean and take his chances. But he didn't quite know how without sounding like some comic book hero, and at the same time keep the lustful tremble out of his voice. He chose his words carefully.

"To be honest with you, Gina, I watch those same old war movies. Only this is the first time I've ever seen the girl play the starring role. What can I say? I was hoping to get you up here and use those same lines to get in your pants. Now I feel like a first class heel. I really do want you to be the girl waiting for me when I get back home from the war, but I guess I blew it as far as you're concerned. You didn't happen to read my mind on the way up here did you?"

"No, I didn't read your mind. It's the same tired old rap used by every boy in America after they get drafted and think they're going to be sent off to fight old folks wars where they might end up dead. They never wait to see if they're going to the front line before giving their spill in the hope the girl wouldn't know the majority of them won't see any combat. I figured you're no different than the rest, but you want to know what? I meant every word I said. I'm yours to do with as you please until you leave next month and forever upon your return."

"Lady, you're too much. But I could never live with myself if I went off to Vietnam, and you found out after I'm gone that you're pregnant. What would you do then?"

"Don't worry about me getting pregnant," she said holding up a packet of birth control pills. "I stole them from my momma's medicine cabinet."

Sometimes it pays to be patriotic, he congratulated himself as he took her into his arms.

For the next month, he was the top dog on the block among his circle of friends. The members of his peer group were certain he would be the first real hero of the community upon his return from Nam. They never took the time to consider that he might not get assigned to Vietnam. Neither did Bob for that matter, even though Vietnam veterans kept telling him he may get sent to Korea, Thailand, Japan, or someplace else where there was no war being fought. Like everyone else in his peer group, he could only think Vietnam. He couldn't win medals unless he went to the war, and since the war was being fought in Vietnam, that's where he wanted to go. From the day he received his draft notice, he tried to visualize what it was going to be like running through the hot, steaming jungle, wasting everything that got in his way. He pictured himself doing all the things John Wayne, Audie Murphy, and other television war heroes had done. Facing incredible odds, hunger, disease, and everything else the war could throw up against him, and he would still come out smelling like a rose. There was no doubt in his mind; he was meant to be a soldier. It never crossed his mind John Wayne and the majority of the other movie stars impersonating military heroes had never even served in any branch of the military services.

A couple of Vietnam Veterans, along with several of his peers outside his circle of friends who opposed the war, told him he should be trying to figure out how to get a deferment or not go into the army at all. One veteran suggested he join the Navy as a way to avoid being sent to Vietnam. Their advice fell on deaf ears, because all he could think about was the medals

PATRIOTISM

he was going to win while helping America put an end to the Vietnam War and communism around the world. If Bob's Dad had been against the war he may have had second thoughts, but that was not the case.

A small voice in the back of his mind kept saying, *a wise man stops and looks, where fools jump in.* He chose to ignore it. He believed it was his destiny and he was ready to face that destiny head on, both physically and mentally. He also visualized after every battle there would be a beautiful woman waiting for him to fill his empty moments until he returned home to his dream girl, Gina, who would be waiting patiently for his return. Not once did he entertain the thought he might get killed. He was sure Larry had gotten careless and ended up coming home in a body bag. He kept telling himself--maybe wounded, but not killed.

As time for him to leave grew near, his momma became more protective than ever. Bob himself became so excited he could hardly wait to leave. Bob's Daddy walked around with his chest stuck out, telling everyone what a fine soldier his son was going to make. "A modern day Sergeant Rock," he said.

Gina had been more than he wished for. When he was with her, she made him feel that fighting for mom's apple pie was truly the ultimate high. His friend Johnny, who wouldn't turn eighteen until that coming November, was trying to get his parents' permission to enlist so he and Bob could meet their destinies together. Whenever he brought up the subject of his daddy signing enlistment papers so he could join the army, his daddy always told him to shut up and stop being such a stupid dreamer.

Although Bob kept telling everyone he was ready to leave, at times he secretly wished the special treatment would last forever. But as the old saying goes, every good thing must come to an end. Friday morning, June 13, 1970, Bob got up early and packed his bag. He'd been told to travel light. He was to catch a Trailways bus from Helena at 8 a.m., which would take him to the Induction Station in Memphis, Tennessee, arriving at approximately 10 a.m.

He was told testing and filling out other paperwork would take several hours. Afterward they would be inducted into the armed forces, given plane tickets, and transported to the airport with a departure time of 2 p.m. The flight from Memphis International Airport in Memphis, Tennessee to Fayetteville, N.C., with one delay en-route, was a five-hour trip. Making adjustment for the bus ride, they should be arriving at Fort Braggs no later than 8 p.m. that evening. *At approximately 1 p.m. this afternoon, I'll be a member of the Armed Forces of the United States of America,* Bob bragged to himself.

Bob went into the kitchen and kept his momma company while she prepared breakfast. As they talked about everything but his leaving, he could tell she was trying very hard to maintain her composure. Ronda and little Harvey came into the kitchen and sat at the table with him.

"How many them VC's you gonna kill, Bob?" little Harvey asked. Bob only smiled at the question.

Ronda asked, "Aren't you scared going all the way to North Carolina by yourself?"

"Naw, besides, I won't be going by myself. When Larry went into the army in Memphis, twenty guys ended up being shipped off right along with him to Fort Sill, Oklahoma. So I doubt if I'll be going to Fort Bragg alone. Even if I was going by myself, I wouldn't be scared because I'm a man now," Bob tried to convince himself instead of his sister.

Bob's daddy had come into the kitchen right after Ronda and little Harvey but said nothing. That could only mean one thing, he was more concerned about his son than he wanted anyone to know. Bob was about to ask his daddy how he was feeling when the phone rang. Ronda answered it.

"It's for you, Bob. It's your hot little mama, Gina, wanting to say good-bye to her soldier boy before he runs off to the war."

"Very funny," Bob said as he took the phone from her. "Hello, baby, what's up?" he asked Gina, trying to sound cheerful.

"Bob, could you pick me up on your way to the bus station? I want to see you off. I've cleared it with Momma and Daddy already. They said it's okay." Gina said.

"Ok, baby. It's six o'clock now, takes half an hour to get to the bus station, the bus doesn't leave until eight, pick you up at fifteen after seven. That should give us about fifteen minutes to smooch before my bus leaves."

"I'll be ready. I love you, soldier," she whispered before hanging up.

After replacing the receiver, his momma told him to come on and eat his breakfast before it got cold.

Bob's daddy said, "I swear that gal just might go with you to North Carolina, the way she's been carrying on. Just think, boy, before this day is over, you'll be the first man in the generations of the Wood family to serve this country. I know we'll be proud of you."

"I hope so. Everyone has been treating me as if I'm going to the White House to be President of the United States instead of going to war. Boy, I would never have thought in a million years Principal White would heap so much praise on me at graduation, army or no army."

"He knows what a fine young man you are. Besides, he's an old army man himself. He knows how hard it is to get ahead without having a high school education. The soldier with the most education is the one who gets promoted first," his daddy explained.

Bob's graduation was not a moment of joy for his momma because of his decision to honor his draft notice. Her prayers that college basketball coaches would come to the school and watch Bob play basketball and offer him a scholarship were answered. She was the happiest momma in the state of Arkansas when college basketball recruiters from the Universities of Arkansas and Kansas State University made trips to their house to talk to Bob about coming to their school on scholarships. He was even invited to visit the schools campuses. All he had to do was tell them when he would be able to visit and they would send him the plane tickets. Bob wanted to be a soldier. His decision broke his momma's heart because he had passed up an opportunity to get a college education, and at the same time delay his entry into the armed forces. She told Bob although she disagreed with his decision, she would support him because he was still her baby. However, her support had not been given before she had her say.

"Bob, what the hell is wrong with you? You have an opportunity to get a college education, and at the same time delay your entry into this god-awful war that no one agrees with but the damn government. Those kids you see protesting on television and burning their draft cards would give anything to be in your situation. And you want to throw it all away because you want to be like those fake soldiers on T.V.," she complained.

"Momma, everything is going to be alright, you'll see. I don't think I was cut out for college and all. Basketball is fun in high school, but I don't want to try and make a job out it. I think I would get bored doing nothing but playing basketball all the time," Bob tried to reason with his momma.

"I'd rather you be bored as hell than know you're in Vietnam dodging bullets. Use your head boy. The war will probably be still going on when you graduate, so you can become a soldier then if that's what you want to do with your life," she countered.

"I'm sorry, momma, I just don't want to go to college," Bob said.

"Joe, will you talk some sense into your son's head before he takes his butt off to this damn war and get himself killed?" Bob's momma pleaded with his daddy.

"You heard the boy, Zelma. He doesn't want to go to college. He's a man now. He can make decision for himself," Bob's daddy supported his son.

"You're just like your son. Neither one of you know what's good for you. Go ahead and take your hard headed butt into the army. I'll pray for you, son," Bob's momma said defeated.

The rest of the meal was consumed in silence. After finishing eating, everyone sat around the table watching the clock.

"Well, I guess it's about that time," Bob said at seven o'clock. After putting his bag in the car, he went back into the house to say good-bye to Ronda, little Harvey and his momma.

"Good-bye for now, sweet lady, and don't worry about me.

I'll be fine. Just you wait and see," Bob said to his momma. "I'll call as soon as I get to Fort Bragg. Collect of course," he joked, trying to make the both of them feel better.

Instead of laughing she burst into tears as she took him into her arms. "You take good care of yourself, you hot dog."

It took all the power he could muster to keep from crying himself. As he was heading for the car, little Harvey called after him, "Hey, big brother, if you don't kill none of them VC's, don't come back home."

"Sure, you're right. I'll get a few of them just for you," Bob assured him, making the little fellow smile. "And you, Ronda, don't break too many hearts while I'm gone. I would hate to have to come back here and bust some heads because you messed over a bunch of boys."

"You worry about yourself, ok?"

He assured her he would.

"Boy, you about ready? If we don't get going, we won't have enough time to pick up that gal of yours," his daddy warned.

Bob never imagined it would be so hard to leave his family. There were tears welled up in his eyes just waiting to burst forth. When they pulled out of the driveway, his momma, sister and little brother were standing on the porch waving. They were still waving when the car turned the corner out of sight of the house. He felt a little better knowing Gina was waiting for them to pick her up so she could be with him until it was time for him to depart for Memphis, Tennessee.

Bob was wondering if his daddy felt as bad as he did when he left home for the first time. As if his daddy had read his mind he said, "This reminds me of the first time I left home," he began. "All I had was the clothes on my back. I didn't know where I was going or what I was going to do when I got there. I hopped trains all over this country before settling here in Helena with your momma. I made it and so will you. You have a hell of a lot more going for you than I had when I left home. You have a high school education and a place to start. So get that "the-world-is-coming-to-an-end" look off your face.

"Thanks, Daddy, I really needed that shot of confidence. I hope I get to be as wise as you are. It seems you always know exactly what to say and when to say it."

"Don't worry, son, you are Joe Wood's boy. It'll come in time."

As they pulled up in front of Gina's house, Bob was hoping Mrs. Samson would be waiting out front. He wanted the satisfaction of saying *I'm sorry I didn't run off to Canada and prove that you're right about the young men of today. I guess it goes to show that even the best predictors are sometimes wrong.* But she was nowhere in sight. She probably would have cast some type of spell on him that would have prevented him from ever getting another hard on as long as he lived, he thought. "Old witch," he said aloud, but not loud enough for his daddy to hear.

Gina was waiting on the side of the road as they pulled up in front of the house. She tried to get in the car before it came to a complete stop.

"Aren't you going to let your momma know you're leaving?" Bob's dad asked her.

"She's probably looking out of her bedroom window. Besides, she knows you don't have time to stop and chat. Let's go, please, Mr. Wood," she said. It was easy to tell she'd been crying by the sound of her voice.

33

They rode to the bus station in silence. Neither one trusted themselves to speak. After purchasing his ticket to Memphis and checking his bag, Bob and Gina went and sat in the car. Bob's daddy struck up a conversation with the old black janitor who kept the bus station clean so he and Gina could be alone to say their good-byes. As Bob had promised, they had approximately fifteen minutes to say their good-byes. Bob spoke first.

"Gina, this past month has been the happiest of my entire life. You're more than I could ever hope for. I'll think of you every waking moment we are apart."

Tears were rolling down Gina's cheeks as she said, "Oh Bob, I swore to myself I wouldn't carry on like this, but I can't help it. I'm going to miss you so much. I feel you are taking away my reason for living. I never dreamed I could love someone as much as I love you. I've been crying ever since you took me home last night. Is there any way I can go with you?" she asked, now sobbing uncontrollably.

He could no longer hold back the tears that had been building ever since he had gotten up that morning. "I wish you could, baby. God in heaven knows I do. I'll write to you every day, and that is a promise," he managed to say between sniffles.

They were locked in each other's arms, crying like two kids who were about to lose their favorite toy, when his daddy came out to the car to tell him the bus was being boarded.

"How much time do I have?" Bob asked, still holding Gina tight in his arms.

"About two minutes at the most. You had better hurry and say your good-byes before you get left."

The idea of missing his bus was very tempting, but he knew there was no way his daddy would allow that to happen. So they walked over to the bus holding hands, hoping all the time that by some miracle he would not have to leave, but knowing better.

While Bob and Gina were saying their final good-bye, the bus driver said, "Last call, young feller. Either you bring her with you or stay here. I have a schedule to keep."

"Well, baby, until I see you again. I'll call you as soon as I can when I get to Fort Bragg. Don't forget, I love you, lady." He then turned to say good-bye to his daddy. He reached out his hand, but to his surprise his daddy embraced him.

"Take care of yourself, son. And make sure you call your Momma as soon as possible. I don't want her worrying about you too much."

"I'll call her first chance I get," Bob assured his daddy.

Bob boarded the bus and found a seat next to a window, where he could wave good-bye to two of the most important people in his life. As the bus pulled away from the station, he felt as if he was leaving a part of himself behind with his daddy and Gina. She looked like an angel standing there with tears running down her face. A scene he would never forget as long as he lived. He no longer tried to hide the tears running down his face from the other passengers on the bus. He watched the town he loved pass by the window through tear-filled eyes. He kept asking himself, *If being a soldier is what I was meant to be, why the hell do I feel so God-damned bad about leaving home?*

Bob's daddy had warned him, after he made his decision to go ahead and serve his tour of duty, that leaving home for the first time would be one of the most difficult periods in his life. Bob never dreamed it would be that hard. He was still feeling sorry for himself when the bus stopped in Marianne, Arkansas, a little town about half way between Helena and Memphis. A young black man about his own age boarded the bus with tears in his eyes. Being he was the only other black person on the bus; Bob motioned for his newfound comrade to sit beside him. He was sure they had at least one thing in common; they were both headed for Vietnam.

"What's happening, man?" Bob asked, feeling better now that he was not the only one on the bus feeling shitty.

"Ain't nothing happening, my man," he answered as he settled himself into the seat next to Bob, " except my rich uncle decided it was time for me to do my part to help protect the South Vietnamese people from the commies of the North."

"My name is Bob Wood," he introduced himself.

"David Cooper. It seems our rich uncle has been pretty busy writing letters lately. I guess they're running out of niggers in Vietnam and need a new supply," he said, sounding like so many of the draft dodgers Bob had heard on the radio or seen on television.

"How do you know we're going to Vietnam?" Bob asked.

"I'm not one hundred percent sure, but there is a ninety percent chance that's where we'll end up if they stick us in the infantry," David answered.

"Well, to be truthful with you, I want to do my part to help those people."

"Aw shit, man. Do you really believe these white people give a damn about the South Vietnamese people?" David asked as if no one in his right mind would believe such a thing. "As small as that country is, all the United States has to do is declare war and fuck those gooks up. But no, they are too busy making money. They don't care if every black person in America gets his ass wasted."

"They have white soldiers over there getting wasted too you know," Bob reminded him.

"That's true," he agreed. "But, do you know that almost half of all the casualties in Vietnam are black, and we only make up twenty percent of the whole Army?" he exaggerated the casualty rate. "What does that tell you, Bob Wood?"

"That too many brothers volunteer for the infantry," he answered.

"Volunteer my ass. Boy, are you in for a rude awakening. Me myself, if I have a choice, I'm going to get me a soft office job where I can sit back and ride the rest of this screwed up war out. I should've withdrawn my savings and hauled ass off to Canada right along with the rest of those smart-ass white boys. They'll probably get away with dodging the draft in a few years anyway."

Bob knew the protestors and demonstrators had taken their toll on the young men in America, but he never knew just how much. The protests never bothered him in the least, because he wanted to go to Vietnam. Surely David did not believe America would let those draft dodgers go unpunished. He was probably pissed because he had been drafted.

"That may be true, but all they're doing is making our country weak. I hope there aren't too many more guys going to the war who feel as you do. I hope I'm not the last young person left who gives a shit about this country of ours," Bob said becoming angry.

"Man, you and this damn patriotism bullshit you're talking is for the birds. You should know regardless of how loyal a nigger is to this country, we as a whole will never get our just reward--that is unless there is a revolution between blacks and whites and we kick their asses." David sounded as if he was just angry as Bob was.

"That's bull shit, David. Thanks to cowardly people like you, black and whites, this country won't last much longer anyway. We'll probably end up speaking some bullshit foreign language like Russian or something. If you don't mind, let's pretend we never met," Bob said.

"That is fine with me damn fool, because you'll probably last about two months once you get to Vietnam. You must think you are John Wayne or some damned body. Those white movie actors get up the next morning laughing at all you fools who think they're some kind of hero. More power to you, damn fool," David spat.

"I may be a crazy fool to you, but at least I'm not a coward," the tone of Bob's voice let David know the conversation between them had ended. David got up and moved to another seat. The remainder of the trip was made in silence. The silence between himself and David continued on the shuttle bus during the ride to the induction station.

Once they arrived at the induction station in Memphis, Bob didn't have time to be angry at anyone. He was too busy taking tests and filling out forms. At least a million he thought to himself. Bob was sure he would spend the rest of the war filling out forms and taking tests. He could hardly wait until it was time for them to be inducted into the Army. After what seemed an eternity, twelve o'clock finally rolled around. He was the proudest young man in America as he took the oath to defend his country. If need be, to the death. For the first time in his short life, there was no doubt in his mind he was a true American. He did not see David again until they were lining up to take the oath. *I hope he ends up so high in the Central Highlands of Vietnam they mistake him for a native,* Bob wished the worst for David. Vietnam Veterans had told him that the Central Highlands was one of the most dangerous assignments in Vietnam.

After the induction, Bob was grouped with fifteen other guys with orders for boot camp at Fort Bragg, N.C. While on the way to Memphis International Airport on an airport bus, Bob thanked his lucky stars David was not in his group. Bob thoughts turned from his dislike for David to his hometown and the people he loved but had to leave. His eyes became misty as he remembered how beautiful Gina looked that morning and how proud his father had been as they saw him off. He was so deep in thought that he wasn't even aware when they reached the airport.

"Everybody off the bus," driver announced, bringing him back to the present.

The fifteen guys traveling with Bob to Fort Bragg for basic training looked scared to death. Except for him, they all looked as if they were headed for the electric chair instead of the war. Since they had already been given airline tickets before they left the induction station, all they had to do was check their bags and get a boarding pass. After checking in, Bob decided to call home since he had some time to waste. Collect of course. The phone rang four times before his mother answered it. She accepted the call and asked how things were going with her soldier boy.

"I'm doing fine so far. I'm at Memphis International Airport waiting for my flight to North Carolina."

"Are you alone?"

"No, ma'am. There are fifteen other guys going there besides myself," he said and asked if she was alone.

"Yes, I am. Ronda is at a friend's house; Harvey is somewhere down the road with one of his little friends, and of course your daddy is still at work. I swear, that man has been bragging about you since you left, saying you'll be the Top Sergeant of the Army some day. How did the induction go?"

"Not bad, I guess. There were about fifty of us total. I thought I would give you a call to let you know that I'm still alive and kicking since I had some time to kill before my plane leaves. Some soldier I am. I haven't been gone a whole day and already I miss y'all," he confessed.

"You'll be fine once you get where you're going and get into a normal routine," his momma assured him.

"I sure hope you're right. I couldn't stand many more days like this one. Well, I had better get off of this phone and stop running up your phone bill. Tell everyone I said hello and I love them. I'll call again as soon as I get to Fort Bragg."

"Okay, baby, we'll be waiting to hear from you soon. Bye-bye."

Now that he had called home, he could start worrying about the problem immediately at hand--how to overcome the fear of flying. He had never flown on a plane before and had no desire to do so. Bob had convinced himself a long time ago that if God had wanted man to fly, he would have given him wings. He kept telling himself he was being childish about the whole thing. His biggest fear was he would get on the plane, and half way to where they were going, he would puke his guts out with everyone on the plane watching. While trying to convince himself that everything was going to be fine, one of the other guys started talking about how scared he was because he had never flown before. The fear Bob felt a moment ago disappeared because he knew if they could do it, so could he. Nevertheless, he couldn't help thinking about the last time he had watched the evening news where a plane had crashed. It had taken days for them to recover all of the bodies. What was it the reporter had said? "The chances of anyone surviving a plane crash are practically zero."

Hell, you only live once. Besides, the only way I can get to the war is by plane, Bob said to himself. His daddy had taught him a long time ago if you can overcome your fear of the unknown, you can do almost anything you set your mind to because fear is the biggest obstacle we have to overcome in our lives. Bob wondered if the ride on this big plane was going to be anything like the crop dusters he had watched for the last nineteen years, an up and down affair.

Bob knew he was just as brave as the other guys who had never flown; still his body tensed upon hearing the announcement their plane was ready for boarding. As he walked down the corridor to the plane, he again thought about the last newscast he had watched on television about a plane crashing, killing all aboard, but he cast the thought aside. He found his seat and sat down. Bob was surprised to find the seats were softer and more comfortable than the ones in his daddy's '55 Chevy. However, he didn't feel as safe. As they taxied out to the runway for takeoff, he thought, *this may be fun*. He wasn't so sure it was going to be fun a short time later as they were speeding down the runway for takeoff. He watched as the buildings sped by and it seemed the pilot made no effort to leave the ground. *We're running out of runway. This thing will never get up in time. I'll be the first soldier in the history of the Wood family to die in a plane crash. And the damn thing never even left the ground.*

Bob's anxiety was relieved as the plane lifted off. Surprisingly, after getting airborne and leveling off, it was one of the smoothest rides he'd been on in a long time. It was nothing like the bumpy rides up and down the dirt roads in his daddy's car. The only discomfort he felt was the pressure on his ears. Not knowing this pressure was normal, he asked the stewardess what he could do to relieve it. She laughed and told him to hold his nose and blow. Pop went the ears and he settled back for the remainder of the trip. He imagined himself being in the cockpit of one of the Old World War II fighter planes, searching the skies for none other than the *"Red Baron."* It would've been billed as the greatest dogfight in the history of World War II. He pictured himself emerging victorious from the battle, bloody and weary, because it would have been a long, tiring one. He was still in his fantasy when sleep overtook him. The next thing he knew one of the stewardesses was waking him to inform him they would be landing in Charlotte, North Carolina momentarily and asked him to please fasten his seat belt. He had enjoyed the flight so much; he could hardly wait to get airborne again.

When the announcement was made that the next plane was ready for boarding, he thought it would be another 727; but instead it was one of those old propeller-type planes he had seen on television bouncing up and down as they flew across the screen. It wasn't even big enough to pull up to the airport on/off boarding gates. They had to walk out onto the tarmac to board the plane. *Oh crap, not one of those rickety old planes*, Bob said.

He never forgot that ride because it seemed every time he dozed off to sleep, the plane hit an air pocket and scared the living you-know-what out of him. For a while he had serious doubts as to whether they were going to make it to Fort Bragg, which was located in Fayetteville, N.C. God must've been looking out for them because they made it in one piece. As they taxied down the runway to the off-loading location on the tarmac of the small single story airport, they could see several Army buses parked in the airport parking lot. While unloading, the guys joked that the Army had supplied each of them with their own private transportation to Fort Bragg. Apprehension was in the air as they headed for the lobby, where they were told someone would be waiting for them, which there was.

A Staff Sergeant Anthony Wilford was waiting for them at the flight arrival gate. He directed them to a designated area as they entered the terminal, without asking if they were new recruits heading for the base. After all sixteen of them were accounted for, they were escorted to the waiting busses.

"I wonder how he knew we were in the Army?" Bob asked no one in particular.

"If you haven't noticed by now, look around. We are the only ones walking around with these big, brown envelopes," the nearest person answered.

"What about our bags?" someone asked Staff Sergeant Wilford.

"After you have been assigned a seat on one of the buses which will be transporting you out to the base, then you can grab your bags. Is that alright with you?" he addressed everyone in the group.

"Sure," half the guys answered.

He's not a bad guy, Bob said, remembering being told the sergeants at boot camp were all mean, heartless bastards. As David had said, "Boy was he in for a rude awakening." A saying he would never forget in his lifetime.

After being assigned a seat, they were allowed to claim their bags. There were already approximately twenty-five guys on the bus he was to ride on. Bob had never in his life seen so many guys with such long hair, except on television. There were brothers with afros bigger than any girl's he had ever dated. And the white guys had tried their damnest to put all barbers out of business. They had hair down to the cracks of their butts and beards which damn near covered their whole face. "Boy the barbers are going to have a field day on these creeps," Bob said under his breath.

It was seven-twenty when they arrived at the Reception Station at Fort Bragg, North Carolina. His name officially changed from Bob Wood to "private everything but a child of God" for the next several months.

Chapter 2
BASIC TRAINING

Upon their arrival at the Fort Bragg Basic Combat Training Reception Station, they were herded into a classroom where they had to fill out another couple hundred forms, in addition to rechecking the forms in their brown envelopes they had filled out while at the induction station in Memphis, Tennessee. While filling out the forms, Bob looked around the room at the number of his fellow recruits. He was surprised to see their rank had grown from sixteen when they left Memphis to approximately one hundred upon their arrival at the reception station at Fort Bragg.

Of the approximately one hundred recruits in the classroom, 99 were starving. The peanuts served on the planes had long served their purpose. The grumbling about that hunger started after one brave soul asked if they were going to get something to eat before going to bed. They were told they would get fed after everyone had finished filling out their forms and not before. As Bob's large intestine was about to devour his small intestine, the officer in charge announced that all forms had been completed and turned in. It was time to eat. They were led over to the mess hall [dining facility] for late evening chow at 10:15 P.M. To Private Wood it was a bedtime snack. It was common for him to be eating this time of night because he ate this time of night after almost every road game during the basketball season.

Bob was so hungry he could smell the bacon and eggs cooking long before they reached the mess hall. When he got inside the building, he couldn't help but notice how hefty the cooks were. He wondered why the army allowed them to get so far out of shape. Oh well, Bob thought, who cares as long as they dish out the grub. Although Bob could clearly see that the cooks were only serving scrambled eggs, Bob was caught off guard when the cook asked him how he wanted his eggs. For an unknown reason, Bob thought the cook may make an exception for him. The temporary mental lapse caused his first embarrassing incident.

"How do you want your eggs, trainee?" The cook asked Bob when he stepped up to the grill.

"Regular, well done, not scrambled please," Bob answered.

The cook laughed and sloshed a glob of scrambled eggs onto his plate.

"I wanted my eggs regular, well done, and not scrambled" Bob said, magnifying his embarrassment.

The cook stared at him for what seemed like an hour, because it didn't take a genius to figure out that he'd made his first mistake and was about to pay for it. The cook kept looking at him as if he had made a derogatory remark about his ancestors, or worse. "If you don't get the hell out of my face, trainee, you won't have enough teeth left in your mouth to chew the god-damned eggs on your plate. Now move on troop. I have other people to feed."

Bob couldn't comprehend why the cook was so upset just because he didn't want scrambled eggs. "I don't know what the hell his problem is. Bastard shouldn't have asked me how I wanted my eggs if he was going to give me what he wanted to give me in the first place," Bob protested, after setting his tray on the table where three of the guys who had come from Memphis with him were sitting.

"Hey, man, you're going to have to get used to that. They like screwing with big guys like yourself because they know you can't whip their asses up in here," one of the guys assured him.

The explanation made Bob feel a little better, but not a whole hell of a lot. It wasn't his fault he had reached a height of 6'4" tall, and the majority of the men in society had not. All he knew was he was ready to start his training to become one of America's greatest fighting men. He didn't have time for an overweight a-hole Mess Sergeant giving him grief on the first day of his arrival at Fort Bragg.

"Alright, you bunch of assholes, lissen up," Sergeant Wilford said entering the dining facility. "This is a damn mess hall, not a conversation center. You came in here to eat, not to carry on a conversation with your buddy. Does everyone understand what I said?"

"Yes, Sergeant," the majority of them answered.

"Good, you only have three minutes to finish that garbage on your plates." He then began timing them by setting the timer on the stop watch he wore on his wrist. Half the guys had just sat down with their plates, the same as Bob. It didn't really matter to Bob that he had been given only three minutes to eat because he had eaten faster than that on numerous occasions back home to be on time for basketball practice or a game. Therefore, it took all of about one and a half minutes to gulp down the eggs, SOS on two pieces of toast, two pieces of bacon, and drink the glass of milk he had on his tray. Bob was starved and wanted to make sure he didn't go to bed hungry that night. He had eaten so fast he didn't even taste the food, but had finished not a moment too soon.

As Bob was taking his tray up to the window where the trays and dishes were washed, Sergeant Wilford started yelling as if the building were on fire. "Get out of this fucking mess hall right now. Where the hell do you people think you are, at the Dairy Queen?" he asked, but didn't wait for an answer. "You have been sitting here for at least five minutes and still haven't finished your meal. I could have eaten a damn elephant by now." His last few words went unheard because people were running over each other to get out of the mess hall.

Sergeant Wilford's assistant, Corporal Samuel Sanders was waiting outside, directing everyone to fall in as they came running out of the building. Very few of the guys knew what he was talking about. Noticing half the guys standing around looking lost, he said, "Fall in means I want four even numbered rows of people standing side by side. You guys can figure that out, can't you?"

"Yes, Sergeant," most of them answered.

"Its corporal, numb nuts," Corporal Sanders corrected them.

After everyone was formed as well as could be expected, they were marched over to the supply room, if you could call it marching because no one was in step with anyone else, and lined up to receive their linen. As they passed the supply window, they were issued two blankets, two sheets, a pillow, and a pillowcase. From the supply room they were marched, or walked, over to their barracks and assigned a bunk. Since he was tired, Bob started to make his bunk while the rest of the guys were standing around bitching about what had transpired

PATRIOTISM

since their arrival three and a half hours ago.

In stepped Sergeant Wilford. "Why the hell is it that out of all you damn people, and only one puke is attempting to make his bunk?" When no one answered, he walked over to where Bob was standing beside his bunk and told everyone to gather around. "This is a classic example of how not to make a military bunk. Now everyone watch closely how I want you to make these bunks every day you're here. Make sure you pay close attention because I'm only going to show you once."

After Sergeant Wilford finished his demonstration on how to make a military bunk properly, he asked if there were any questions. Although 99.9% of them couldn't make the bunk the way he had showed them to save their lives, no one asked any questions. Bob was wondering if Sergeant Wilford was going to leave his bunk made so the other guys could use it as a guide.

Bob's wondering mind was answered when Sergeant Wilford said, "You think you are going to get over, don't you, trainee? Old Sarge got your beddie all made for you and all you have to do is jump in and go to dream land. Wrong," he screamed and tore the covers off the bunk. "All right girls, lissen close. You have ten minutes to make these bunks the way I just showed you. And if they're not right, you'll wish you had never met me. Well, what the hell are you girls waiting on? For me to hold your hands?" he asked when no one moved.

Until that night, Private Wood had never in his life had to make his own bed. Also, he'd never heard a person yell as loud as Sergeant Wilford had, not even his high school basketball coach, Mr. Flowers, and he was loud. Sergeant Wilford returned approximately ten minutes later as promised and conducted what he called an inspection, but to everyone in the barracks it was a search and destroy mission. Every bunk in the barracks was torn apart. They were instructed to keep making the bunks until he was satisfied they were made correctly.

An hour later and convinced that they would never make the bunks to his satisfaction, Sergeant Wilford said, "All right, girls, even though your bunks look like crap, I'm going to let them go for tonight. But tomorrow we'll get them right if I have to kick the living shit out of every one of you. We will get them right tomorrow, won't we, girls?" he asked tauntingly.

Only half the guys answered. Bob thought Sergeant Wilford had been loud in the mess hall, but it had sounded no-where near as loud as he shouted this time in the smaller confines of the barracks.

"I said, we'll get them properly made tomorrow, won't we girls?"

This time everyone in the barracks answered as loud as they possibly could. Bob could have sworn the whole building shook. And as if he had not scared the living crap out of them, he became calm again.

"Because these barracks are old and made of wood, which is all dried out, there is a constant fear that one of you stupid trainees will set fire to the place and burn everyone up. So we have what we call a fireguard. And guess who the fire guards are going to be?" Sergeant Wilford asked without expecting an answer. "You are, every swinging dick. We start with A and go through Z. That way everyone gets a chance to make sure their buddy doesn't get burned up. Everyone whose last name starts with A through G, I want to see you over here. The rest of you hit the sack."

About ten guys went over to where Sergeant Wilford had

indicated; the rest got into bed. Sergeant Wilford explained that each person would stand watch for an hour and then wake the next person on the list. A temporary duty roster was made out and posted on the bulletin board so that the person on duty would know who they were to wake up at the end of their one-hour shift. After Sergeant Wilford finished briefing the fire guards for the night, he asked if anyone had any questions about anything before he left for the night. When there were none, he said tauntingly, "Good night, girls. I'll see you in the morning."

After making sure Sergeant Wilford was gone and out of hearing distance, the guys let off a little steam.

"Who the hell does he think he is calling us a bunch of girls," one faceless person in the dark protested.

"Yeah, if they think I'm going to put up with this shit for eight weeks, they can kiss my ass," put in another. And that was the way it went until everyone fell asleep.

The last thing Bob remembered before falling off into a deep, dreamless sleep was asking himself, *Is this truly what I want to be, a piece of crap to be stepped on?*

The next morning Bob and his fellow recruits were awakened at 0400 hours military time, an ungodly hour by civilian standards. They were instructed to make their bunks as they had been shown the previous night. After numerous attempts to make the bunks as instructed, and failing to do so, they were marched over to the mess hall. This time when asked how he wanted his eggs, Bob said, "Whatever you have," which happened to be scrambled.

From the mess hall they were marched over to the barbershop. Being an intelligent individual, you would think Bob was capable of putting two and two together, with the incident in the mess hall and the barber asking him how he wanted his hair cut. However, being he was with the first group to get their haircut, he didn't have the faintest idea of the pranks the barbers used to get a laugh. The tactic the barber used to get his daily laugh on Bob's behalf was unfair and humiliating.

"How do you want your hair cut, trainee?" the barber smiled.

"I guess bald, sir," Bob answered, knowing bald was the customary military hairstyle.

"Dammit trainee, I asked how you wanted your damn hair cut. I don't want to hear no I guess shit. Now, how do you want your hair cut?" the barber asked again.

Feeling somewhat intimidated, Bob requested the style he had worn throughout high school. "High and tight, sir," Bob answered.

"As you wish," the barber grinned. He then took his clippers and cut a swat right down the center of Bob's head, all the way to the scalp. Everyone in the barbershop laughed as if it was the funniest thing they had ever seen in their entire lives.

Bob had never been so humiliated in his whole life. While sitting there in that chair steaming he swore, *From now on, no matter what they ask, my answer will be whatever is right. Why in hell didn't I stick by my original answer? Why didn't I see this coming anyway?* He asked himself.

From the barbershop the new recruits were marched over to CIF (Clothing Issue Facility). There they were issued a duffle bag, fatigues which didn't fit, combat boots that weighed ten pounds, and an assortment of other ill fitting clothing. They would grow into them, they were told by the issuing personnel. After everyone had received his issue of clothing, it was one o'clock in the afternoon and everyone was starved.

"Hey, Sergeant Wilford, what time do we eat?" Bob asked,

raising his hand to be noticed. The second he saw the look on Sergeant Wilford's face, he knew he had made his third mistake.

"Oh, is the little girl hungry?" Sergeant Wilford asked in a sarcastic tone. "Come on out here and daddy will feed you."

Oh man, here I go again, Bob mumbled to himself as he made his way out to the front of the formation.

Upon reaching Sergeant Wilford at the front of the formation, Bob was handed a baby's bottle and instructed to suck it. Bob didn't care what Sergeant Wilford did to him he wasn't about to suck that bottle. Bob had been told by veterans that the army Drill Sergeants did this sort of thing all the time to teach new recruits to always think before asking questions or shooting off their mouths. Bob didn't care what Sergeant Wilford's reasons were, he was not going to be humiliated in front of his peers by being made to suck a baby's bottle. He had thought the incidents in the mess hall and barbershop would be the last laughs at his expense. He wouldn't have minded being made to do push-ups or sit-ups, but he sure in hell wasn't going to suck that bottle.

"You suck that damn bottle, puke, or your ass is mine. Do you understand?" Sergeant Wilford asked threateningly.

"Whatever is right, Sergeant," Bob responded, sticking by his guns.

"Are you going to suck that damn bottle or not, trainee?" Sergeant Wilford asked, pressing the brim of his Smokey-the-Bear hat against the upper portion of Bob's forehead.

"No, Sergeant, I'm not going to suck this bottle, no matter what you do to me. I'm now a soldier of the United States Army, not a baby," Bob said.

"Then you drop and push Fort Bragg away," Sergeant Wilford hissed, pissed off because he had been cheated out of his daily laugh. Sergeant Wilford had told them earlier that every time they screwed up they would be made to do push-ups until he got tired. And of all the exercises in the world, Bob was weakest at push-ups. While the rest of the guys stood around snickering at him, he did as many as he thought he could, apparently not enough to satisfy Sergeant Wilford.

Sergeant Wilford said, "Look at the little girl. She's tired already. What is your name trainee?"

"Bob Wood, Sergeant," he answered. Every muscle in his arms was aching.

"Well, Private Bob Wood, by the time you leave Fort Bragg you'll be able to do a hell of a lot more push-ups than you can do right now. Just to show you what a good sport I am, I'm going to let you get up after only ten more push-ups," Sergeant Wilford laughed.

At that moment Bob knew his name had officially change from simply Bob Wood to Private Bob Wood. He didn't know where he got the strength from to do ten more push-ups, but he did them.

"Alright, trainee, get up. And the next time you have a question, make sure you ask for permission to speak. Is that understood?" Sergeant Wilford asked.

"Yes, Sergeant," Private Wood screamed at the top of his lungs. Lesson number three he recorded in his memory bank: keep my big mouth shut.

After being told to recover and get back in formation, every muscle in his arms was totally shot. He was sure when they got to the mess hall he wouldn't be able to lift his spoon to feed himself. His theory was totally debunked because shortly after

PATRIOTISM

Private Wood fell back into formation, they were marched over to the mess hall, where he was amazed that the hunger pains in his stomach made him forget about the pain in his arms. Later that evening they had to fill out more forms and correct some of the forms they had filled out earlier upon their arrival the previous day. Sergeant Wilford told them that would be the last order of the day and they would be allowed to relax right after dinner (supper in the south). After dinner they were marched back to the barracks, thinking they had survived their first full day at screwed up Fort Bragg, N. C.

Upon reaching the barracks, Sergeant Wilford said, "All right, you piles of shit, when I fall you out, I want you to go inside and stand beside your bunks. I want to make sure you have made them the way I showed you yesterday. Is there any question before I fall you out?"

Everyone wanted to say, '*Yes you dip shit, how can you fix your mouth to say something that stupid, knowing full well you told us our bunks looked like crap before we left the barracks this morning?*' But none of them dared ask the question that was on their minds.

After tearing up every bunk in the place again, Sergeant Wilford volunteered four individuals to go with him on a special mission, and informed the rest of them he would be back at 1800 hours to re-inspect their bunks. It was 1700 hours then. After he left, it was again time for the guys to let off a little steam.

"Man, that Sergeant Wilford is one crazy fucker," noted Dean Jones, who turned out to be the clown of the platoon. "If that bastard ever tells me to drop and push Fort Bragg away, I'm going to tell him where to get off."

55

Everyone agreed with Jones, knowing full well they were talking out of their ass because their mouths knew better.

"If I were you, man, I wouldn't have done those last ten push-ups. I would have told him to kiss my black behind," Larry Larking added.

It went on and on until around five forty-five. It was then they finally realized Sergeant Wilford would be back to re-inspect in a very short time. They rushed to make their bunks, knowing all the bullshit they had been talking was nothing more than just that.

While they were standing around bitching, Private Wood had made his bunk and was positive it would pass Sergeant Wilford's inspection. He took this time while everyone was busy making their bunks to speculate on what had occurred since their arrival at Fort Bragg and what would be expected of them the remainder of basic training. It was during this time he realized Sergeant Wilford was preparing them for the training ahead, and later Vietnam. Therefore, he wouldn't fight the harassment, mental abuse, or physical punishment. He would welcome everything they threw at him because he figured to survive in combat, you had to be physically fit and mentally sound. Private Wood didn't care if he had to work seven days a week; nothing was going to lower his morale. He planned on being the best-damned soldier the Army had ever seen and dammit, he was going to be it. *I am an American fighting man, and as such, I must be the best trained soldier in the world*, he said to himself with such conviction that he looked forward to Sergeant Wilford's inspection.

Private Wood's newfound dedication was about to be tested. Sergeant Wilford entered the barracks and right away, everyone could tell he was pissed about something. Private Wood figured he didn't like working late, or someone had chewed him out for something.

"Alright, you fucking dirt balls, the first thing we're going to do is pack our civilian clothes in the boxes I have outside so they can be shipped back to your homes first thing Monday morning. There'll be no more civilian clothes worn for the period of time you're undergoing your basic combat training. Then I'll inspect your bunks. Well, what are you shit heads waiting on? Move it!" he shouted as if they could read his mind.

Private Wood was the first one out the door and back in with his box. He was also the first one to finish packing and addressing his box. He sat on his bunk and watched as some of the guys strained to get the content of two or three suitcases in the one box they had been allowed initially. They were allowed to get as many boxes as they needed after Sergeant Wilford had his laugh. After everyone finished packing and addressing their boxes, Sergeant Wilford began his inspection of their bunks. As they expected, he started tearing up bunks, throwing pillows that way, blankets this way, and sheets all over the place. Private Wood stood patiently waiting for Sergeant Wilford to reach his bunk. He knew he was ready for his first challenge since his arrival at Fort Bragg. As Sergeant Wilford approached his bunk, there was a noticeable change in his attitude. It seemed he resented the fact there might be a bunk made exactly the way he had instructed it to be.

"Well, hello, Private Bob Wood. Do you think your bunk will pass my inspection?" Sergeant Wilford asked with a smile on his face.

"I'm sure you as a sergeant in the United States Army will

be fair regardless of the outcome of your inspection," Private Wood answered. His answer seemed to have further infuriated Sergeant Wilford because he was more pissed than when he first came into the barracks.

"I didn't ask for a wise ass answer, you fucking jerk. I am fair. It's you dumb ass trainees who make things around here miserable." Sergeant Wilford then proceeded to inspect the bunk. He spent twice the amount of time inspecting Private Wood's bunk as he did the others. Finding no deficiencies, he turned to Private Wood and hissed, "Since you don't have anything to do, after I finish my inspection you can come with me. I need some help around the orderly room." After tearing up the last two bunks, he informed the rest of them he would be back again in half an hour to re-inspect.

For an unknown reason, Private Wood felt he had nothing to fear as he walked along side Sergeant Wilford to the orderly room. He knew there were other bunks that should have passed Sergeant Wilford inspection. But he didn't dwell on it. The only possible conclusion Private Wood could reach why his bunk was allowed to pass was Sergeant Wilford intentionally let his bunk pass inspection because he needed someone for a detail.

The help Sergeant Wilford needed was cleaning the orderly room, which consisted of sweeping and mopping. He would instruct Private Wood to wax and buff the floors the following morning. Sergeant Wilford stared at him as he cheerfully walked along beside him on their way to the orderly room. Sergeant Wilford didn't like black soldiers, and he gave them hell the whole time they were at the reception station. Now here was a black boy who talked white, and had an air about him that said he was just as good or better than any white man. Sergeant Wilford felt he had to do something about that confident attitude, because he knew other black soldiers would eventually follow his lead. Who in the hell wanted an army of intelligent niggers? That meant they would want to be in charge of their own destiny soon.

Although black officers were few and far between, Vietnam had produced more black noncommissioned officers than Sergeant Wilford cared for. Principally because he felt inferior to black men who had gone through so much shit in their lives and were still able to compete with him. On several occasions while he was stationed in Vietnam, black soldiers were promoted ahead of him although he had more time in grade and more time in service. He refused to admit to himself that the black soldiers who had been promoted ahead of him were better soldiers. He was saddled with that white privileged syndrome. Still, as far as Sergeant Wilford was concerned, all black soldiers were good for was being cannon fodder or bullet catchers.

Private Wood was finished by the time Sergeant Wilford returned from his re-inspection of the barracks. Private Wood was no stranger to sweeping and mopping floors thanks to his parents. He never had to make his bed or cook his meals, but when he worked with his daddy evenings and on Saturdays, he had to keep the workshop clean. The detail only took an hour to complete.

Upon his return, Sergeant Wilford was disappointed to see Private Wood had finished the detail. He had planned on using the incomplete detail to emphasize that black soldiers were incapable of completing the simplest of tasks in a timely manner. He was forced to change tactics. "I see you're finished already."

"Yes, Sergeant Wilford. It wasn't that much to do. Is there anything else you need done?" he volunteered.

Private Wood's cheerfulness set Sergeant Wilford off, because the intention of the detail was to demoralize him. "I want your black ass back in this orderly room at 0400 hours in the morning," he said, starting to turn red in the face.

"Is that four o'clock in the morning, Sergeant Wilford?" Private Wood asked, not sure of military time.

"Yes," he hissed, "that is exactly the time I meant. Let me ask you a question, Private Wood. Do you hate white people telling you what to do? Because I sense a note of hostility toward me under that calm exterior of yours."

The question caught Private Wood completely off guard. He couldn't figure out how the hell Sergeant Wilford got the notion that he hated white people. All he was doing was what he was being told to do. It took him a few seconds to collect his thoughts before he answered. The black veterans also told him that many of the army's white leadership, both officers and noncommissioned officers, tried to treat black enlisted soldiers as if they were all uneducated, stupid, or plain dumb, just because they talked differently than white soldiers do. Private Wood had listened closely to his momma and daddy debate racism and the Civil Rights Movement with both black and white people on the farm. He also listened closely to his two favorite black leaders, Dr. King, and Malcolm X, so as to get an idea on how to answer such questions.

Because he knew it was only a matter of time before he would be thrown into the racial debate, he spent hours upon hours in front of his bathroom mirror practicing his answers and

PATRIOTISM

delivery to possible questions he might be asked. He wanted to insure he would be able to express himself clearly and intelligently when answering questions he might be asked about black people wanting equal rights in America. Private Wood's favorite area of discussion was debunking the myth that black people hated white people.

"Sergeant Wilford, I don't know what you expect me to say, but if you think I have anything against you or anyone else of a difference race, creed, or color, you're wrong. You're a sergeant in the United States Army, something I have dreamed of becoming for the last two years now. I know you have paid your dues to get where you are today, and I'm willing to pay mine," Private Wood answered honestly.

It was obvious Sergeant Wilford had never heard a black trainee say such a thing. He turned even redder than before. "You let me tell you something, black boy. If you, or any other black soldier, think being in the Army is going to change anything for you black people in America, you're sadly mistaken. You black people will never be fully accepted in America's society. You people have always been doormats for white people to step on and you always will be. So I don't want to hear any more of your smooth talking bullshit. I guess the next thing you're going to tell me is you want to go to Vietnam to help the poor South Vietnamese people stamp out communism."

Sergeant Wilford had slandered all black people in America, and Private Wood wasn't about to let that pass without letting him know where he stood on the race issue. Regardless of what Sergeant Wilford would do to him afterward, he would have his say.

"Permission to speak, Sergeant," Private Wood asked between clenched teeth.

"Permission granted, but don't take too long. I have to get up early in the morning to kick you trainees in the ass," Sergeant Wilford smiled knowing he had hit a nerve.

"Sergeant Wilford, you're not the first white person I've had to tell me that and I'm sure you won't be the last. For your information, Sergeant, I do want to go to Vietnam and help those people learn the American way of life. And as far as the military's concerned, I'm going to be one of the best damn sergeants to ever wear the uniform. If it means I have to contend with people like you, so be it. I have made up my mind I'm going to be the best damn soldier, black or white, this Army has ever seen. I don't give a damn if I'm hated by every other soldier in the whole damn Army." Private Wood said no longer caring if he was put in the shit house for the remainder of the time he had left at Fort Bragg. Nor did he care if Sergeant Wilford was offended by his bold stance.

All Sergeant Wilford said was, "I will see you at 0400 hours in the morning. Be here or your black ass is mine. Now get out of here before I do something bad to you," he said, redder than Private Wood had ever seen a white person get.

After leaving the Orderly Room, Private Wood felt he had encountered the first enemy of his military career and won. It was unfortunate this particular enemy wore the same uniform as himself. He was looking forward to engaging the enemy in Vietnam because they wore a different uniform and lived by a different set of rules. Unfortunately, the racist enemy from his own country would be the only enemy he would encounter during his military career.

The run-in with Sergeant Wilford awakened his memory of

a similar incident back in his hometown. He was going through the checkout line at Mr. Grimes' corner store when Mr. Grimes had asked, "Are you ready for the infantry, Bob?"

"I'm not going into the infantry, Mr. Grimes. I want to get into a field that is directly related to the civilian job market, such as a military policeman or heavy equipment operator. Anything along that line," Bob answered.

"Don't get your hopes too high, boy; everyone knows black soldiers aren't mentally competent enough to take on such jobs. No, boy, you stick with what you people know best. Fighting."

Bob had been pissed to no end. "You know something, Mr. Grimes, you may be right. I'll need all the Infantry training I can get so when the race war starts here in America, I'll know what I'm doing. God knows there's a lot of you white people we have to kill. Maybe the Black Panthers will want me to train them in the art of war," Bob said. He picked up his groceries and walked out. Bob got no more advice from Mr. Grimes. Mr. Grimes did however tell Bob's daddy about the incident.

His daddy laughed and said, 'Maybe he'll keep his big mouth shut from now on. No one asked for his opinion in the first place."

Private Wood knew he would be asked a million questions upon his return to the barracks, so he was ready with all the answers. They met him at the door wanting to know what had happened to him at the orderly room. No, Sergeant Wilford did not kick his ass. Yes, he got his ass chewed. All he had to do was sweep and mop the floor. He had to report to Sergeant Wilford at 0400 hours in the morning. No, he wasn't going AWOL. No, he wasn't afraid Sergeant Wilford had it in for him. Tiring of all the questions, he put an end to them by saying, "I don't care what Sergeant Wilford, or anyone else says or does. I'm going to be one of the best soldiers Fort Bragg has ever seen. So if you guys don't mind, I'm going to bed. I have to get up early in the morning or daddy Wilford is going to spank my pretty black behind for being late."

Private Wood was a busy young man for the next three days at the reception station. He was put on every shit detail that came up. He did everything he was told to do with a smile on his face. Sergeant Wilford knew he was wasting his time trying to make Private Wood mad, but he still screwed with him every chance he got anyway. Sergeant Wilford, for reasons unknown, never raised the race issue again.

From the reception station they were loaded onto cattle cars, eighteen-wheelers with holes in the sides, and transported to their basic combat training unit, Company C, 5th Battalion, 1st Combat Training Brigade. They were unloaded and divided into four platoons. Private Wood was a member of the 1st platoon, 2nd squad, spot #17. The drill instructors responsible for training them for duty in Vietnam were Drill Sergeant David McCoy and Drill Sergeant Drew Morgan. Staff Sergeant McCoy was the senior drill instructor, so Private Wood had very little dealing with Drill Sergeant Morgan. Their indoctrination into the Infantry philosophy of kill the Viet Cong started the minute they stepped off the cattle trucks.

"Alright, you dumb fucking trainees, lissen up," Staff Sergeant McCoy began. "I have only eight weeks to prepare you fucking people for duty in Vietnam. And I'll be god-damned if I'm going to send a bunch of dummies over there to get themselves killed or to embarrass the United States Army. So you fucking shit heads had better pay attention to what we have to

PATRIOTISM

teach you, because if you don't, Charlie is going to get your ass. So if I have to open up your dumb ass heads and pour this training into it, you will learn and you will learn it well. I'm going to give you sons of bitches five minutes to go into that first barracks, to your immediate rear, find yourselves a bunk and wall locker, secure your belongings inside those lockers and have your asses back out here in the same spot you're standing in right now. Are there any questions before I fall you out?" There were none, so they were given the command to fall out. As always since his encounter with Sergeant Wilford, Private Wood was the first one to complete the task given. Sergeant Wilford had told Sergeant McCoy and Sergeant Morgan, in the gaining command, that Private Wood was bad news and they had better keep an eye on him. He said Private Wood's super soldier bullshit rhetoric was not to be believed.

"You must be Private Bob Wood, the super soldier," Drill Sergeant McCoy said more to himself than to Private Wood upon his return to the formation area.

"Yes, Drill Sergeant," he answered as loud as his diaphragm would allow.

"So you want to be the best damn soldier the Army has to offer, huh? Okay, you silly fucking patriot. You're the platoon sergeant for the first platoon. Whenever they fuck up, that means you fucked up. Therefore, if anyone within your platoon gets dropped for any reason, you'll have to drop right along with him. Do you think you are man enough to handle the job?"

Private Wood stared Drill Sergeant McCoy straight in the face and said, "If I can't handle the job, Drill Sergeant, no one can." So, on that note his basic combat training began.

Private Wood had to put in some long hours, but he never

complained. He was constantly put on the spot because someone in his platoon was always screwing up. After the first couple of weeks passed, he could tell his drill instructors were becoming more and more confident in his ability to lead his troops. The mental abuse and physical training never ceased, but he knew it was for their own good and he had to constantly remind his fellow trainees of that. They were like sponges, soaking up all the knowledge the drill sergeants had to offer. Both drill instructors had served in Vietnam, so they were teaching from experience, not from an Army manual, which they pointed out at every opportunity. Private Wood and his fellow trainees were constantly reminded, after screwing up somewhere, that without a doubt if they made the same mistake in Vietnam, they would be very dead. This made them try harder to get it right the next time.

As their training cycle came closer and closer to its end, they all wondered where they would be going after graduation. They had been told they would be reassigned to another post for Advanced Individual Training (A.I.T.) to obtain their Military Occupational Skill (MOS) and to further prepare them for Vietnam. The day before graduation, early that morning before formation was held, Private Wood was told to report to Drill Sergeant McCoy ASAP. Usually that meant someone in his platoon had messed up and he was about to get his butt chewed. But this time he was in for the biggest surprise of his short military career. He double-timed over to Drill Sergeant McCoy's office and reported.

"Private Wood, you're one of the best damn recruits I have ever had the pleasure to train. There is no doubt in my mind you can go to Vietnam and not only survive, but be the closest

PATRIOTISM

thing to an American fucking hero I have seen since the war began, because you pay attention to details and learn from your mistakes. No matter what you were made to do because of someone in your platoon screwing up, you never complained. And you always set the example you wanted your men to follow, even though you knew it would make you unpopular with some of the soldiers in your platoon. Because of those leadership qualities, you've been promoted to Private E-2 under the military's accelerated promotion system. Here are your stripes. I want them sewn on prior to graduation tomorrow. Congratulations to you, trainee," he said, extending his hand.

Private Wood grabbed both the stripes and Drill Sergeant McCoy's hand at the same time. "Thank you very much, Drill Sergeant." It was the first time he had been talked to as a fellow soldier instead of a dumb ass trainee since his arrival at Fort Bragg. He didn't know whether to thank Drill Sergeant McCoy again or leave his office.

Private Wood was standing there staring at the stripes he held in his hands when he heard the far away voice of Drill Sergeant McCoy. "What the fuck are you standing around here looking stupid for? Get the hell out of my office. I don't have time to sit around here watching you gloat. I want to see the other three trainees you recommended for promotion, one at a time. Now get the hell out of my office."

After leaving Drill Sergeant McCoy's office, Private Wood ran back to the barracks to show off his brand new stripes. All the members of his platoon congratulated him and swore he deserved nothing less than Private First Class. In his excitement he temporarily forgot he was to send the other three soldiers he had recommended for promotion to see Sergeant McCoy. At the time Private Wood had been told to submit the names of the three best soldiers in his platoon for consideration for promotion, he thought it was just a formality all acting platoon sergeants had to go through. Naturally he submitted the names of three of his squad leaders. Now that he had been promoted, it was a real possibility his three choices would also be promoted. He didn't dare tell them in front of the whole platoon who they were and why he chose those three over them.

Throughout the day, while tightening up loose ends before graduation, trainees from all four platoons reported to their respective Drill Sergeants to be promoted. All the acting platoon sergeants were promoted first, then the three guys recommended by each of the acting platoon sergeants. Private Wood hoped Drill Sergeant McCoy had not told them he was the one who had recommended them for promotion, although he felt they deserved it as much as himself. In all honesty, he had made it known to Drill Sergeant McCoy that he felt everyone within the platoon should be promoted just for making it through basic training. They had all worked so hard to make their platoon the best they possibly could. But Private Wood was not to get off the hook that easy.

Private Ronald Hobbs, the first one he sent to see Drill Sergeant McCoy, upon his return to the barracks let the cat out of the bag. "Hey, Wood, thanks for recommending me for promotion. Drill Sergeant McCoy told me all about it. Who are the other two guys you recommended for promotion?"

Questions flew at him from all directions. He held up his hand for silence. After the questions died down, he explained. "Drill Sergeant McCoy instructed me to submit a list of individuals, three to be exact, from within the platoon I felt deserved a promotion more than the rest. I told him I felt we should all be promoted for completing this hard-ass course, but we are in the Army, and we do things the Army's way whether we like it or not. Therefore, since there were only three sets of stripes to be given out, I chose Hobbs, Simms, and Gregory. I felt it was only fair since they have been my squad leaders since we got here."

"What the fuck about me, Wood?" Matthew Allen growled. "I was one of your fucking squad leaders too you know."

"Yeah, but you kept my ass in more hot water than you kept me out of. So I didn't recommend you."

Private Wood's answer pissed Allen off. "You want to know something Wood. I hope we end up in Vietnam together motherfucker. You'll never recommend anyone else for anything," Allen growled.

"Allen, you might as well shut the fuck up because you don't scare anybody. Just in case you have forgotten, let me remind you. If not for me, you wouldn't even have qualified with your M-16. Who would you say stands the better chance of getting who?" Private Wood asked. Allen started to say something but Private Wood held up his hand and said, "One more word out of you and you can take your complaint to Drill Sergeant McCoy." Allen retreated but was grumbling the whole time.

Having to tell his colleagues he'd chosen others within the platoon over them left a sour taste in Private Wood's mouth. Of the three he had recommended, only one was Black. And that was why Allen was so pissed off. It gave the appearance Private Wood preferred his fellow white soldiers instead of his own people. But it didn't really bother Private Wood because he had learned from his daddy you don't base your feeling on the merits of a man's skin, but by the merits of the man.

Graduation day was a day to behold. Like himself, the young men who'd been fortunate enough to get promoted walked around with their chests stuck out as if they were the most important soldiers in the Army, possibly the whole world. They were strutting around like prized peacocks on a farm. After the ceremony they were marched back to their company area to receive their orders and new duty assignments.

"Private Bob Wood, 95B, Military Police, Fort Gordon, Georgia."

Private Wood heart skipped a beat. His spirit sank to the lowest depth of his short military career. Although he had told everyone back home he would try to be anything other than an infantryman that was now what he wanted to be, because all of his television heroes had been infantrymen. The first chance he got he would let Drill Sergeant McCoy know. Maybe he could help him get his orders changed. There was nothing he wanted more than to be an infantryman. He didn't want to be a damned military policeman.

When Private Wood finally got the chance to ask Drill Sergeant McCoy why he had been chosen to be an MP, Drill Sergeant McCoy joked, "I guess it's because you're big and ugly. Also, they must think you'll make a good MP." When Private Wood continued to insist he wanted to be in the infantry, Drill Sergeant McCoy became agitated. "Look at it this way, Private. As a military policeman you'll have the most difficult job any person in the military can have. They play one of the biggest roles in the military, both during war and peacetime. You'll get your chance to win all the medals you want and then some, if that is what you're belly aching about."

PATRIOTISM

Private Wood wasn't happy about being chosen to be an MP, but Drill Sergeant McCoy's assurance he would still get his chance to win some medals made him feel a little better. Private Wood also realized Drill Sergeant McCoy was just saying what he wanted to hear to get him off of his back. He made up his mind to pursue the matter once he got to Fort Gordon, Georgia.

As Bob had promised before he left home, Private Wood had written both his momma and Gina almost every day and called collect at least once a week. They were so proud of him for getting promoted so quickly. They were even happier that he wasn't going to be an Infantryman. The only disappointment was that he did not get to go home and show off his hard earned stripe before going on to Fort Gordon, Georgia.

Saying good-bye to the guys he'd come to know so well was almost like saying good-bye to his family. We'll get together in Vietnam in a couple of months or so, they promised each other, knowing full well they would probably never see each other again.

At 1535 hours, Friday, 27 August 1970, Private Wood was on his way, on a chartered bus to Fort Gordon, GA for Advanced Individual Training (A.I.T.). During the trip he kept trying to convince himself Drill Sergeant McCoy was right about the military police playing a major role in the war in Vietnam, but it was a losing cause. The closer he got to Fort Gordon, the more depressed he became. There were thirty-six guys on the bus with him and not one was from his platoon. The only thing he'd ever heard about the military police in Vietnam was they rode around in their jeeps behind enemy lines and screwed with the real fighting men when they got a chance for a little R & R from beating the bush, or they played nursemaid to every VIP that came to the country to fuck off for a few days. He convinced himself there was no way he could win medals in the war guarding embassy's, fence lines and VIPs. He would do his best to get put out of the military police corps and into the infantry where he felt he belonged.

The trip from Fort Bragg, N.C. to Fort Gordon, GA was short because he had fallen asleep while trying to figure out what he could tell his commander at Fort Gordon that would enable him to be transferred over to the infantry. Private Wood hadn't realized how tired he was. The last thing he remembered was thinking how nice it was going to be not having a drill sergeant breathing down his neck at every turn. But as he had been told once before, boy was he in for a rude awakening. When they pulled into the company area, the first thing he saw was a Smokey-the-Bear hat, which could only mean one thing. A.I.T. had its share of drill sergeants too.

Chapter 3
A.I.T.

They hadn't been off the bus ten minutes when a Drill Sergeant Wilson said, "I need five volunteers for a special mission." No one volunteered because they knew from Basic Training it meant he needed someone for a work detail. So Drill Sergeant Wilson picked five people at random. Private Wood happened to be one of the five he picked for that special mission, KP (kitchen personnel) duty, something he never had to do while in basic but was very familiar with. This only added to his growing depression. He had planned on getting settled in as soon as possible so he could think things out. Maybe he'd even get a chance to talk to someone about getting out of the military police corps. Now it would be nine or ten o'clock that night before he got out of the mess hall. They double-timed over to the mess hall where a big, fat, sloppy looking mess sergeant was waiting for them.

Private Wood was the only black among the five Army-style volunteers, but he didn't think that mattered, that is until the mess sergeant said, "You black privates make damn good dishwashers, because you're used to it. So you, Private Wood, are my pots and pans man."

Private Wood was instantly pissed off because of the remark. "Permission to speak, Sergeant," he requested.

"Permission granted. But don't take up too much of my time, trainee. I don't have much time to listen to a lot of bellyaching."

"Sergeant, do you actually mean the only reason you picked me to wash dishes is because I'm Black?" Private Wood asked.

"You let me tell you something, you fucking puke. Don't ever question my reason for doing anything ever again, you understand? You sound like a fucking trouble maker." The cook said as if he had a reason to be mad.

"Yes, Sergeant," Private Wood answered, feeling the whole world was against him because he wanted to be an infantryman and do his part to help win the war in Vietnam.

It was amazing how in just a few short hours he had gone from being an outstanding trainee to a fucking troublemaker. It was almost too much for his young mind to comprehend. For the first time since he'd been in the Army, there were tears in his eyes that were not caused by homesickness. It took all the will power he could muster to keep from crying and saying to hell with trying to be patriotic. While bending over the hot, soapy water, washing pot after pot, pan after pan, the DJ in downtown Augusta played the record "Nine Pound Steel" sung by Joe Simon. It was one of his favorite songs, but for the first time he understood what it meant.

> "I never see the morning sun,
> I'm here because of the wrong I done
> This old jail is so cold.
> I need your love more and more."

After the song finished playing, Private Wood realized he didn't have it so bad after all. Immediately he felt much better. At least he was not in prison. Therefore, the fat, overweight slob could only screw with him at the most for eight weeks, and he would be gone to Vietnam to win his medals. Private Wood planned on somehow convincing his drill sergeant he should be put in a leadership position if he didn't get the transfer he was hoping for, be it platoon leader or squad leader, it didn't really matter. He had enjoyed the leadership role he'd played as platoon sergeant while in basic training. And if possible, he would continue serving in leadership roles until he sewed on his real sergeant stripes. But it wasn't to be. They had already chosen the acting platoon leader and squad leaders while he was on KP. He was disappointed at not being in a leadership position, but he wouldn't let that dampen his newfound spirit.

Private Wood's mind switched from thinking about leadership positions to whomever he had to talk to, to get reclassified. He would explain to whomever he talked to that he was not unhappy because of Fort Gordon, or the military wanting him to be an MP, he just felt he did not belong at the Military Police School because what he really wanted was to be an infantryman. He spent Sunday trying to think of some good reasons why he should not be an MP. The only two things he could think of were he did not want to be an MP, and MPs didn't win enough medals or do enough to help win the war. Now all he had to do was convince someone he was serious, regardless of how weak his reasons were.

During the initial in processing into the company at Fort Gordon, Private Wood ask one of the clerks what he had to do to request to be transferred to the infantry. He was told he had to get his drill instructor to set up an appointment for him to talk to the commander. He was assured that it was no big deal because new recruits were shipped out to infantry units all the time.

The following Monday during a ten-minute break after being issued field gear for playing war games later on, Private Wood got his chance to let his feelings be known to someone other than his fellow trainees. Drill Sergeant Wilson was standing alone under one of the shade trees a short distance from the building where they were gathered. He approached with confidence. The drill sergeants in AIT were nowhere near as vicious as the ones in basic training.

"Drill Sergeant Wilson, could I talk to you a minute, please?" Private Wood asked.

"Sure, trainee, what's on your mind?"

"Well, I don't want to piss anybody off, but I feel they put me in the wrong MOS and I want out. Although I was drafted, I came into the Army with the intention of helping to win the war in Vietnam. I feel being a military policeman won't allow me that opportunity," he explained.

"Correct me if I'm wrong, trainee. You want out of the Military Police Corps and into combat arms, the infantry or maybe artillery. Then you want to go to Vietnam and kick Charlie's ass single-handedly. Right?" Drill Sergeant Wilson asked, looking at him as if to say I've heard all this bullshit before.

"Yes, Drill Sergeant, to a certain extent." Private Wood was beginning to think he had made a mistake in talking to Drill Sergeant Wilson.

"Let me give you some advice, dumb shit. At least fifty percent of all the casualties in Vietnam are minorities. Whether they are there by choice is not the point. What I'm trying to get across to you is they don't need any more black heroes getting their asses shot off in Vietnam. Stay in the Military Police

Corp, they need bright young men like yourself. Then maybe some of the injustices being done to the black soldiers in the military will cease."

What Drill Sergeant Wilson said made a lot of sense, but he still wanted to talk to the commander before giving up on the idea of becoming an infantryman.

"Drill Sergeant Wilson, I appreciate what you're telling me, but I would like to talk to the commander before I get too far into the cycle. I would like to hear what he has to say," Private Wood was bold enough to say.

"Let me ask you a question, private. Would you rather be in a position where you can help your fellow black soldiers, or black people as a whole, and be viewed in a positive light, or do you want black soldiers to continue to be viewed as nothing but hired killers?" Drill Sergeant Wilson asked.

"I would rather be in a position to help my fellow black soldiers and be viewed in a positive light. You make it sound like fighting for America's way of life is not a positive thing," Private Wood said.

"Do you really think the guys in Vietnam are fighting for America's way of life? Give me a break. The majority of them are draftees that want no part of this war. Others were given a choice of going to jail or joining the military. They're nothing more than expendable equipment that will be of no use to anyone when they get home. A lot of those soldiers, black and white, are going to end up on the streets hooked on that shit they're shooting in their veins over there to cope with the possibility that they may never make it home alive. Is that what you want? As an MP you will be provided the opportunity to get a job with a police department anywhere in America when you get out of the military, which would allow you to continue to help your people. So as I see it private, you have to choose whether you want to be cannon fodder, a bullet catcher, or have a genuine chance to make a difference for your fellow black soldiers. I say you should take this opportunity to show the world that black soldiers are just as intelligent as white soldiers. The Military Police Corp will give you that opportunity," Drill Sergeant Wilson argued.

"Why is that important to you, Sergeant Wilson? You're the first white person since I've been in the army I've heard say anything about it being important that black soldiers show a positive image to the world. Why is that?" Private Wood asked.

"I had a black friend in the Nam from Mississippi. He put himself in harm's way for the rest of us in the platoon every day we were patrolling the bush. We knew he was one of the best soldiers to ever wear the uniform, but the world didn't because he was out of sight, out of mind in the jungle of Vietnam. One morning, about a week before he was schedule to leave the country, he asked me to do him a favor. The favor he wanted from me was to tell white people in America that black soldiers in Vietnam were dying to better the lives of their black families, because America doesn't care about them. However, if in the process what they accomplished on the battlefield helps white America, so be it.

He told me I was the first white person who had ever treated him as a human being, and he wanted me to know he appreciated it. We did everything together. They called us salt and pepper. That night Charlie threw a grenade inside our tent and he jumped on it and saved the lives of about twelve guys, myself included. When our platoon leader submitted his name for the

Congressional Medal of Honor, I went with him to the orderly room back at headquarters. While waiting in the orderly room I overheard the white unit commander tell the Lieutenant niggers weren't worth the paperwork. Fighting for America's way of life, are you sure you want things to remain as it is? Don't risk your life for anything unless you're going to get something in return," Drill Sergeant Wilson said, shaking his head remembering his friend.

Private Wood felt Sergeant Wilson's pain, but he was determined to make a name for himself on the battlefield. "Sergeant Wilson, I appreciate what you're saying but I think every man has to follow his own destiny. I feel mine is on the battlefield," he said.

"I'll see if I can arrange for you to talk to the commander in the next couple of days," Drill Sergeant Wilson said and walked off.

For the next couple of the days, Private Wood could not concentrate on what he was supposed to be doing. Instead, his mind kept going back to the conversation he'd had with David Cooper en route to the induction station in Memphis. He stated almost the same casualty percentage as Drill Sergeant Wilson, minus including other minorities. Plus the story Drill Sergeant Wilson told him made him rethink his position about the war.

Damn, is there a possibility David was right about too many of us being sent over there to fight the war? That we should get office jobs and let the White soldiers fight the war for a change? Damn you, Sergeant Wilson. I had everything all figured out. I was going to get out of the Military Police Corps somehow, get into the infantry, win some medals, and do whatever else it took to help win this stinking, fucking war. And then I had to screw around and ask you for advice. Well, I don't care what you, or that coward, David, says. I want to be able to set my grandkids on my lap and tell them how I did my part to help win the war in Vietnam. And when they ask to see my medals, I will be able to show them. How the hell am I going to win these medals if I'm not involved in the fighting? Private Wood figured all of his friends back home would be disappointed if he was not the first real life hero Lakeview, Arkansas had ever seen in the flesh.

Drill Sergeant Wilson saw the potential of Private Wood becoming a first rate soldier. He didn't want him to waste his intelligence beating the bush if he didn't have to. So when he set up Private Wood's appointment with the commander, his suggestion was that they try and change his mind about going into the infantry. Drill Sergeant Wilson was not ignorant of the fact that Captain White didn't particularly care for black soldiers, but he liked to consider himself a fair man, so he took the advice of his Noncommissioned Officers seriously.

Drill Sergeant Wilson said, "Sir, I have a bright young black private in my platoon that think he want to become an infantryman. I think he can better serve the military as an MP."

"What makes you think that sergeant?" Captain White asked.

"I think he would be the type of black kid that will set the example we want other black soldiers to follow. He's gung-ho, but in the 'do right' patriotic sense," Drill Sergeant Wilson said.

"Patriotic. Huh? You don't see many patriotic draftees these days. Okay Sergeant Wilson, I'll see what I can do," Captain White said.

Captain White wasn't in the dark when it came to Sergeant Wilson wanting black soldiers to get fair treatment from the command. He had also heard the story about his black friend jumping on the grenade to save his life. For the sake of Sergeant Wilson he would try and keep Private Wood in the command, but he wouldn't go out of his way to do so.

Private Wood's appointment with the commander was set for 1900 hours several days later. He felt this was his last chance to get out of the MP Corps, although he was no longer one hundred percent sure if that was what he really wanted anymore. He arrived at the orderly room ten minutes early as instructed. He was shown how to report to the commander. Private Wood wanted to tell them he already knew how to report to a commander, but he didn't want to make waves. So he pretended to follow their instructions. After his block of instruction on how to report to the commander was completed, Private Wood was told to report to the commander. He knocked on the door and waited to be invited in.

"Come in, trainee," Private Wood heard Captain White say. He entered and reported as instructed and was told to have a seat. "Now why don't we get straight to the point, trainee. I have talked to Drill Sergeant Wilson about you and he feels you have the potential to be a damn good MP. So why do you want out?" he smiled.

"Well, sir, it's like I told Drill Sergeant Wilson. I think I could better serve my country by being where the action is and being part of that action," Private Wood said.

"Do you really expect me to believe that patriotic bullshit you're saying?" Captain White asked, but did not give him a chance to answer. "The Military Police have one of the most important jobs in the Army during both war and peace time. Plus, if you decide to get out after your two-year hitch is up, you can get a job with almost any police department in the United States. Most privates like you who request to go to Vietnam are already killers at heart and see the war as an opportunity to kill some people and not go to jail for it. Are you one of those types, trainee?"

"No, sir, I'm not," Private Wood answered, trying to conceal the anger building up inside of him. Again he was made to feel there is no place left in America for a patriot, not even in the damn Army. It took all the control he could muster to continue without pissing the commander off, intentionally anyway. "Sir, I cannot make you believe anything you don't want to believe. I came in here, sir, with the intentions of basing my decision on the advice you would give me," he said between clenched teeth.

"And what decision have you reached?" Captain White asked.

"If this is the type of attitude I'm to encounter from my superiors for the next two years, sir, I want out of the army period. I don't think I'm capable of adjusting to the army," Private Wood answered, expecting to get thrown out on his ears.

"What's your name again, trainee?" the captain asked, the tone of his voice changing dramatically.

"Private Bob Wood, sir."

"I'm very impressed with you, Private Wood. I like a young man who knows what he wants to do with his life and is not afraid to let people know when they are interfering with those plans. We need smart young men like you in the corps to help improve our image. There is no doubt in my mind that whatever field you eventually end up in, you'll perform your duties to the best of your ability at all times. I apologize for placing you in the same category of a dumb trainee who doesn't know what he really wants. Also, I apologize for labeling you as a born killer. It would be a pleasure to say as your commander, 'Yes, sir, I had the privilege of training that fine young soldier,' he said, changing tactics. "There is no doubt in my mind that if you continue on the present trend, you will go a long way in this man's army. Well, have I helped you choose the field you want to go into?"

"Not completely, sir. But if you answer my last question, it'll make my decision easier," Private Wood said ignoring the sugar coated bullshit.

"Shoot, hit me where it hurts," he said, leaning forward in his chair.

"Sir, I know the military police in Vietnam guard embassies, perimeter fences, deal with POWs, and perform basic law enforcement missions, but what is the role of the military police in the bush?"

Captain White thought for a while before answering. "If you're asking me whether the military police go out into the jungle and beat the bush, the answer is no. Where we, the military police, earn the majority of our medals and casualties is from running convoys behind enemy lines and guarding the rear flanks. I know it's not what you want to hear, but that's it in a nut shell." After he finished speaking, he searched Private Wood's face for some type of reaction, but Private Wood's face remained blank. When he said nothing, the Captain added, "One thing I can promise you, unlike the infantry, long after the war is over, there'll still be a lot of people depending on you for their safety. And for some, even their lives will be in your hands. Take it for what it's worth. Are there any more questions?"

"Yes, sir, just one. Can I talk to you again about this?"

"Sure, just go through Drill Sergeant Wilson and I'll see you tomorrow," the Captain promised.

Private Wood came to the position of attention in front of the Captain's desk, saluted, did an about face, and walked out of the office thinking the good captain thought he was a damn fool who could easily be persuaded to do anything he was told as long as he used sugar coated bullshit.

When Private Wood walked out of the captain's office, Drill Sergeant Wilson said, "Black soldiers need you in law enforcement, private."

After Private Wood left the orderly room, Captain White call Drill Sergeant Wilson into his office and asked, "Do you believe that shit? That black ass private sounds whiter than I do. What do you think about him sergeant? Should we try to keep him in the Corp, or ship him off to Fort Benning to become an infantryman that will probably be sent to Vietnam to get his ass blown off?"

"I think he'll be a hell of a soldier sir. He's intelligent as hell for a black soldier. We might be able to use him to help control some of these racial problems the military are having around the world right now," Drill Sergeant Wilson suggested.

"You mean as a mediator between white and black soldiers?" Captain White asked.

"Yes, sir. He seems to be a good communicator," Drill Sergeant Wilson agreed.

"Ok, we'll keep him in the Military Police Corp. Leave it up to me to convince him it's for the sake of his people that he remains an MP," the Captain said, dismissing Drill Sergeant Wilson.

Private Wood laid awake most of the night trying to convince himself that it didn't matter if he was a military policeman; he would not be able to stop any of the injustices being committed against his Black brothers, as Drill Sergeant Wilson had suggested. But every time he would think the infantry was the only way to go, he would think about what Captain White and Drill Sergeant Wilson both said about long after the war was over, people's lives would still be in his hands if he chose to make the army a career. The more he thought about it, the more he started to believe that maybe he would be able to correct some of the injustices being committed against his Black brothers if he became an MP. He liked the sound of that. And last but no way least, he'd been assured that even if he was not in the infantry, the possibility of his winning medals in Vietnam was still good. At the end of the second meeting with Captain White, his mind was made up. He would be the best damn military policeman the Army ever produced. With his head on straight and again pointed in the right direction, he was back to being his old hard working, dedicated self again.

 Private Wood took solace in the fact that being an MP would make it easier to get into law enforcement if he decided that was what he wanted to do if he got out of the army at the end of his draft commitment in two years. His family was thrilled to death that there was going to be a cop in the family and that he was not going to be a regular bush beater. Little Harvey didn't care what he was, as long as he killed some of them VC's. Gina said it was the best news she'd heard since he'd been in the army. Now instead of picturing himself running through the jungle wasting Charlie, he would be leading convoys deep behind enemy lines. And after the war was over, he would be involved in high-speed chases and shootouts. As before, he could picture himself getting wounded, but never killed. His favorite fantasy was where he would capture the most wanted man in the history of the United States. His picture would be in all the major newspapers in the country. That would make his family and Gina so proud of him. He would receive the key to whatever city he happened to accomplish this feat in. It would also give him a chance to show off the medals he won while running convoys and route recon patrols behind enemy lines in Vietnam.

Because he was so articulate when it came to his training, and he wouldn't be satisfied unless everything was as close as possible to being perfect, he had very little time for a social life. It seemed to everyone that other than taking the time to go to the gym on weekends, he was a hermit. In basic training he was kept busy because someone in his platoon was always screwing up. Now that he didn't have that responsibility, he kept himself busy by reading paperback novels, his MP training manuals, Army Regulations and Field Manuals he got from Drill Sergeant Wilson.

After the fourth week of training they were allowed to stay out overnight on weekends. He enjoyed the peace and quiet when there were only three or four guys in the barracks beside himself. He would lie there and fantasize about what it was going to be like when he got home standing tall and proud. He could hardly wait to see the look on his parent's faces when they saw him standing there at the door looking like the true life Sergeant Rock, although he only had one stripe. After the hugging and kissing and how-have-you-been was over, he would then get caught up on the latest gutter gossip about the gutter people he ran around with from his daddy. His next stop would be to say, 'Hello, Gina, daddy is back in town.' Boy that was going to be a day to remember. He always smiled when he thought of trying to explain to little Harvey why he had not killed any of them VC's yet.

Everything was going as Private Wood had planned until the sixth week of training. He received some disturbing news from Gina. She said her mother was trying to get her to join a Job Corps Center somewhere in Texas because she was out of school and was not doing anything with her life. If she went, she would be leaving, according to his calculations, four days before he got home. He called Gina the same day he got the letter and was reassured she would be waiting patiently for his return home. Satisfied he could continue his fantasies about Gina upon his return home, he returned to training as usual.

With three days left before graduation, Private Wood felt on top of the world. He was sure he would be promoted to Private First Class upon graduation, because he had volunteered for all the details everyone else had shied away from. The company commander and drill sergeants constantly told him what an outstanding soldier and military policeman he was turning out to be. Private Wood was an expert marksman with the 45 cal. pistol, the M14 and M16 rifles, and at throwing hand grenades. He constantly assisted his fellow soldiers during PT [physical training] runs so they would not fall out of formation. He filled out his military police reports as if they were going to be used in a real court of law. During war games he volunteered to walk the point, or to be the M60 machine gunner, knowing in real combat he would be the enemy's number one target during a firefight in Vietnam. Private Wood also assisted his acting platoon sergeant in correcting their fellow soldiers when they screwed up, as well as helping them when they needed help with the many tasks they were required to complete prior to graduation. As in basic training, the unit leadership was impressed that he completed all given assignments without complaining once. However, he was not promoted, but he took pride in knowing he was graduating at the top of his class.

Private Wood was looking forward to mail call that day, because if his calculations were right, he should be getting letters from his mother and Gina; the last two he would be receiving while stationed at Fort Gordon, Georgia. When the mail clerk called his name that afternoon at mail call, he was overjoyed. *Damn, even right about the mail,* he thought to himself. One of the letters was from Johnny, his high school buddy. Johnny started out by saying his daddy still wouldn't let him join the army although he graduated from high school and was now eighteen. But the real reason he had written was to let him know Gina had joined the Job Corps in Arlington, Texas and would be leaving in two days, which meant she left the day before he received the letter. He threw the letter in his wall locker and ran to the nearest phone booth and called her house.

Mrs. Samson answered the phone. "Hello, this is the Samson residence."

He was so shook up he could hardly speak. "Mrs. Samson, this is Bob. May I speak to Gina please?"

"Didn't she write or call, and tell you? Gina left yesterday for a girl's Job Corps Center someplace in Texas. I forget the name of the place. I'm sorry I had to be the one to tell you the bad news. I tried my best to get her to write and tell you so you wouldn't get too upset," she crooned, trying hard to sound as if it was Gina's idea to join the Job Corps.

"When will she be back?" Bob knew she probably wouldn't

tell him even if she did know, which he knew she did.

"Oh, deary me. I really don't know at this time. I would say at least a year," Mrs. Samson said.

"Well, I hope you're happy, you old bitch," Bob yelled into the phone and hung up. He knew he would have to apologize to her when he got home, but for now he would let the gossipy old bitch fume until he got home. His momma would insist that he did. There was no doubt that Mrs. Samson was sure to tell her what her son had the audacity to call her.

Private Wood called home. Collect of course, to get reassurance from his family that everything was going to be all right. As far as he was concerned at that moment, his leave would only be half as enjoyable as he had expected it to be.

The night before graduation one of the guys snuck off base and brought back a couple of gallons of bootleg whiskey. They took it out behind the barracks and chased it down with coke cola and 3.2 beers. Private Wood got so drunk they had to put him to bed. He drank wine with members of the basketball team, and few 3.2 beers while there at Fort Gordon, but he had never gotten that drunk in his life. The next morning he was sure if he made a sudden move in any direction, his head would fall off. He learned that morning, drinking to forget was very, very stupid.

"Never again will I be that stupid," Private Wood swore to himself as his stomach did a flip-flop, a promise he would make to himself numerous times in the future.

As in basic, after graduation they formed up outside the orderly room to receive their orders and next duty assignment. The orders were handed out in alphabetical order.

"Private Alvin T. Wacer, Vietnam," the sergeant announced.

Since his name was next on the list, Private Wood was sure he would be getting orders for Vietnam also.

Private Wood said to Wacer, "I guess I'll be seeing you in Vietnam because I'm next on the list."

"Don't be stupid, Wood. You had better hope you get sent someplace else," Wacer cautioned.

Private Wood couldn't believe his ears as the sergeant read his orders. "Private Bob Wood, 199th Replacement Company, Yongsan, Korea."

Private Wood was in a daze as he went up to receive his copies of the orders. He read them again and again. There had to be a mistake. He had made it very clear he wanted to go to Vietnam. After everyone had received their orders and were on their way to the barracks to grab suitcases and AWOL bags to go home, Private Wood stayed back to ask his First Sergeant if there was any way he could get his orders changed to Vietnam. The First Sergeant told him there was nothing they could do. He would have to wait until he got to Korea to get his orders changed. Private Wood felt he'd been betrayed.

"God-dammit, three damn strikes against me since I've been in this man's Army," he said aloud, not caring who might hear him. "First they talk me out of fighting them to get into the infantry. Then Gina's bitchy-fide old mother ran her off to a Job Corps Center someplace in Texas, and now to top it off, they are shipping my ass off to Korea." It was enough to make a grown man cry. He would definitely pursue this matter upon his arrival in Korea. The only good news he received was that he would be home for three whole weeks before leaving for Korea.

Private Wood had made reservations for a flight to Memphis, Tennessee, the previous night before going drinking with the

PATRIOTISM

guys out behind the barracks. From Memphis he would catch a Trailways Silver Eagle bus home. Johnny was to pick him up at the bus station in Helena.

It was approximately 8:45 P.M. when he stepped off the bus. Johnny was standing there waiting for him. Man what a sight for sore eyes. They hugged like lost lovers.

Chapter 4
HOME AGAIN

"Hey, hey, hey, look at the bad soldier boy. Man, you look great. These girls are going to cream in their pants just looking at you in that uniform," Johnny exclaimed, admiring how well Bob looked in his green class A uniform. "So where do you go from here?" Johnny asked.

"The first thing I'm going to do is go home to see the family and see what Momma cooked for supper. I haven't had a decent meal since I've been in the army," Bob informed his friend.

"What kind food do they serve yall?" Johnny asked.

"Man, I've never had potatoes in so many ways. They feed us baked potatoes, mashed potatoes, hash brown potatoes, French fried potatoes, chive potatoes, and steamed potatoes. They must have gotten their recipes from the Irish people. Then they have this stuff they call cream chip beef on toast that is served every single morning. We soldiers call it SOS, which stands for Shit On a Shingle. It looks like someone jerked off on a dirty plate. But I have to admit, it tastes pretty good," Bob laughed.

"What else? I know that's not all they feed y'all."

"Naw, everything else is standard food like steak, pork chops, chicken, corn, bean, etc., but no soul food. You talk to them white boys about ham hocks, chitlins, and collard greens they act like they never heard of it. Talking about they don't see how anyone can eat that stuff. Half of them white boys are from the south and know damn well they eat the same thing we do. Anyway, you see I'm not starving," Bob said.

"I don't believe you didn't tell your momma and daddy you were coming home today. They're telling everyone you won't be home until tomorrow. I was wondering why you wouldn't be home until Saturday if you graduated from your training Friday morning," Johnny said.

"I told them my unit wouldn't let me leave until Saturday morning because they messed up some of my paperwork. I want to surprise them, okay?"

"Sure, good buddy. I was surprised when you called me." Johnny patted Bob on the back.

"Man, it feels good to be home. It feels like I've been gone forever," Bob said looking around. It seemed the town was smaller somehow.

Johnny wasn't interested in how Bob felt to be back home. He wanted to know when the killing would start. "Since you didn't write to keep me updated on your military plans, when're you going to the Nam to kick some gook ass?" Johnny asked.

"Those jive ass suckers are sending me to Korea, but only for a little while. As soon as I get over there, I'm requesting a transfer to Vietnam. Sergeant Wilson, the drill instructor I had in AIT, talked about how much pussy I'm going to get while I'm stationed in Korea. Hell, from what I hear the bitches in Vietnam have pussies too," Bob informed his friend of his intentions.

"That's my man. Ain't no sense in being a soldier if you can't help win the war," Johnny said getting excited.

"That's what I've been trying to tell the two commanders I've had so far. But they kept acting as if I'm some kill crazy

Black man trying to satisfy an appetite at the expense of the Army," Bob said angrily, remembering how everyone had reacted when told of his desire to help win the war in Vietnam.

"I don't understand what you're saying. You mean they drafted you into the Army but don't want you to fight for your country?" Johnny asked incredulously.

"It seems these White people in America would rather see these White boys burn their draft cards than listen to a brother talk about patriotism," Bob spat the words out, remembering numerous conversations he had with other Black and white trainees in basic and AIT, on the subject of patriotism. "But I tell you one thing, this is one dedicated soldier they won't keep out of the action," Bob swore.

"I hear you, brother. Just make sure you make it to Nam so they can see the Blacks in America are still patriotic even if they ain't," Johnny said getting more and more angry with each word he spoke. "Hell, if it wasn't for my old man, I would've been stepping off the bus with you instead of picking you up."

"Hey, it's not too late. Go ahead and join up and I'll see you in Vietnam in a few months. But screw Vietnam for now. I have some people to surprise. Did you tell anyone you were coming to pick me up?"

"Naw, I told my old man I was going to play basketball at the school."

"I knew I could depend on you, good buddy. Let's go. I can't wait to see the family."

After pulling away from the bus station, Bob could tell there was something Johnny wanted to tell him but didn't quite know how to go about it. Bob also knew he'd get around to telling him whatever it was he wanted him to know. It was amazing how after a four-month absence and a ton of bullshit, they were still on the same wavelength.

"Gina asked me to tell you something for her before she left," he began after they were a mile or so down the road. "That's if you want to hear it," he said cautiously.

"Sure, why not? I know she didn't want to leave before I came home. Boy, that mother of hers is a real bitch," Bob said, not expecting the bomb Johnny was about to lay on him.

"I hate to throw a wrench into that smooth running confidence of yours, but it was Gina's idea to go to the Job Corps," Johnny informed him.

Bob didn't want to believe what he had heard, but he was positive his good friend wouldn't joke about a thing like that. As much as he hated the thought, he could not help but think Johnny had made a pass at Gina and she had turned him down and told him to fuck off. And this was his way of getting back at her. Since he very seldom jumped to conclusions without the facts, he would give Johnny the benefit of a doubt to explain what he meant.

"You want to clarify this shit for me, John?" Bob asked with raised eyebrows. The only time he called his friend by the short version of his name was when he was pissed.

Johnny was well aware of this. He answered Bob's question with a question. "What did she tell you?"

"She said her mother was pressuring her to do something with her life. That since they couldn't afford to send her to college, the Job Corps was the next best thing; but no matter what her mother said, she wouldn't leave until I got home. She gave no indication why I shouldn't believe her. I was sure she would be waiting for me when I got home. And I fell for the whole line of bull shit," he said angrily. Bob had tried to keep the anger and pain he felt out of his voice, but he knew he hadn't succeeded by the look on Johnny's face.

"Hmm, I see. I don't know if you want to hear what else I have to tell you. You sound pissed already," Johnny said.

"God-dammit John, don't play games with me man," he hissed, madder than a demon in hell. "I want to know if I was so much in love I was too blind to read between the lines."

"Okay, okay, she said her momma told her what it was going to be like being married to a soldier and she doesn't think she could handle it. There would be too much required of her, especially the waiting for you to come home from Vietnam. Going from day to day not knowing if you are alive or dead. Or you may come home with only one leg, one arm, or maybe a vegetable for the rest of your life. She said even if you did escape injury in Vietnam, you would always be gone some place training. Gina said she felt she would end up raising your kids by herself. She stressed the point that she loves you more than anything in this world, but she said no deal," Johnny finished.

As usual when faced with a situation such as this, Bob didn't want to jump to a final conclusion until he talked to Gina himself. What Johnny had told him made a lot of sense, but he thought she should have told him herself. Hell, he'd been thinking the same thing since basic training. In the past she had never hesitated to let her feelings be known to anyone. Well, no matter what he had to do, he would get Gina's phone number at that Job Corps Center from Mrs. Samson, so Gina could tell him with her own mouth why she didn't want to be his girl. She was probably pissed because he didn't come home after basic training as he'd promised.

"To hell with Gina for now, I have a family to surprise," Bob said more to himself than to Johnny. "Screw her for now," he said, this time directly to Johnny. "I can't wait to see the look on Momma's face when she sees me at the door," Bob put his hurt feelings on hold.

Johnny filled him in on what was happening in the community, but Bob was only half listening. In his mind he could still hear Drill Sergeant McCoy calling cadence. *Ain't no sense in going home; Jody got your girl and gone. Am I right or wrong' you're right. Are we weak or strong? We're strong!* Well, Bob didn't feel strong right then. From a distance he heard Johnny asking if he was all right.

"What you say, Johnny?"

"I asked if you're feeling all right. I've been talking for ten minutes now and you haven't heard a word I said."

"I'm sorry, Johnny, I guess I miss the girl more than I thought."

"I can dig where you're coming from. Did you get a chance to play any basketball these past four months?" Johnny asked.

"Sure, I played a little bit. But most of the time I was too beat to do anything other than perform my duties, take a shower and go to bed."

"It's a good thing you got to play at least a little bit because every brother around here is waiting for you to show up at the court tomorrow. They say now is the time to beat the schoolground super star because the only games you have been playing are war games."

"I'll show them tomorrow how much I have forgotten. When it comes to round ball, I'm still the best around here," Bob assured his friend.

PATRIOTISM

"I'll pick you up around eleven tomorrow morning. All of the guys will be at the school ground waiting for you."

When they pulled into his driveway, Bob could hardly wait to get into the house. He was out of the car before it came to a complete stop.

"They sure are going to be surprised to see you," Johnny winked with a big grin on his face.

"Right on, brother, well here goes nothing." Bob knocked on the door and after what seemed an eternity his momma asked who was there.

"Someone you haven't seen in four months and you missed him very much," he said, giving her a clue.

She picked up on his hint right away. She threw open the door and took him into her arms, all in one motion. "Oh my God. When did you get back?" she asked, still hugging him.

"Hey, you don't think I would go and see someone else before I came home to see my favorite family, did you? I had Johnny pick me up so I could surprise you guys," Bob said.

"Hey, everybody, it's Bob. He's home," his momma announced. "You told me you wouldn't be home until tomorrow," she said.

Everyone was happy to see Bob and have him home again. He'd never been so happy about getting home before in his life. In fact he was so happy he temporarily forgot to be mad at Gina. He loved being the center of attention again after four months of being called a maggot, dumb ass, or a loser. He even received a hug from his daddy, which again surprised him. His daddy was bursting with pride at seeing how well his son looked in uniform.

"My boy, an American fighting man," his daddy said proudly.

Bob could hardly wait to get his daddy alone to talk about Gina. But he knew it would be a while before he got the chance. His daddy would be able to tell him the real reason Gina had dumped him, if she had indeed dumped him.

As expected, the first thing out of little Harvey's mouth was, "You kill any of them VC's yet?"

"No, not yet little buddy. I just finished training. Give me a chance, okay?"

"All right, but don't wait too long or them soldiers will done killed them all," little Harvey cautioned.

After some of the excitement of his surprise homecoming died down, Bob started calling all of his friends to let them know the kid was back in town for a few days. He was looking forward to seeing them out on the court the following day, and the girls on the sideline cheering him on.

Later that night, after everyone was in bed and asleep, Bob couldn't sleep. The excitement of the day and the disappointment of Gina not being there waiting for him caused temporary insomnia. He watched television until it signed off the air. He lay awake thinking of how his life had changed in just four short months, from a high school kid to a trained killer. But he was proud to be a soldier. He thought of what that White dude said a long time ago, "I regret I have but one life to give for my country." However, he would soon be faced with how things are run in the real world. He finally fell asleep around 4 a.m.

The Wood family, as most country families were early risers. Therefore he only got a couple of hours of sleep because little Harvey woke him up at 6:30 a.m., advising him the Army must've made him lazy because he used to get up every morn-

PATRIOTISM

ing no later than 5 a.m., and here it was almost 7 a.m. already.

"Hey big brother, wake up. Wake up man. The army done made you lazy," Harvey said shaking him.

"What you want, little turd?" Bob asked.

"Momma said it's time for you to get up for breakfast. Why you sleepin so late anyway? What time you get up in the army? It cain't be too early the way you sleepin late and all at home," Harvey finished.

"If only you knew kiddo. What's for breakfast?"

"Momma cooked bacon, eggs, toast, orange juice, oatmeal, and brown taters. Man, you should leave home more often. We get the good stuff when you come back," Harvey said.

"Momma and Daddy always feed us good and you know it," Bob said tapping him on the nose.

"Yeah I know. Let's go eat," he said.

After breakfast he laid around on the floor with Ronda and Harvey watching cartoons and horse playing all morning until Johnny stopped by to pick him up.

"Man, from what I heard this morning, everyone who ever picked up a basketball will be at the playground to get a shot at you," Johnny informed him as they were on their way to the school ground.

"Whatever is right," Bob laughed.

As soon as they reached the school ground, before Bob even got out of the car, he was ribbed to no end about how he was going to get slam dunked through the basket because they knew he hadn't had time to play any round ball. And as much saltpeter he had eaten in the past four months, he had to be gay by now.

Bob biggest rival on his high school basketball team was Jimmy

True, aka June Bug. He was also the biggest trash talker to ever enter a gym.

"Looky here, my man, you may as well get your rusty ass out of car cause I'm going to embarrass the hell out you. Since you haven't been on a basketball court in a while I'll take it easy on you for the first six or seven points, and then I'm going to stuff your ass through the hoop." June Bug laughed.

"Shit Bug, you can't beat me on your best day. As a matter of fact, you can't even carry my jock. I'll beat your ass after I've been dead for a couple weeks," Bob countered.

"Man, I let you win those one on one games we played before Uncle Sam drafted your ass. I could've whipped your ass anytime I wanted to. I didn't want to take away your confidence before games," June Bug said.

"My confidence? Negro, please! Lets get it on."

"Hey, I ain't never beat this Negro. The way I figure it I ain't never going to get a better chance. I get him first," Nathan Crawford, aka 'Spoon' said. He got his nickname because he was always eating peanut butter with a spoon.

"Spoon, please. You can't beat yourself one on one," Bob laughed.

"I've been practicing, brother. I'm gon kick your ass," Spoon said.

"I'll tell you what. We play sudden death one on one. First one scores win. Let's see, there's about twelve of y'all, it shouldn't take too long to beat all of y'all. And to make things interesting, each of you get the ball first. I have to give each of you a chance to win," Bob said.

"Man you one crazy SOB, we're gonna kick yo ass," June Bug said taking the basketball from Spoon and stepping onto the courts.

PATRIOTISM

Bob took off his shirt and blew kisses to the girls gathered around the outdoor court. The majority of the girls that had been his classmates came to the playground to watch him play, as he knew they would.

When the girls commented on how well he looked, he said, "The better for you to have and to hold, you beautiful creatures."

No one mentioned Gina. Bob didn't know whether it was because they didn't care she was gone, or they were just sparing him the pain of talking about her, but he was grateful. Because he had to prove himself all over again on the basketball court, he was devastating. Bob made moves he didn't even know he could make. Every time he scored a basket, the girls cheered and clapped. It brought back memories of the past basketball season at Lakeview High where he was chosen the Country Superstar of America by his teammates. The majority of them had been disappointed he hadn't accepted one of the scholarships he was offered, but accepted the fact it was his life and it was up to him what he did with it.

When they left the school ground, he had Johnny take him around the community to say hello to the older neighbors, except for the Samson residence. He had to have a talk with his daddy before he stopped by there. Bob waited until after supper (dinner for people in the Army) before asking his daddy if he could talk to him about something.

His daddy smiled and said, "I was wondering when you would get around to asking me about that gal. Let's go over to Jim's Cafe and talk about this over a beer."

That was the best idea Bob had heard all day. When they got to the café, Bob ordered a beer for himself and a shot of whiskey for his Daddy. Bob waited for his daddy to start the conversation about Gina. As Bob knew all too well, his daddy would say nothing until he was good and ready. His daddy talked about how well the crops were doing, how much he was missed around the farm, and how proud he was of him. Everything except what they had come there for. Bob knew better than to press him before he was ready to talk about her. Finally after what seemed a lifetime, his daddy got around to talking about Gina.

He said, "That gal of yours really do care about you, boy. She knew you wouldn't believe anyone other than myself, so she asked me to tell you how she felt about having to leave before you got back home. The girl really wanted to wait until you got back before she left, but her family, Mrs. Samson mostly, kept pressuring her until she had to choose between satisfying her family's wishes or waiting for you to get home. And you know my feeling when it comes to strong family ties."

"Damn, Daddy, you mean to tell me Mrs. Samson couldn't find it in her cold ass heart to wait three damn days until I came home before shipping Gina off to the wide plains of Texas? Damn old bitch acts as if I was going to try and talk Gina out of going to the Job Corp or something. Hell, I wanted Gina to do something with her life while I'm away. I don't expect her to sit around the house doing nothing for a whole damn year, or however long I'll be gone," Bob said.

That wise old look came into his daddy's face and Bob knew he was in for some realistic advice, the last thing he wanted right then.

"Let me ask you a question, son," he began, ignoring the spew of profanity which escaped Bob's lips. "What if she had gone against her momma's wish and waited on you. Do you realize how much hell Gina would go through after you left? Would that have made you happy, knowing what she was going through and you not being here to lend her your shoulder to cry on?"

"Crap, I get your drift, Daddy. Don't you ever get tired of being right all the time, old man?" Bob asked, toasting his daddy with his beer.

"You don't have to be old to be wise," his daddy assured him. "If you take the time to look at both sides of any situation, more often than not, you'll make the right decision. On the other hand, if you go off half-cocked, well I don't think I have to say anything more on the subject. However, I do want to point out that you have gotten in to a very bad habit of using four letter words when looking for a way to express yourself. Cussing don't make you a man. It's respecting yourself and those around you that make you a man. So before you leave here to go to Korea I want you to apologize to Mr. and Mrs. Samson for calling her a bitch. If you're mad at someone for doing something to you that you don't like, you don't call up someone else and call them out of their name because of it." Bob's daddy went back to sipping his drink, letting Bob complete the rest of the lecture in his mind.

"Yes sir, I will. And I apologize for embarrassing you and momma. I also apologize for the cussing I just finished doing" Bob said.

Bob finished off the rest of his beer and his daddy his shot of whiskey. They had fresh drinks in front of them before either of them spoke again. Bob's daddy broke the silence.

"I know it was a blow to your male ego to tell your woman

to wait for you and she doesn't. But you have to realize the women of today feel they're capable of making decisions without the help of their male counterparts. I've been telling you this shit for a long time now. But no, you keep right on sticking up for this ERA bullshit. Do you still feel the same now that you've gotten a taste of the real world?"

"To tell you the truth, I would like nothing more than to find out where she is and go there and beat the you know what out of her," Bob said.

His daddy took a piece of paper out of his shirt pocket and handed it to him. "Now is your chance to do just that. The same day she reached the Job Corps Center, she called and gave me her address and telephone number to give to you."

Bob read the note to himself, "Arlington Job Corps Center for girls, Dorm #2406 room 214, Arlington, Texas. Telephone number (214) 274-2253. You don't miss a trick, do you?" Bob said, amazed at how his daddy was always able to figure out a way to control every situation faced by his family.

"I figured she owed you that much. So let's forget about that damn woman long enough to get drunk." And on that note they proceeded to get totally blown away, at least Bob did. He made the mistake of trying to match his daddy drink for drink.

Bob's last conscious thought after getting home and going to bed was to call Gina the first chance he got the following day.

An old saying in the farm community was there was no drunk like a bootleg whiskey drunk, but after the drinking bout with his daddy, he wasn't sure if that was true. Bob woke with a headache worse than the one he had experienced while he was in AIT. Only this time not only did he have to deal with the headache, there was also Little Harvey.

"Hey, big brother, how you feeling this morning? Daddy said you got drunk last night. Is that true?" he asked.

Although Harvey had spoken in a normal little boy's tone, to Bob it sounded as if he had shouted at the top of his lungs. "Dammit little turd, do you have to shout?" he asked too loud.

A pained look came into his little brother's eyes and he looked as if he was about to cry.

Bob took the little fellow into his arms and said, "Hey, I'm sorry I shouted at you, little buddy. It's not your fault I acted like a fool and drank myself silly last night. What do you say we go to Dairy Queen after breakfast for a pineapple sundae," he offered, trying to get back on his little brother's good side by offering him his favorite ice cream treat.

"Sure," Harvey answered, forgetting he had been shouted at for no reason. He left Bob's room with a big smile on his face.

Bob stumbled into the kitchen where the rest of the family was already buttering biscuits. His momma had prepared all of his favorite breakfast food, but to his disappointment his stomach rebelled against it. He sat there toying with his food.

Ronda said, "Boy, I never thought I'd see the day when big brother couldn't eat. I guess this means Thor, the family dog, finally gets some leftovers. You must have drunk half the booze in Arkansas last night."

"Go ahead and laugh. I hope to repay the comment someday," he said pretending to be mad.

Bob's daddy laughed and said, "Leave the boy alone. He just can't hold his liquor right now. He'll be okay in a couple of years."

Little Harvey was the first one to finish eating. He said he wanted to be sure he was ready when ice cream time rolled around.

Not being able to eat anything, Bob lay back down to clear his head and settle his churning stomach before taking Harvey to Dairy Queen. A couple of hours later he was awakened by his little brother informing him it was time they went and got the ice cream before it got too late. It was ten-thirty. As they were getting ready to leave the house, Ronda asked if she could tag along. Bob seized this opportunity to get back at her for the comment she'd made earlier regarding his hangover at the breakfast table.

"No, you can't go with us," he said, trying to sound upset with her. "You may tell everyone there I got drunk last night and couldn't eat breakfast this morning."

"Aw, come on, Bob" she protested. "You know I was kidding."

"Well, maybe this time. But you'd better watch your step next time, you hear?" he said acting serious. All went well at Dairy Queen.

That evening at six o'clock Bob decided it was now or never. He had to talk to Gina. His hands were sweating as he dialed her number and waited for someone to answer the phone.

"Arlington Job Corps Center's Blue Block Area, may I help you please?" a female voice asked.

"Yes, may I speak to Gina Samson in dorm #2406, room 214 please?"

"Hold on. I'll see if she's in," the lady said and placed him on hold.

As he waited, he mentally rehearsed what he was going to say. He was still deep in thought when her voice jolted him back to reality.

"Hello, this is Gina Samson speaking. Who is this?"

"Hello, Gina, this is Bob. I said I was not going to call you, but I guess you have a bigger hold on me than I care to admit. The way I have it figured, I owe you the chance to explain why you lied to me," he said in one breath, wanting to get it all out before he lost his nerve.

"I'm glad you called. And I'm even happier to hear you say you still love me, because I love you more than words could ever say. I cried myself to sleep every night for a week after you left. I didn't have the heart to tell you I wouldn't be home when you returned. I figured you were going through enough crap already without me adding to it. Please don't let this come between us and spoil the good thing we have going," she said sounding homesick.

He could hear her sniffle at the other end of the line. He longed to hold her in his arms and tell her all was forgiven. But his male ego wouldn't leave it at that. "Look Gina, the only person I believe was telling the truth about how you felt or feel about leaving, was Daddy. Whether you believe it or not, you made it hard for me by not letting me know what you had planned on doing, or why you were doing it," he lied.

"I wanted to wait for you, but momma kept putting pressure on me. She wanted me to do something with my life. She said if I didn't go ahead and join the Job Corps, she'd do everything within her power to keep us from getting married. She said if we really love each other a year wouldn't make that much difference. I didn't believe her, and still don't, but I gave in just the same. Please don't think I'm weak because I gave in to my momma, or that I don't love you because I do. Your daddy said it would probably be best if I went ahead and joined the Job

Corp if I wanted to maintain the strong family relationship that all families should have. If I made the wrong decision, please forgive me. God knows I love you more than I could ever put into words. Will you still love me when you get back from Vietnam, Bob?" she asked, hoping with all her heart he would say yes.

"You sure don't make it easy. But I guess I'll always love you. All I want to know is why you thought I wouldn't understand why you made the decision you made. Did you really think I'd be so narrow minded I wouldn't be able to understand what you were going through, being alone and all? I would never do anything to hurt you or our families. I don't like it, Gina. Not one little bit," he said, trying to sound as if he was still angry.

"I'm truly sorry, Bob. I was afraid if I told you on the phone what I was planning to do, you wouldn't love me anymore. It'll never happen again. I promise, ok?"

Bob still wanted her to think he was pissed but was giving in to her. He still loved her very much. "I guess it's okay this time. Don't do this to me again," he warned. He didn't tell her right away he had been assigned to Korea instead of Vietnam.

"I won't," she promised.

"Why did Johnny tell me it was your idea to join the Job Corp?" Bob asked.

"Because that's what I told him. I couldn't tell him my momma was treating me like a little girl," Gina explained.

They talked for at least an hour before she was told she had to get off the phone so someone else could use it.

"Bob, I gotta go. Someone else needs to use the phone," Gina informed him.

"Ok, but I forgot to tell you that I'm going to Korea, not Vietnam. So you can stop worrying about me getting killed over there," Bob updated his status for her.

"That's good news. Well, I better get off this phone because the dorm lady is starting to give me some dirty looks," Gina said.

"Ok baby, I'll call you later", Bob assured her.

Bob called her every day he was home to tell her how much he loved and missed her. He even went by her house and apologized to Mrs. Samson for calling her an old bitch. He told her he only said it because he was upset with Gina for leaving without letting him know she was leaving before he got back. Mrs. Samson accepted his apology and told him to stop by again before he left for Korea.

Mr. Samson told Bob if he ever called his wife a bitch again, for any reason, when he got back home he'd better be ready to fight. Bob assured Mr. Samson it would never happen again. After all he would be their son-in-law when he got back from Korea. He couldn't believe he had been let off the hook that easy, but he was glad they had not made a scene about his stupid outburst.

His saying good-bye to his family and friends this time was not as painful as the first time but nevertheless painful. In a way he was glad Gina was not there to see him off this time because he didn't ever want to go through another tear-jerking scene as before. That was one of the main reasons he visited her only one weekend while he was home. As much as he wanted to jump in his daddy's car and drive up there before he left, he knew it would only make it harder for him to leave her again. This time as the bus pulled away from the station, he felt much better because he was on his way to show the Korean people, and later Vietnam, what a fine soldier the United States Army had produced.

Chapter 5
THE REAL WORLD

Private Wood reported to the transfer station at Fort Lewis, Washington in September 1970 to begin his military career as a Military Policeman. He thanked God he was no longer a stupid trainee. There he was billeted with approximately forty other guys en route to Korea. Surprisingly, the majority of them said they wished they were going to Vietnam. They were told to associate only with the personnel within the first three buildings because they were all going to Korea. The soldiers in the other five buildings were on their way to Vietnam. That way they could avoid any complications that may arise because of the different assignments. Private Wood didn't understand why the different assignments should create a problem, because they were all in the same Army. The reason became perfectly clear why they were separated when they called the first formation, which they were all required to attend, to let them know when their flights would be leaving. The Korea bound personnel were required to wear the Class A uniform, the Vietnam-bound personnel were in jungle fatigues.

As soon as they were formed into their respective groups, the Vietnam-bound individuals started calling Private Wood's group a bunch of pussies and war dodgers. Tempers flared, insults were exchanged, and a full-scale riot damned near broke out right there in the formation area. Private Wood had been so offended, he was sure if he hadn't been restrained he would have beat the shit out of half the ass holes by himself.

After order had been restored, Private Wood and twenty of the other guys in his barracks en route to Korea were informed that they would be leaving at 0200 hours that night; and all of the Vietnam-bound boys were leaving at 0800 hours the next day. As he was heading back to his barracks, Private Wood heard his name called from the vicinity of the Vietnam-bound personnel heading back to their barracks. He looked in that direction and was surprised to see Private David Cooper approaching.

When Private Cooper reached where he was standing Private Wood said, "Hey, David, what's up?"

"Well, I'll be damned. I do everything in my power to keep from going to Vietnam, and where the hell am I going? And here you are all fired up and ready to win the war single-handed, and where are they sending you? Korea. Where you can lay back and ride the war out. Kiss my ass. How did you do it?" Private Cooper asked, as if Private Wood had anything to say about where he was to be assigned.

"I've been requesting to go to Vietnam ever since I got to basic training, but they keep telling me to put in my request at my next duty station. I don't know what else to do," Private Wood said sharply.

Private Cooper took a long, hard look at him and said, "Don't be a fool, home boy. I know you're patriotic and all that shit, and I was a little hard on you when we were on our way to Memphis, but I meant well. You don't realize how lucky you are. I'm scared shitless I won't be coming back home from Vietnam. I guess you were right. I'm a coward when it comes to the possibility of me dying on the battlefield," Private Cooper said sadly.

Private Wood instantly felt sorry for wishing he would end up so high in the Central Highlands of Vietnam he would be mistaken for a native. Although Private Wood had never been to a war, he believed that type of attitude would get Cooper killed.

Private Wood said, "Come on, man. You sound as if you have given up on life already. What wrong with you, man? Didn't they teach you anything in basic or AIT? I know damn well you have what it takes to survive this stinking war and return home to the people who love you. Even if you give up on yourself, you owe it to your family to survive. So get off this bullshit I'm-going-to-die-in-Vietnam kick. If death is what you want, commit suicide. God, I wish I was going to Vietnam with you."

"So do I," Private Cooper said and walked away.

Private Wood stood there dumbfounded, trying to figure out how David could go through all that combat training and give up on life so easily. One thing was for sure, if he didn't change his attitude, he was a dead man waiting to be buried.

Though Private Wood swore he would not lose any sleep over Private Cooper, he did not sleep a wink. He lay in his bunk trying to figure out the logic behind the Army's way of thinking. There he was ready and willing to go to Vietnam and they send him to Korea. And on the other hand, Private Cooper would've given anything to keep from going. And to phrase it as Private Cooper had, *Where the hell are they sending him?*

Private Wood was wide-awake when they were told to start preparing for their flight to Korea. He had thought about trying to get his orders changed while he was there at Fort Lewis, but decided to wait until he got to his unit in Korea to request a transfer. Private Wood prayed to God that somehow fate would fix it so he got to Private Cooper before the Viet Cong did. But it wasn't meant to be. He never saw Private Cooper again or ever heard what happened to him.

The plane trip to Korea was definitely a new experience, an experience Private Wood would never forget. He had learned in school that three-fourth of the earth's surface was covered with water, but he never thought he would get a chance to see so much of it. The lakes back home, which they thought were big bodies of water, were but a raindrop compared to the Pacific Ocean.

The flight took approximately nine hours to reach Yokota, Japan. Private Wood never imagined there were so many ways to sleep in an airplane seat. Every time he woke up, or was awakened by one of the stewardesses asking him if he wanted something to eat or drink, he was in a different position. He enjoyed the stopover in Japan. He walked around looking at all the latest model of watches and stereo equipment. He didn't have enough money to buy anything so all he did was window shop. He did send his family and Gina post cards from the airport.

From Japan to Korea the flight took only an hour and twenty minutes. After what seemed only a few minutes, in comparison to the flight from Ft. Lewis, WA, to Yokota, Japan the captain of the plane said, "Ladies and Gentlemen, welcome to Korea the Land of the Morning Calm."

When Private Wood looked out of the plane window he couldn't believe his eyes. All he could see were rice paddies and straw huts, the exact same scenery all the guys who'd been to Vietnam had described to him prior to his leaving home. He

PATRIOTISM

wondered if the captain and his crew had made a navigational error and they had ended up in Vietnam anyway. Private Wood knew that was next to impossible, so he sat back and stared out of his window, waiting for the plane to land so he could get a closer look at this strange looking land.

As they taxied up the runway at Osan Air Force Base, Private Wood could see guys, both Army and Air Force, waiting in the lobby to catch their flight back to the world, as he soon learned that was what they called returning home from Korea. He assumed they were going home. Why else would that many guys be at the air base airport for? To his surprise he hadn't thought about home too often since he left. After getting off the plane and entering the lobby, he walked around killing time until his duffle bag was unloaded. Private Wood felt like a giant among the Korean people working there. He wondered if all the Korean people were that short, and the women as beautiful as the ones there at Osan, AFB. After securing his duffle bag, he checked in at the Army Reception Desk and was directed to the army busses that were waiting to transport them to the 199th Replacement Center.

From Osan Air Force Base, they were transported to the 199th Replacement Company in Ascom. They were told they would have to wait there until they received orders from Eighth Army Headquarters before proceeding to their permanent duty station, which would take about two days. Again the first order of business upon reaching the replacement unit was filling out another ton of paperwork. When the paperwork was done they were issued linen and assigned a bunk to sleep and a locker to store their gear.

They were told not to leave the compound, as he learned all

installations in Korea were called, and go to the village, which happened to be right outside of the main gate. Private Wood had no intention of going anywhere or getting comfortable until he was in Vietnam. However, some of the guys were overcome with curiosity at what secrets the village held for them, so they snuck out later that evening anyway. They came back with wild tales about how they bribed the MPs on the gate to let them through because they didn't have passes, and about the women and other people they met out there. What they had to say didn't interest Private Wood one bit. So while everyone who was afraid to leave the compound sat around listening to them tell their stories, he lay in his bunk reading one of several novels he had purchased while at the airport in Japan.

During this down time, Private Wood found out that several of the guys there had been waiting for orders going on two weeks now. So Private Wood didn't believe the people who worked there at the Replacement Company knew when they would be leaving. Private Wood didn't mind it taking a while for him to receive his orders because it gave him time to prepare his reason for a request for a transfer.

Whenever orders came down from the 8th U.S. Army Headquarters, the orderly room personnel would call a formation, which everyone had to attend whether leaving or not. The replacement company averaged about four formations a day.

The formations had become monotonous and the days started to blend together. Private Wood started to get a little edgy because some of the guys who came in after him had their orders and had gone already. On the fourth day, he and nine other guys who came into the country with him received their orders, assigning them to Company C, 728th MP Battalion, Yongsan,

Korea, right near Seoul, the capital of Korea.

Upon arrival to their unit, they were in-processed at the orderly room and told to stick around. The commander, Captain Gregory Hicks, wanted to welcome them personally to the unit. This was great news for Private Wood because he would be afforded the opportunity to make his feelings known to the commander without the hassle of trying to set up an appointment to see him. Private Wood had rehearsed what he was going to say to his new commander for the past four days. He had no way of knowing Captain Hicks was a card-carrying member of the invisible empire of the Ku Klux Klan from Mississippi. He was the typical blue-eyed, blond hair, all American looking officer who had graduated from Duke University with a degree in Political Science.

Captain Hicks had a habit of showing his lack of concern when his black soldiers came to him with complaints of racial discrimination by the White NCOs in the unit, or shown by the local Korean store and bar owners. Captain Hicks always managed to somehow make it appear the black soldiers were at fault in all the complaints forwarded to the 8th U.S. Army Headquarters. Captain Hicks was so good at politics, he had been considered for the position to head the newly established 8th United States Army Race Relation Command, which was to investigate all complaints of racism and reports of discrimination throughout the Korean Peninsula.

Captain Hicks wanted the position badly, because he felt he could use the office to convince the Army brass in Washington that the racial problems the Black soldiers in Korea were experiencing were directly caused by their inability to adapt or intermingle with people outside of their own race. He harbored the thought that the Army would be better off if Black and White troops were still segregated.

The newly arrived troops were called into the commander's office one at a time. Private Wood was the last one to be called in. "Private Wood reports, sir."

"Have a seat, Private Wood, and tell me something about yourself. Where you come from, what you think of Korea, what you think of the Army so far, and stuff like that", Captain Hicks said with an obvious Southern accent.

"I was born and raised in Helena, Arkansas, took basic training at Fort Bragg, North Carolina, AIT at Fort Gordon, Georgia, and now I'm here. From what I've seen of the country so far, it's not too bad, I guess," Private Wood answered, intentionally not commenting on how he felt about the Army at this particular time in his short career.

"I'm from Mississippi myself. I guess that makes us neighbors back in the world. Well, what do you think of the Army so far?" Captain Hicks insisted.

"Sir, may I speak freely about my true feelings toward the Army without having to worry about repercussions?" Private Wood asked.

Captain Hicks shifted in his chair and was now sitting as if he was about to be smacked up side his head and had to be braced to prevent the force of the blow from knocking him out of his seat. "Go ahead, Private, and let it all hang out. I'm sure it's nothing that ain't gon down befo," he said giving his best impression of how he thought all black soldiers talked.

Private Wood ignored the insult. "Well, sir, when I was first drafted I thought I was going to be an infantry soldier. Upon completion of basic training I was told I was to become a

Military Policeman. When I questioned them as to why I was chosen to be an MP, they said it was because I was big and ugly, which wasn't funny to me," Private Wood said.

"So you don't want to be an MP?'" Captain Hicks interjected.

"The Military Police Corp wasn't my first choice, sir. So off to Fort Gordon, Georgia, I went for AIT, convinced I would not be happy until I got orders assigning me to an infantry unit and later Vietnam. The first opportunity I got after getting to Fort Gordon, I explained my feeling to the commander about wanting to do my part to help stamp out communism. He insinuated I was nothing more than a bloodthirsty hoodlum using the Army as a license to kill. After assuring him that wasn't my purpose for wanting to go to Vietnam, that there are still patriotic Americans left in this troubled nation of ours, he withdrew the statement. However, his withdrawal of the statement didn't lessen the blow to hear one of America's military leaders make such a statement. It was beyond my comprehension, sir. It also made me wonder if I wanted to become a part of this Army establishment. He finally convinced me the military police play a major role in the war in Vietnam. So I completed my training and here I am".

Captain Hicks was so stung by Private Wood's oratorical skills he sat temporally dumbfounded. He didn't know what to make of this black private. Gathering his wits he said, "Excuse me, Private. You've repeated this desire to go to Vietnam to both commanders you've had since you were drafted?" Captain Hicks asked.

"Yes, sir. That's what makes me wonder if I want to be a part of the Army establishment. My company commander at

Fort Gordon convinced me the military police play a major role in the war in Vietnam. I completed my training and here I am. You've been around for a while, sir, maybe you can tell me why it's so strange that a black soldier in America wants to help his country win the war in Vietnam," Private Wood said. That look of doubt he'd seen on the faces of his previous commanders was now on Captain Hicks'.

"Well, son, let me put it to you this way," Captain Hicks began. "Although I'm impressed with the way you express yourself, I find it very hard to believe any black soldier is willing to go to Vietnam where he may be killed or get his nuts blown off for a country in which he may never be treated as an equal to his white counterpart. Are you sure your only reason for wanting to go to Vietnam is to serve your country? Did you by any chance have a friend killed over there and you feel you should avenge his death?"

Private Wood had gone from being diagnosed as a born killer by his commanders in the states, to an avenger of the death of a friend by Captain Hicks. The words of the war protesters and draft dodgers came to mind. Their argument was the crooked politicians were making a lot of money off the war and had no desire to see it end anytime soon. The war was a plan by the war mongers to dominate the world. Although he didn't agree with them, he was beginning to understand why they felt as they did. This argument always pissed the powers to be off when they heard it, so Private Wood used the argument to aggravate Captain Hicks. He felt the vibrations of his anger start at the base of his spine, working its way up to his brain and eventually out of his mouth.

"Sir, now I know why young men in America are burning

PATRIOTISM

their draft cards and saying screw the army, the country, and the world. This war isn't about patriotism or trying to stamp out communism. It's about making money and who will control the world. As long as the war continues the corrupt politicians and military leadership included, continue to make money and don't really care how many soldiers die in the war. For your information, sir, equality for black people in America is right around the corner, and in the far distance I see a Black man being elected president of the United States. Let's say within the next fifty years or so. Therefore, I could care less whether you, or any other white person in America, likes me or not. And as far as your acceptance of me as a full-fledged citizen is concerned, the Constitution of the United States of America has already given me that right. All I'm requesting from you, sir, is a transfer to Vietnam. Whether you believe me or not, my reason for wanting to go to Vietnam is as I have stated from the beginning. It is to help win the war there. I'm not trying to impress anyone in America or the military. I just want to do my part for my country. So as you can see, sir, I don't think too much of the Army," Private Wood finished, knowing he would be put on the Captain's shit list.

"I'll say one thing for you, Private, you certainly know how to argue your case. But let me tell you one thing, you smart-ass, White-talking black son-of-a-bitch. I'm going to keep you right here in this stinking country with me. And I'm going to insure you don't make it above specialist four. But I'm going to work your black ass as if you were the sergeant major of the fucking army. You black soldiers aren't competent enough to perform above the rank of Specialist 4 anyway. And as far as a black man being elected President of the United States of America in the next fifty years is nothing but wishful thinking on your part. Who's it going to be? The so-called black leaders today can't even run their neighborhoods. How in the hell do you think they'll be able to run the country? The first thing they should do is get black people off welfare and out of the unemployment line, and then do something about the crime element that controls your neighborhoods before reaching for such lofty goals. Until that is done black men can forget about even thinking about being President of the United States. Even if a black man did come along with a chance to win, he'll probably end up dead," he said, showing Private Wood he wasn't used to a black private talking to him in that manner. Captain Hicks also knew he could say anything he wanted to as long as there were no witnesses, which was his style. And who in his right mind would take the word of a black private over the word of a white commander?

Private Wood was about to tell Captain Hicks how he felt about people like him, but was told to keep his smart-ass mouth shut or he would spend the rest of his military career behind bars. So he sat there while Captain Hicks chewed his butt out for another five minutes or so.

Finally Captain Hicks said, "If you ever cross my path again, you smart-ass nigger, your black ass is mine. Now get the hell out of my office and see Specialist Mayberry, the unit clerk, so he can direct you to the supply room for linen and MP gear. I'm going to get your ass on the road as soon as possible." He called Specialist Mayberry into the office. When Private Wood stood to leave, the Captain added, "You can forget about that transfer you requested. Your black ass is mine. Specialist Mayberry, get this damn private squared away so he can get to work as soon as possible," Captain Hicks instructed Specialist

Mayberry.

Private Wood left the captain's office mad as hell because he hadn't been allowed to defend himself against the verbal assault. While on their way to the supply room, Specialist Mayberry asked Private Wood what the hell he'd said to piss the old man off.

"What the hell happened Wood? I've never seen the Old Man so pissed off before," Specialist Mayberry said.

"You're a white soldier, and as such, you would not understand," Private Wood said.

"Wouldn't understand what?" Specialist Mayberry asked.

"Wouldn't understand how hard it is to function in a white man's world," Private Wood said.

"I don't get it," Specialist Mayberry said.

"And you never will," Private Wood assured him.

Private Wood could tell Specialist Mayberry was offended, but he wasn't feeling too friendly right then. He wanted to tell Specialist Mayberry his anger wasn't directed toward him but couldn't find the words. After he was issued linen and MP gear, Private Wood was escorted to his barracks and shown where he was to sleep for the next thirteen months. Specialist Mayberry told Private Wood he would see him in the orderly room after he put his gear away. He stuffed the gear into his wall locker and went to the orderly room to retrieve his duffle bag. Specialist Mayberry told him to wait, the First Sergeant wanted to talk to him.

I wonder what he wants? Private Wood asked himself as he sat staring at the walls of the orderly room. After a fifteen-minute wait, he was told the First Sergeant would see him now. He knocked on the office door and was told to enter. *If these people think they can scare me they are sadly mistaken,* Private Wood was thinking as he entered the First Sergeant's office. To his surprise, the unit First Sergeant was black, from Birmingham, Alabama.

"Have a seat, Private Wood. I'm First Sergeant Tucker. I'd like to have a little talk with you and welcome you to the unit and Korea," he said with a big smile on his face. After Private Wood was seated he continued, "I hear you and the old man had a disagreement a few minutes ago. Would you like to tell me what happened?" First Sergeant Tucker asked.

Private Wood knew he couldn't tell the First Sergeant everything that was said. So he picked the reason the argument started. "I asked the commander if it was possible for me to get a transfer to Vietnam, because I want to do my part to help America put an end to the fighting there. When he said no, I guess I got a little mad and said something I shouldn't have said. Every commander I've talked to since I've been in the Army about going to Vietnam has basically told me the same thing. I must have a personal vendetta for wanting to go to Vietnam. But I don't. Why is it so hard for the Army establishment to accept the fact that patriotism still exists in America?"

First Sergeant Tucker studied his face for a while before he spoke. "You know something, Private Wood, if I had my way around here I would ensure you ended up so high in the Central Highland of Vietnam they would mistake you for one of the locals. However, you're stuck here with us for a while. Maybe later on if you don't change your mind, come back and see me. I'll personally try my best to get you that transfer to Vietnam. What do you say to that?"

Private Wood didn't believe a word the First Sergeant said.

But to avoid another argument, Private Wood said, "Yes, First Sergeant, that would be fine. When should I check back with you?"

"I would say in about a month or two. We should have enough people in by then to let you go."

Being the First Sergeant is the enforcer in the unit in these situations involving enlisted soldiers, he waited for the First Sergeant to lower the boom on his behind. The First Sergeant had to know that he had said something out of the ordinary to tee the captain off. All the First Sergeant said was, "you're dismissed" when Private Wood didn't move.

From the orderly room Private Wood took his duffle bag to the barracks to get settled in. As he was unpacking and hanging his clothes in his locker, the houseboy, Mr. Kim Dae Won, whose name he had been told by Specialist Mayberry, came over to where he was.

"Hey, you no have to do. You pay me eight dollars a month and I do everything for you. I shine you boots, makey you bed, takey you clothes to the laundry, and pick them up. I prepare everything for all inspections. Everything. I even find you very nice girlfriend so you no catchey VD," Mr. Kim said in broken English.

"All that service for only eight dollars a month?" Private Wood asked, thinking he was being conned even though Specialist Mayberry had told him the same thing earlier.

"Sure, me number one houseboy and I thinky you be number one GI."

They shook hands on the deal. And so began a lasting friendship, even to this very day. While he was sitting there watching Mr. Kim finish unpacking his clothes and hanging them in his locker, the incident with Captain Hicks came to mind.

Here I go again beating my head against the wall. Maybe I should just keep my big mouth shut, go ahead serve my thirteen months and get the hell out of Korea with whatever rank I happen to make while I'm here. That would make everyone happy. But Private Wood knew he wouldn't take the easy way out when he knew, or felt, he was right about something. He had been raised to stand up for what he believed to be right. His daddy always did and would expect no less of him.

Later that evening, around 1930 hours, [7:30 p.m]., the 7am-to-7pm shift came strolling into the barracks carrying five cases of beer.

"Hey, look what we got here," he counted Private Wood and the other guys who came in with him, "Ten new turtles," the first guy through the door announced.

The turtle tag came about because of the helmet liners the MPs wore while on duty. It was shaped exactly like the shell of a turtle. It was painted black with big MP letters and rank insignia on the front, and the 728th MP logo on the sides in white.

"Now maybe we can get a couple of days off every once in a while." one of the other guys chimed in.

Private Wood was very impressed with the appearance of their uniforms. Even after a full day of work, their uniforms looked better than his did before he put it on. Their pistol belts had a big brass buckles with the U.S. Army brass insignia in the center and four small MP cross pistols emblems around it. The buckle were very impressive indeed. It made him feel good to know he was assigned to a unit with individuals who took pride in their appearance.

PATRIOTISM

After introductions were over, they started telling the newbies the do and don'ts while stationed in Korea. They repeated the same thing they'd been told while at the 199th Replacement Company in Ascom. Half the girls had some type of venereal disease for which there was no cure. The thieves, better known as slicky boys, would steal the watch off your wrist while you were walking down the street without you even knowing it. Don't get caught black marketing. And the food, especially the kimichi, was not to be touched.

One of the White guys, to prove his point about the effect of Venereal disease on the baby maker, went so far as to pull his pants down and whip out his penis to show newbies they weren't trying to bullshit them about the VD part. His penis looked like a rotting piece of meat not even a starving dog would touch. He informed them what they were looking at was shankrods in the advanced stage. Luckily for him there was a cure for that type of VD. Private Wood had to admit that seeing what VD does to the baby maker was a lot uglier in person than on a movie screen.

"So how would I know what women not to mess with?" Private Wood asked

"The army has an agreement with the Korean government which allows our medics to give all the hookers physical examinations monthly. If any of them have VD they're giving penicillin shots, have their VD cards stamped with a red dot, and are supposed to be taken out of circulation for 2 1/2 weeks. Penicillin is suppose to kill the virus in two weeks, so the doctors add a few days to make sure it's given time to work. Sure some of the girls slip through the crack, but as a whole the system works. You guys will learn about the hooker card system when you start working the gates. Shank-man over here got burnt screwing around in an off limits village. Now he has to worry whether his dick is going to fall off later in his life," Specialist Goober explained.

"I guess that means the girls in the off limits villages don't have VD cards," Private Wood said.

"You're a sharp dude," Specialist Goober laughed.

After the conversation died down they all changed clothes and headed for the day room (Recreation Room) with their beer. Private Wood and the other guys were invited to join them, but Private Wood declined. He had some letters to write.

Korea gave him a weird feeling. It was the first place he'd ever been in his life where everything was not run or owned by some White person. Everywhere he had been so far, Osan, Ascom, and now here in Yongsan, the installations were dominated by the Korean people. It was a feeling he would soon learn to love, but right now he had more depressing things to think about. He was given two days to finish in-processing in the unit and he would then be put to work.

Although Private Wood didn't particularly want to be a military policeman, he couldn't help but feel proud the first day he was preparing for duty as he stared into the latrine (bathroom) mirror at his reflection staring back at him. His uniform was starched and pressed. He was sure there was so much starch in his pants they would've stood in a corner by themselves. And his pistol belt buckle and boots were highly shined. The .45 caliber pistol at his side gave him the feeling he had the power to control life and death, that he could stop crime and corruption single handedly. He admitted to himself, all in all, he felt big and bad. The anti-war rant he went on in Captain Hicks' office was just that, but the laws of the UCMJ [The Uniform

Code of Military Justice] he had sworn to uphold was very real. His stance when it came to enforcing those laws would pit him against his fellow soldiers and his leadership.

    Private Wood was assigned to the night shift, second squad, 7pm to 7am, the action shift he'd been told by his squad leader, Staff Sergeant Gary Pearson, during his initial in briefing. Private Wood was also informed that most of the time after midnight it would be extremely boring if he happened to be working one of the gates, mainly because of the curfew. The curfew was established after the ceasefire agreement at the end of the Korean Conflict. Korean Military and Civilian Police checkpoints were set up throughout the country to prevent the North's insurgents from entering the South. Private Wood was also told that after a while he would have a very difficult time keeping himself motivated because all of the troops would be back on post at midnight and there would be very little to do once the curfew kicked in. He found it hard to believe he would have problems keeping himself motivated, except maybe when missing home or Gina.

    Private Wood and the other two new turtles assigned to the same squad were told since they had to work the gates they should hope to get assigned on gate #2, #7, or #12. These were the gates the Korean girls went through to get to the clubs on the compound. Gate #2 was near the Castle Club where most of the black soldiers hung out. Gate #7 was near the Lower 4 Club where most of the white soldiers hung out. And Gate #12 was called the high-class hooker gate because it was located near the officer's club. It was at one these gates the MPs would pick up the strays that didn't hook up with a GI to take home for the night. It would be a while before Private Wood would get to work either one of those gates.

After guard mount he was assigned gate guard duty at gate number 36. Specialist David Schultz, a member of the squad, laughed and told him if he was lucky he may see a couple of Americans soldiers pass by before it got dark. Otherwise, it would be just him, one Korean National Policeman (KNP), and one Korean Security Guard (KSG). All they were doing down there was guarding a hotel being renovated to be used by the Army as an R & R (Rest and Relaxation) center for the guys stuck up at the demilitarized zone (DMZ) when they got passes to come to Seoul to get away from the hostile environment for a few days. The Naja Hotel, he was told was its name.

"Why do they put an MP down there if all they're doing is guarding a half-finished building?" Private Wood asked.

"Don't ask me," Specialist Schultz said and walked away.

Private Wood was sure Specialist Schultz had exaggerated, but he was to find out differently. Also, he was to become very familiar with that particular gate.

"OK, Private, let's go. I wouldn't want you to be late for your first day on the job," the patrol supervisor, Sergeant Brad Davis, said.

As Private Wood climbed into the small jeep, he smiled to himself, thinking of how Drill Sergeant Wilson, back at Fort Gordon, had constantly told them how lucky he was to have a job that only required him to ride around in a big sedan and give tickets. *If this is a big sedan, I must be the Pope*, he smiled to himself.

They rode for half an hour through traffic before Sergeant Davis said, "Well, here we are, Private Wood, your place of duty for the next twelve hours. Come on in and I'll brief you on what you're supposed to be doing while you're on duty here."

When they entered the guard shack, Private Patrick J. Cooney, the off-going MP, was still asleep in the bunk that had been provided for the Korean Policeman who sometimes slept there instead of going home after getting off shift at midnight.

"You'd better get off your ass Cooney if you want to be relieved," Sergeant Davis said, kicking the bunk to wake him up.

Private Cooney slowly got up and retrieved his weapon and helmet that was hanging on the wall by the entrance door of the guard shack.

Sergeant Davis glared at him and said, "The next time I catch you asleep on duty I'm going to burn your ass, you worthless piece of shit."

"Aw, come on sarge you know damn well there ain't a fucking thing to do here but sleep, get drunk or get high." Private Cooney said sleepily.

"That's pure bullshit and you know it. Get your sorry ass in the jeep and wait until I finish briefing this new private," Sergeant Davis instructed.

"That shouldn't take too long," Private Cooney quipped as he was going out the door with his weapon and helmet in his hands.

"Don't mind Cooney, he's nothing but a screw-up. That's why they stick his worthless butt out here. They don't want the public to see what a sorry excuse for an MP we have in him," Sergeant Davis explained. He then introduced him to Mr. Yi, the KSG on duty at the time, and Mr. Lee, the KNP. "I want you to understand one thing and never forget it. You are the man in charge out here. All these Korean security guards and Korean National Police work for you. I don't care how old they are, or how long they've been working out here. You're still the boss and they do what you tell them to do whether they like it or not. You understand?" Sergeant Davis asked.

"Yes, Sergeant," Private Wood answered.

"I know this particular job don't appear to be very important, but it is, or they wouldn't have an MP out here guarding the place. "That hotel," Sergeant Davis pointed to a half-finished building, half surrounded by a brick wall, "has a lot of construction material in it and we don't want the slicky boys ripping us off," he said.

"How long have they been working on the hotel?" Private Wood asked.

"About six months now," Sergeant Davis answered.

"And have there been any incidents of material getting ripped off?" Private Wood asked, trying to comprehend why an MP was needed way the hell out there.

"No, not so far. But God knows it's not because of the MPs they put out here to guard the damn place. It seems the only people they put out here are new privates, like yourself, or the unit screw-ups like Cooney. Don't ask me why because I don't know. I'll probably be back out here sometime tonight to check on you and see if everything is all right. If not, I'll see you in the morning after you get relieved. Are there any questions before I leave?" Sergeant Davis asked.

"Yes, there is one question I wanted to ask. How long will I have to work out here before I get to go on the road?" Private Wood asked.

"That's up to Sergeant Pearson. Normally you are switched around from gate to gate until you get your driver's license before you get to work the road. You should have it in a month or so. Any other questions?" Sergeant Davis asked.

"No, Sergeant, thank you." Private Wood heard Sergeant Davis call Private Cooney a good-for-nothing fuck off as he was driving away. And so began Private Wood's tour of duty in the "Land of the Morning Calm."

After being in the country a while, he enjoyed working with the KNPs and KSGs because they were extremely nice to him. They would give him anything he asked for, within reason. And he in turn did the same thing for them. Private Wood actually liked working gate #36 because of the friendship he established with all the KNPs and KSGs, but three straight weeks of gate #36 without a day off was beginning to get to him. He was ready for a change in scenery, even if it was another gate. It had gotten to the point where everyone had started calling the Naja Hotel, Private Wood's Hotel.

After guard mount at the beginning of the fourth week, Private Wood approached Staff Sergeant Pearson. "Sergeant Pearson, could I have a word with you before I go out to the gate?" he asked.

"Sure, Private. I already know what it's about. It's about you getting off of gate #36, but what the hell? I guess I owe you an explanation as to why you've been on that particular gate all this time. That's what it's about isn't it?" Sergeant Pearson asked.

Taken aback somewhat Private Wood said, "Yes, Sergeant, that's what I wanted to ask you about."

"Well, come back here in the briefing room where we won't be disturbed." As soon as they entered the briefing room, Staff Sergeant Pearson transformed from a caring squad leader to a first-rate ass hole. "I wondered how long it would be before you brought your black ass to me crying about where I've been assigning you to work. I'll listen, but I'll tell you right now, it won't do any good. Three weeks and already you're trying to tell me where you want to work."

Private Wood could tell all Staff Sergeant Pearson was trying to do was intimidate him, but he wouldn't be intimidated by anyone in the unit, hell, in the whole damn Army. "Sergeant Pearson, you can call it anything you want to, but I have asked everyone in this platoon if it was common practice for one person to work the same gate for so long. I don't think I have to tell you what they said. Now I want to hear what you have to say. Maybe you have a very good reason for keeping me hidden from the public's view, but I can't think of one to save my life," he said, staring Staff Sergeant Pearson straight in the eyes.

"They said only turtles with no balls and screw-ups work gate #36 that long, right?" Private Wood nodded. "Well, I guess you're wondering what category you're in. Neither right now, as far as I'm concerned. It was requested you be assigned duty at that particular gate, and you are to stay there until further notice. I'm afraid I have no say so in the matter," Staff Sergeant Pearson confessed, opening himself up for ridicule.

Private Wood could not believe his ears. Here was a staff Sergeant in the United States Army standing there telling him, a private, that he had no say so where his people worked. He knew what he was about to say was going to piss Sergeant Pearson off for real, but he didn't really care because he knew who had made the request. Also, he had no respect for a spineless son-of-a-bitch that didn't have balls enough to stand up for his troops. He'd only been an acting platoon sergeant in basic training, but he'd be damned if he didn't stand up for his troops.

PATRIOTISM

"Sergeant Pearson, every non-commissioned officer I've encountered since I've been in the Army ran his platoon or squad with minimum outside interference from his company commander," he began. "I've been told time and time again that any platoon sergeant or squad leader who lets someone else run his people doesn't belong in that position or deserve the stripes he's wearing. For three weeks now I've sat at that damn gate and watched the stars come out at night and go away the next morning without doing anything similar to military police work. And frankly, Sergeant Pearson, I'm tired of that. I wouldn't even mind working one of the other gates here on main post. At least I would get a chance to check passes. And if I'm lucky, maybe every now and then I could catch someone stealing. That's not what I call exciting military police work, but it beats the hell out of sitting on gate #36 watching a building grow. And now you tell me, a private, that you, a staff sergeant in the United States Army, aren't competent enough to run your own squad," Private Wood finished, watching Staff Sergeant Pearson's face going from red to redder.

Staff Sergeant Pearson was so pissed off he was visibly shaking. "You let me tell you one thing, you smart-ass private, that is exactly why you're on that gate every night right now. You're too smart for your own damn good. And to make things worse, you're a black ass private. Boy, as far as I'm concerned, you'll rot down there," Staff Sergeant Pearson said with a self-satisfied smirk on his face.

"You can't do a thing about it anyway, now can you, Sergeant? You only do what you're told and nothing more. Am I right, Sergeant?" Private Wood asked and started for the door.

"You get your smart black ass back over here. I'll tell you

when you can leave," Staff Sergeant Pearson said.

Private Wood walked back over to where Staff Sergeant Pearson had indicated and said, "I guess I was right or you wouldn't be so pissed off."

"You get the hell out of my face right now before I knock your god-damned head off," was all Staff Sergeant Pearson said, clenching and unclenching his fists.

The next night Private Wood was assigned guard duty at gate #10 on the main post. He still hadn't had a day off, but he decided he had better not push his luck. He would wait until he felt the time was right before asking for a day off. So far, all he had time to do was eat, sleep, go to the gym a couple of hours each day and write home. He'd been working such long hours he didn't realize how little he was missing home and Gina. Two months after arriving in country he obtained his military vehicle overseas operator's license and was allowed on patrol.

Private Wood had accepted the fact that racism was rampant in places like Arkansas and Mississippi back in the world because they were southern states that were still fighting the civil war. So he was surprised at the racial hatred that was so prevalent there in Korea between some black and white soldiers. He got a taste of that animosity up close and personal his first night on patrol. It was a night he would remember for the rest of his life, because the ugliness of the situation was displayed on both side of the spectrum of human emotion. Private Wood even found himself in conflict with his patrol partner, Specialist Four Marvin Thomas, who later became his gym buddy. Private Wood and Specialist Thomas were patrol partners that night and they were dispatched to the 8th Army Enlisted Men's Club in reference to a disturbance. They were told to secure the scene until other patrols arrived. With hearts pounding, they arrived at the scene. Soldiers, both black and white, were running in every direction. There were trails of blood leading either into or out of the club but they couldn't tell.

"Hey soldier! You," Specialist Thomas yelled at a soldier who didn't run, and happened to be white, "What the hell is going on here?" Specialist Thomas asked.

"Ask the coons, they're the ones going around cutting people with razors and shit," the soldier said and started to walked off.

Because of the racial slur, Specialist Thomas forgot he was supposed to be above reacting to taunting behavior. "Get your ass back here, white boy. You and your friends probably started this shit in the first place with your white racist attitude," he said.

Before Specialist Thomas got a chance to question the soldier, other MP patrol units arrived at the scene, along with an ambulance. Sergeant Davis yelled at them to just get the soldier's name and unit for now, they would talk to him later. It was reported a bleeding soldier had run behind one of the building near the club. Specialist Thomas and Private Wood were told to go and see if they could find him. The building was a short distance from the club. As they turned the corner of the building, there sat a white soldier leaning against the building. He was covered with blood.

"Damn, man. Are you alright?" Private Wood asked, knowing it was a stupid question the moment it left his mouth. "Where're you cut?"

"Man, of all the MPs in this damn country, it had to be a couple of niggers who get to me first. Well you niggers have done enough for me for one night. I would rather die than have another nigger touch me," the hurt soldier said, and spit blood and mucus in Private Wood's face.

Private Wood jerked back as the blood and mucus hit him

between the eyes. His first reaction was to pull his nightstick and grant that dying white man his wish, but he believed in his job and knew he had to take the bad with the good. Specialist Thomas on the other hand, had been called the "N" word once too many times.

"Come on Wood, man. Lets put this cracker out of his misery," Specialist Thomas said and pulled a razor out of his back pocket.

"Thomas, are you crazy? Man, you're going to get us busted and thrown into the stockade. What're you going to do? Kill every white person in the world who calls you a name?" Private Wood asked getting between Specialist Thomas and the soldier, while wiping away the blood and mucus that had started running down his face.

"I don't need your help, nigger. Let him go ahead and kill me if he has the guts," the soldier whispered, almost too weak to talk now. Blood was running out of several deep cuts on his arms and chest.

"Fuck this, I'm going to kill this bastard," Specialist Thomas said, trying to get around Private Wood to cut the soldier's throat.

"I can't let you do this man. You'll have to cut me too," Private Wood stood his ground.

"Well, you go ahead and do your thing. I won't raise a finger to help that Klu Klux Klan bastard," Specialist Thomas spat putting the razor back in his pocket.

By this time the soldier had passed out from the loss of blood. Private Wood called for medical assistance on the radio. While waiting for the medics, Private Wood bandaged the soldier's wounds as best he could with the bandages from his and Specialist Thomas's first aid pouches.

Upon the arrival of the medics, Private Wood and Specialist Thomas went back to the club and took statements from numerous individuals and gathered all the evidence they could from the scene. They were told to return to the station to write their report. Though it was a very difficult report to write Private Wood felt they did a good job, with Sergeant Davis' help, explaining what had happened at the club. It was impossible to know for sure what had actually happened because every story told to them was different.

Back in the barracks that morning after getting off duty, Private Wood went over to where Specialist Thomas was sitting on his bunk and said "You know I can't let this pass, man. I don't think anyone's safe with you running around out there with a gun at your side and a razor in your back pocket," Private Wood said.

"You mean ain't no white boy safe with me running around with a gun at my side and a razor in my pocket. Look man, I don't know what happened. I just snapped, ok? I ain't never reacted like that before. That white boy ain't the first one to call me a nigger. Let me ask you a question, Wood. It didn't bother you when we went up to that white boy to try and save his life and he said he'd rather die than to have one of us touch him? Didn't it piss you off just a little? I thought you were going to go off when he spit in your face."

"I would a liar if I said it didn't bother me, but that's exactly how they want us to react. I won't give them that satisfaction. Besides, we were told during training to expect this type of shit, especially from white soldiers," Private Wood said.

"Wood, I know you're right and I swear I'll never lose it again. Give me a break man. If you ever see me lose control again, then you can bust me out. How bout it man?" Specialist Thomas said.

"You know by agreeing to let you off the hook I'm going against what I believe in. You'll never get another break from me, and if that soldier files a complaint against you, I'm not going to lie for you man," Private Wood said.

"Fair enough, Wood. You don't know how I feel right now. I'm supposed to be training you and it's you who has to save my butt. This is embarrassing as hell, but thanks for taking charge out there and keeping me from ending up in prison over a messed up cracker. I owe you big time. Here, you get rid of this damn thing for me will you," Specialist Thomas said handing Private Wood the razor. Fortunately for Thomas, the soldier never filed a complaint against him and Private Wood never told on him.

When he was on patrol duty, Private Wood was a happy camper because he enjoyed busting the drunken assholes and the low life thieves that lived among their fellow soldiers. He wouldn't admit it to himself, but also enjoyed giving white officers' wives traffic tickets because they thought they were above military justice because they were civilians. Whenever the conversation came up about issuing citations, one particular officer's wife he gave a ticket to always came to mind.

It was against the Provost Marshall's policy to hide from motorist to catch them speeding, because it was a common complaint that the MPs were hiding behind something when people were given tickets for speeding. Private Wood was sitting on the side of the road where vehicles exited the officers' housing area running radar when this white lady shot past him at a high rate of speed. She had to see him sitting there because she drove right past his patrol car. There were no trees or any other obstructions. When Private Wood pulled her over she was irate. Private Wood walked up to the car and asked to see her driver's license.

"Do you know who I am?" she asked.

"No ma'am, but when you give me your driver's license I will," Private Wood said.

She took this as a smart-ass remarks and said, "Very funny nigger. It's bad enough we let you people serve with our white troops, now you think you're as good as us. Why don't you just leave me the hell alone, and let me go. When Colonel Heath hears you gave me a ticket, he's going to fry your ass," she said.

"Ma'am if you don't give me your driver's license I'll have to call my patrol supervisor, and you'll be delayed much longer," Private Wood tried to reason with her.

"I'm Brigadier General Hutchison's wife. Didn't you see the star on the decal? I suggest you let me go," Mrs. Hutchison said.

"Yes ma'am, I did see the decal. I'll let you go after I issue you a citation for speeding 35 in a 20 mph zone," Private Wood informed her.

"Look, you uppity nigger private. You better let me go or else," she threatened.

Private Wood got on his radio and requested his patrol supervisor come to his location.

Upon hearing him requesting his supervisor come to his assistance, she handed him her driver's license and said, "Here boy. Write your goddamned ticket and see where it gets you. I'm going to enjoy watching my husband bust your uppity ass. You give a nigger a badge and a gun and they think they own the damn world."

Before Private Wood finished writing the ticket, Sergeant Davis arrived on the scene and asked what was going on. Private Wood briefed him on who he had stopped and why. Sergeant Davis freaked out when Private Wood told him who she was.

"Private Wood, man, are you crazy? You're planning on giving General Hutchison's wife a ticket?" Sergeant Davis asked incredulously.

"She was speeding, Sergeant," Private Wood said as if it was that simple.

Seeing a white sergeant on the scene, Mrs. Hutchison got out of her car and came over to where they were standing and played the innocent southern belle. "Sergeant, I want you to discipline this black private. First of all he was hiding with that radar gun, and second when he pulled me over, he was rude to me. When I asked him if he knew who I was, he said he didn't give a damn he was going write my white ass up for speeding," Mrs. Hutchison lied.

Although Sergeant Davis knew Private Wood would never say anything like that to anyone he stopped, that automatic mind set to protect white women from black men kicked in. "Private Wood, did you insult General Hutchison's wife? If you did, I'll have your ass busted," Sergeant Davis said.

"Sergeant Davis, you know for yourself I would never disrespect an American citizen. She was speeding and when I asked for her driver's license, she refused to give it to me so I called you. That's all there is to it," Private Wood explained.

"So you're calling Mrs. Hutchison's a liar, is that it?"

"I'm not calling her anything. She was speeding and I'm giving her a ticket for it just as I would anyone else who I stopped for speeding," Private Wood said.

"Let her go, private," Sergeant Davis, said.

"I can't do that, sergeant," Private Wood refused.

Upon hearing this Mrs. Hutchison said, "Sergeant, I know you're not going to let a black private tell you what he's not going to do."

Sergeant Davis knew the PM policy was the MP writing the ticket was the only one who could tear it up. "I said let her go, private," he said.

Private Wood finished writing the ticket, gave Mrs. Hutchison's her copy and asked Sergeant Davis if he was finished talking to him.

"Don't worry Mrs. Hutchison, Colonel Heath will take care of the ticket. Let me have it. The PM has this policy that only the MP writing the ticket or the PM can tear it up. I'll deal with Private Wood," Sergeant Davis assured her.

"Someone need to put that smart ass nigger in his place," she said, got in her car and drove off.

"I'll see you at the station, Private Wood, now," Sergeant Davis said going to his jeep.

Private Wood thought it was amazing how white men believed everything a white woman said when a black man was involved, even though they know the white woman is guilty and is calling the black man a nigger right in front of them. When he got to the station Sergeant Davis took the ticket, along with Private Wood, to see Master Sergeant Snoop.

Master Sergeant Snoop said, "Either you tear it up or I will."

"Tear it up Master Sergeant Snoop, I won't," Private Wood refused.

"Okay have it your way," Sergeant Snoop said tearing the ticket into pieces.

"Is that it Sergeant Snoop?" Private Wood asked.

"Yeah that's it this time, but you pull another stunt like this and I'll let Sergeant Davis deal with you," he warned. Sergeant Snoop only said that to lift Sergeant Davis' spirit, because he was embarrassed by a private.

The following day General Hutchison stopped by the Provost Marshall Office to shake the hand of the private who had the balls to give his wife a ticket. He said it made his day when he found out it was a black private who had busted her butt. Brigadier General Hutchison was the Deputy Commander of the 8th U.S. Army. He was known for being a no non-sense, hard-ass individual who believed in a soldier obeying his chain of command on all levels. It didn't bother the general to bust an individual on the spot and give his rank to the lower ranking person if the person in charge didn't take corrective action against the lower ranking individual who had disobeyed him right away. Private Wood's squad was in the middle of guard-mount when the general showed up at the station. He was told to report to the PM's office ASAP. Private Wood didn't know what to expect as he entered the Provost Marshall's Office. Master Sergeant Snoop told him to have a seat, and went to let the PM and the general know he was there. Private Wood was thinking this was it; his ass would never see another stripe as long as he was in Korea. Master Sergeant Snoop came out and told him to report to the PM.

"Private Wood reports as ordered, sir," he reported looking around the office to see if Mrs. Hutchison had accompanied her husband.

"Private Wood, this is Brigadier General Hutchison. He wanted to meet the private that had the gumption to give his wife a ticket," Colonel Heath informed him.

"I hope it's a pleasure to meet you, sir," Private Wood said nervously.

PATRIOTISM

The general laughed and said, "So you're the big black buck private who scared the hell out of my wife. She said she didn't see you because you were hiding behind a bush, and when you approached her you was very rude to her. What do you have to say for yourself private?"

"Sir, not once did I disrespect your wife. I haven't been an MP that long, but I know better than to do that. As far as hiding, sir, I was sitting on the road right outside of the entrance to your housing area where everyone exiting could see me," Private Wood defended his action.

"Are you calling my wife a liar, private?" the general asked.

Private Wood couldn't tell if the general was pissed or not. "No sir, I'm not calling your wife a liar. The only thing I can say is we have a difference of opinion on what occurred sir," Private Wood said.

"Was my wife rude to you?" the general asked.

Private Wood knew he was skating on thin ice with this question, but he answered it as best he could. "Well, sir, let's just say she wasn't happy about being pulled over and given a ticket," he said.

"You don't remember what she said to you?" the general asked enjoying the game he was playing with Private Wood.

"Yes, sir. I remember everything she said to me, and the names she called me. But I was told in MP School to expect that sort of thing, so I don't hold anything against her. It comes with the territory sir," Private Wood answered.

"Colonel Heath, you got yourself a good soldier here," the general said to Colonel Heath. Then to Private Wood he said, " I just wanted to shake your hand young man for having the balls to do the right thing."

"Thank you, sir," Private Wood said shaking the general's hand.

"I wanted you to know, you'll never have a problem with me soldier as long as you're doing your duty and treating everyone with respect. By the way, my wife told me what she called you, and it made her mad you didn't react to it. Keep up the good work," General Hutchison said.

Private Wood exited the office, and that was the end of that episode. However, Private Wood wasn't so naïve that he hadn't notice the general never said the ticket should have been processed.

Sergeant Davis had been as nervous as an eight-point buck staring down the barrel of a 30-06 during hunting season when he heard that General Hutchison had called Colonel Heath and told him he would be over to talk to him about the sergeant and private who had the balls to give his wife a ticket. Sergeant Davis saw his stripes going out the window when the general arrived. Private Wood was ready to give up his one stripe, because he wouldn't beg anyone to keep it. Private Wood figured the worse thing the general could do to him was have him sent to Vietnam. After the general left they all told Private Wood he was lucky this time, but he had better stop pushing his luck. Private Wood wasn't allowed to run radar in the officer's housing area again for a long time.

Private Wood enjoyed working the main gates because it gave him a chance to meet a lot of different people, people from all over the world. And to his surprise the only difference in them was that they were of different nationalities, had different shades of skin color and spoke different languages. Otherwise they were mostly the same, chasing the almighty dollar to make life as easy as possible for themselves and their families. If they liked you, they would go out of their way to help you. If they didn't, it was screw you. The majority of the people who dealt with Private Wood liked him, although he gave very little quarter where the law was concerned. He was constantly told what a joy it was to work with and talk to him. Still he didn't want to get too comfortable, because he was still determined to get transferred to Vietnam.

Private Wood finally got a day off after 32 days on the gates and road. Everyone wanted to know what he was going to do on his day off. He told them he was planning on going to the gym and maybe catch a movie on main post. They wanted to know why he never went to the ville to mess with the ladies.

"Even though most of the ladies are beautiful, I can't afford to catch anything I can't get rid of before it's time for me to go home," he explained. "Besides, you guys are taking damn good care of them without my help. Just keep up the good work," he teased the guys in his squad.

Private Wood had been invited to a number of the girls' hooches while working the gate, but he always declined, telling them he would be too tired when he got off the next morning. *You can sleep my hooch,* they would say. His name changed from Private Wood to Private Cherry-boy to all the girls in Itaewon and the surrounding villages, which meant he would be considered a virgin until he went to the ville and got himself laid. Although there were smaller villages surrounding the compound, Itaewon was where 99.9% of clubs were.

Specialist Thomas said, "Come on, my man. I've been over here for ten months now and I ain't caught nothing. I'll turn you on to Miss Chin. I know she's clean. And man can she screw. I'm going down to her friend's hooch after we leave the gym tomorrow."

"Thanks, but I don't think so," Private Wood declined.

"Well, give me a holler if you change your mind."

Private Wood spent his day off as he had planned.

After getting back from the gym and taking a shower on his day off, Mr. Kim was looking at him curiously. "Why are you looking at me like that, Mr. Kim?" Private Wood asked, knowing Mr. Kim had been wanting to ask him something for quite some time.

"Why you never go village? Always stay barracks. You no like Korean woman?"

"No, Mr. Kim, it's nothing like that. It's just that I'm engaged to a girl stateside and I don't want to take a chance of catching something I may not be able to get rid of before I go home."

"You think all Korean woman got VD?" Mr. Kim asked sounding insulted.

"No, I don't think all Korean women have VD. I just don't want to take the chance of finding one that do."

"You want cherry girl? I can get for you."

"No thank you, Mr. Kim. What I would like is for you to teach me how to speak Korean."

"You want learn speaky Korean?"

"Yes, ok?"

"Okay, I teach you number one Hangul. I think you be number one soul brother."

From that day forward he had a friend for life. Mr. Kim was a very good teacher. Although he spoke broken English, he was a very intelligent man. Every day Private Wood would try out what he had learned on some of the girls who passed through one of the gates. They would laugh and tell him to keep practicing; he would learn to speak very good Hangul someday. It was a very hard language to learn, but he learned to speak it pretty well.

Private Wood's momma constantly reminded him how happy she was he was sent to Korea instead of Vietnam. He didn't have the balls to tell her he was in the process of trying to get transferred over there. Meanwhile, his tour was on cruise control, and he was biding his time for that transfer First Sergeant Tucker was working on for him.

Private Wood should've known everything was going too good to last for very long. He hadn't had a run-in with Captain Hicks or Sergeant Pearson in some time. He hadn't apprehended anyone who wanted to kill him, or given a ticket to upset anyone since the last incident with Mrs. Hutchison. Sergeant Davis was always telling the other young squad members they should try to be more like Private Wood. He even had an appointment to see the First Sergeant about his transfer to Nam. But like that old clique', all good things must come to an end.

While working gate #2, a Korean woman without an American dependent ID card attempted to exit his gate, loaded down with goods from the Post Commissary. Private Wood knew this was highly unusual for a Korean National without a dependent ID card to attempt something this bold, knowing she would be thrown in jail for black marketing. Still he was very excited because this was his first big black market bust.

The KNP and KSG popped his bubble by telling him that the lady was none other than Staff Sergeant Pearson's yobo (girlfriend). She was taking the food to their hooch in Sam-got-chee, the village a short distance outside the gate. If he knew what was good for him, he would let her pass through without delay.

Being the dedicated young military policeman that he was, he didn't care if it was the president's girlfriend. She was breaking the law and he wouldn't let her off that easy, or Sergeant Pearson for that matter. So he reported what he had to the Desk Sergeant, not knowing that Staff Sergeant Pearson was filling in for the regular desk sergeant, who had been placed on quarters half an hour earlier for some type of illness.

"Oh, that must be Cha. She's my yobo. I picked up some stuff from the commissary earlier and I had her come up to the PMO and pick it up and take it to our hooch," Staff Sergeant Pearson explained.

"She didn't come through this gate sergeant," Private Wood said.

"I know that. She came through gate #5. I told her to go through your gate because its closer to my hooch," Sergeant Pearson explained.

"Sergeant Pearson, do you realize Miss Cha doesn't have a dependent ID card?" Private Wood asked, knowing it was a dumb question.

"Sure, I know it, you dumb shit. And if you have any sense at all you would stop harassing her and let her go," Staff Sergeant Pearson threatened.

"Sorry, Sergeant, but she broke the law and I have no choice but to bust her for it," Private Wood responded standing his ground.

"Do what, Private?" Staff Sergeant Pearson asked, not believing he had heard right.

"You heard me right, Sergeant. I've sworn to uphold the law and that is exactly what I intend to do."

"I'll be right there, Private. We'll handle this little matter face to face," Staff Sergeant Pearson growled and hung up.

The whole time they were waiting for Staff Sergeant Pearson to arrive, Miss Cha kept calling him all kinds of names, none of which he understood at the time. But he knew whatever it was she was saying couldn't possibly be terms of endearment. He was prepared for the worst as Sergeant Pearson drove up in the patrol supervisor's jeep. When Private Wood attempted to explain why he was doing what he was doing, Staff Sergeant Pearson held up his hand to silence him.

"Step outside the gate shack, Private Wood, and let's have a talk."

As they were leaving the shack, Miss Cha said something in Korean to Staff Sergeant Pearson. He said something back to her and motioned him outside to the jeep. Once they were seated inside the jeep, Staff Sergeant Pearson spoke in a fatherly tone.

"Private Wood, you're the first black private, or white one for that matter, I've ever encountered who has his shit together. But let me enlighten you as to how things work around here. Almost every MP in the company has a yobo, including the First Sergeant. And since we don't eat most of the Korean food, we buy our own from the commissary or PX annexes and take it to our hooches. Sometimes, like today, we don't have the time to take the stuff to our hooches, so we get our yobos to come up and get it. Since we're all doing the same thing, I don't mess with their yobos and they don't mess with mine. I know that doesn't make it right, but that's how it is. And if you happen to get yourself a yobo you want to shack up with, you'll be allowed the same, what should I call it, courtesy. We MPs have to stick together. Maybe I should have notified you in advance that she was coming through your gate. Would that have helped?" Staff Sergeant Pearson asked.

"No, Sergeant. I feel it's wrong to bust other people for the same thing we're knowingly allowing each other to get away with. I believe in unity within the unit, but I won't be a part of this yobo courtesy thing," Private Wood said.

"I'm sorry you feel that way, Private. But my yobo is taking my food to our hooch whether you like it or not. You can always request to see someone higher up in the chain of command."

He got out of the jeep, went inside the gate shack, said something to Miss Cha, kissed her and sent her on the way. He was coming out of the shack as Private Wood was going back in. He said, "You have the making of a damn good cop, Private. But you have to realize one thing, you're in Korea, and over here we don't always go by the book. Sometime you have to change the rules to fit the situation. All I have to say is you'd better be glad it wasn't the First Sergeant's old lady. Live and learn, son," Staff Sergeant Pearson advised and walked away.

After Staff Sergeant Pearson left the guard-shack, the KNP and KSG laughed at him and said it was no big deal, that the MPs yobos do it all the time. Private Wood swore they wouldn't do it all the time while he was working the gate. He may not be able to bust their yobos, but they would get so damn tired of having to come down to the gate for them, they would eventually only give them food and stuff from the PX to take to their hooch when he wasn't on the gate. A couple of days after the yobo incident with Sergeant Pearson's yobo, he was told to see the First Sergeant when he got off duty.

PATRIOTISM

Hot damn, it must be about my request for that transfer to Vietnam, Private Wood thought to himself. After finishing his breakfast, he went to the orderly room and was told to go ahead and knocked on the First Sergeant's office door. He was told to enter and have a seat.

"Good morning, Private Wood. It seems the only time I get a chance to talk to you is after you have managed to stick your foot in your mouth," First Sergeant Tucker said.

"I don't know what you're talking about, First Sergeant," Private Wood said, trying to recall everything that had occurred involving himself within the last twenty-four hours.

"What I'm talking about, Private Wood, is you telling Sergeant Pearson you wouldn't care if the commander's or my yobo came through your gate with something from the commissary or PX, you would bust her. Which in all reality means you would be busting us. What do you have to say about that?"

"Well, First Sergeant, I don't really know what you expect me to say. So I guess I'll tell you the same thing I told Sergeant Pearson. I'm told my job is to enforce the law. And nowhere in the UCMJ (Uniform Code of Military Justice) or Provost Marshal's SOP (Standard Operating Procedures) does it state Military Policemen are exempt from abiding by the laws they have sworn to enforce. So if that means I have to take some heat for doing my duty, so be it," Private Wood stood his ground.

The First Sergeant had a strange look on his face as he spoke. "I guess we'll have to do something about that then, won't we?" First Sergeant Tucker asked, not expecting an answer. "By the way, I called personnel about your request for a transfer to Vietnam and they said it would be a waste of time and paperwork to put it in right now. So you're stuck here with us. For how long I don't know whether you like it or not. Do you have anything to add before you're dismissed?"

"No, First Sergeant" Private Wood answered. But as an afterthought he added, "I guess by me having to serve my whole tour here in Korea puts me in one hell of a position."

"It doesn't have to. I've heard a lot of good things about you so far. I would hate to see you get screwed over just for being ambitious, if you get my drift," First Sergeant Tucker said with a wink.

"Yes, First Sergeant, I understand you very well. However, the law is still the law," Private Wood concluded.

"Very well, Private, you're dismissed. But remember one thing, Gate #36 gets very lonely and awful boring after a while," First Sergeant Tucker threatened.

Becoming angry because of the threat of putting him back on gate #36 permanently, Private Wood said, "First Sergeant, you can tell Captain Hicks and anyone else who doesn't like me that they can't scare me. I don't care if I'm left on that gate for the remainder of my tour. I don't get off on racial slurs, but you can tell these rednecks around here they won't get the satisfaction of seeing me go against what I believe in just to be on patrol. Gate #36 can be fun once you know that'll be your permanent place of duty. Ask Private Cooney." Private Wood hadn't intended to say as much as he had, but what the hell. He couldn't take it back even if he had wanted to. So he waited for the First Sergeant's reaction.

"Up until now I've tried to talk to you without hurting your feelings, Private Wood, because I have heard a lot of good things about you since you have been here. And I respect you for that, but now you're stepping on my toes. And I don't give a shit about hurting people's feelings. You're fast becoming a real pain in the ass, not only for the commander but for me as well. I'm going to make you a team player or lock your smart-alecky ass in the stockade," First Sergeant Tucker hissed almost out of breath.

"My intention is not to piss you off First Sergeant, or the commander, but I'm going to perform my duties to the best of my abilities. I know I can't apprehend anyone's girlfriend but I won't let them through my gate with stuff that other soldiers girlfriends get busted for. I'm going to perform my assigned duties to the best of my abilities, regardless of what or where those duties might be, and I'll do it without fear. You want to know something, First Sergeant? Ever since I've been a little boy, I dreamed of some day becoming a sergeant in the United States Army. Why? Because all my life I have heard it is the sergeants who are the backbone of the Army. You're the ones who called the shots on the battlefields to save your men's lives and get them back home safely. You're the ones during peacetime who trained and assigned all duties and details to your men to prepare them for the next war. You're the ones who ran your squads as you pleased as long as the mission was being accomplished, as long as no laws and regulations were being broken while you were doing it. I always thought sergeants were the proudest soldiers to ever wear the uniform."

The First Sergeant was so moved by what Private Wood said, his attitude changed. He too had dreamed of being a sergeant and doing the wonderful things Private Wood described. He didn't want to discourage him from trying to reach his goal of becoming a sergeant by telling him about the pain of being in that position during times of war. While serving in Vietnam he had watched some of his soldiers die, begging for help that no amount of stripes could provide. It hurt sometimes to be reminded of the good men and friends he lost under his supervision during his two tours of duty.

"And now?" First Sergeant Tucker asked.

"I still believe it would be an honor to someday be a sergeant. However, I don't think I could deal with commanders who wanted to run my squad or platoon. As long as I accomplished the mission and stayed within the regulations, he shouldn't have too much to say. That seems to be a common occurrence here in Korea. Is it this way throughout the Army?" Private Wood asked, putting the First Sergeant on the defense.

"No, it's not," First Sergeant Tucker answered looking slightly embarrassed. "But you have to understand that Captain Hicks as the commander, and his lieutenants, also has some say so on how things should be run in his unit."

"First Sergeant Tucker, all I ever wanted since I've been in the Army is to be assigned to Vietnam. I know the possibility exists I might get my ass blown off, or worse, be crippled for the rest of my life. I've seen both happen right there in the states. Why not let me choose where I want to take my chances?" Private Wood asked sincerely.

"It doesn't always work that way within the military system, son. It makes me proud to know there are still young men in the army today who are not afraid to risk their lives in defense of America abroad. There ain't many young men like you, black or white, willing to do that. Because of that courage, someday you young black men should be able to change the army establishment's ways of thinking, not only toward black soldiers and other minorities, but also how the army should be run as a whole. The only thing about that is it's going to take time. Do you have what it takes to fight the system even though you'll be giving up miles to their inches? And at the same time be one of the best soldiers in this man's army?"

Private Wood didn't hesitate to answer his question. "I have what it takes to stick with anything I believe in."

"Well, why don't you start right now at your level and let me worry about the commander. I've been dealing with his type all my life. Make me proud of you, son. I'm going to put my ass on the line for you every day until I leave here."

"First Sergeant, if you can keep the White power off my behind, I'll do the rest. The only thing that I ask is that I be allowed to perform my duties in accordance to the laws and regulations of the army," Private Wood said.

"Dismissed, Private," First Sergeant Tucker smiled, forgetting a minute ago he wanted to snap Private Wood's neck.

When Private Wood left the First Sergeant's office, he felt he had taken his first step toward reaching his goal of becoming a sergeant in the U.S. Army. He felt he was on the right track again and was serious about learning to work from within the army establishment, no matter how screwed up he felt it was, to make things better for all minorities. He knew the only way he could change anything was to be diplomatic while lodging his complaints. Therefore he had a lot to learn, especially how to control his temper and stop flying off the handle so much whenever he got pissed off.

Private Wood figured if he was to learn diplomacy, he might as well start at the top. He went through Staff Sergeant Pearson and got an appointment to see Captain Hicks several days later. His reason for wanting to talk to Captain Hicks was to find out where he stood with the good captain, and to see if he was serious about him not being promoted above specialist. He knew Captain Hicks would probably get pissed having to answer the questions of a private, but he considered it a learning experiment in diplomacy 101. He conditioned his mind for the confrontation with the captain as he knocked on the captain's office door.

"Come in, Private Wood. Have a seat. I suppose you're here in reference to your request for that transfer to Vietnam."

"No sir, I'm not here to talk about the transfer. What I wanted to talk to you about is the disagreement we had the first day I arrived at the unit."

Upon hearing this, Captain Hicks cut him off by saying "You have to realize I've never had a private, black or white, with enough balls to tell me I was interfering with his plans. Therefore, I said a few things I didn't really mean. God knows we have enough racial problems going on right now to last a lifetime. What do you say we bury the hatchet? I know you said some things you didn't really mean yourself. So what do you say?" he asked, extending his hand.

Private Wood shook the captain's hand, but he was not to be put off that easily. "That's fine with me, sir, but there's something I wanted to say." They both sat back down.

"Ok, Private, shoot."

"Well, sir, I initially came in here to apologize to you for going off half cocked, and to ask you a couple of questions if its okay with you."

"Apology accepted," Captain Hicks interjected before Private Wood could continue.

"One of my questions is were you serious when you said

PATRIOTISM

I would not be promoted above specialist four because black soldiers don't have the mental capacity to function above that rank?" Private Wood asked.

"Of course not. I think First Sergeant Tucker is one of the finest First Sergeants I've ever had the pleasure to work with. And as far as you're concerned, from what I've been hearing from Staff Sergeant Pearson and the Provost Marshall, you should be a sergeant, E-5 by the time you leave here. I guess I was trying to scare you into conforming to the way I felt a private should act. What is your other question?"

"Can I count on you to back me while performing my everyday military police duties?" Private Wood asked.

"I don't know what you're getting at," Captain Hicks said guardedly.

"What I'm getting at, sir, is there seems to be a bending of the rules where we, the Military Police, are concerned when it comes to Korean Nationals taking American goods off the compound. To be perfectly honest with you, sir, I don't agree with it. As I see it, either we grant that courtesy to everyone or we obey the law and let no one do it, which I don't see happening. So, when I'm on duty, enforcement of the law trumps everything else, except when an MP has to return to the unit after curfew. It seems my fellow MPs get kicked out of quite a few hooches for not paying the business girls [hookers]."

"Hmm, I see you're talking about the yobo incident with Sergeant Pearson," Captain Hicks said looking thoughtful. "Now let me ask you a question, Private Wood. Who do you think is going to cover your ass when you have to break up a bar room brawl? Or five or six guys jump you at one of the clubs while you're off duty because you're an MP?"

"To be honest with you, sir, as far as the bar room brawl is concerned, I was hoping that all of the MPs assigned to this unit are professional enough not to let their personal feelings interfere with performing their duties. At least that's what we were taught to do in AIT. I assure you, sir, I'm capable of taking care of myself when I'm off duty," he assured Captain Hicks.

"I'm glad to see you have confidence in your ability to handle any and all situations you may have to face while stationed here. However, there comes a time when we all need a friend," Captain Hicks theorized.

"Thank you, sir, for those words of wisdom, but I'm sure everything will work out just fine. All I ask is that I don't get shafted for doing my duty."

"You have my word on that," Captain Hicks promised.

"Oh, and one other thing, sir, I don't like being called a nigger, whether it's out of anger or not," Private Wood added, catching the captain off guard. Captain Hicks reacted as Private Wood thought he would.

"Look here, wise ass, up until now this conversation was developing into a meaningful discussion. I see that wasn't your intention. So let's lay the cards on the table and call a spade a spade. I'm your superior officer, and as such, I have the power to control your ass. So play ball by my rules or you don't play at all. You'll find yourself in the dugout, if you know what I mean. I truly intended to let dead dogs lie because everyone keeps telling me what a fine soldier you are. Don't make me change my mind," Captain Hicks warned.

"Sure, sir, do as I'm told, not the right thing because it may be my superior who is doing something wrong," Private Wood further antagonized the good captain.

PATRIOTISM

This really pissed the captain off. He said, "I'm going to watch you very closely my friend. And when you screw up, I'll be standing right there to rub salt in the wound. Dismissed, Private. I don't want to see you in my office again unless it is for an Article 15," Captain Hicks said.

Private Wood left Captain Hicks' office smiling to himself because he had gotten his point across. Chocolate-coated bullshit wouldn't work on him. He also knew he would have to watch his back at all times from then on. He figured with First Sergeant Tucker's help and guidance, he should make it through his tour without too many problems. In diplomacy, Private Wood theorized, you had to know people's true feelings. That way you know how to deal with them. Captain Hicks showed his true colors, and he wasn't to be trusted. Private Wood stood by his convictions whenever he was on duty, and as a result no one challenged him. However, with everyone else, life continued as usual.

Three months in country, to his surprise, he was promoted to Private First Class (PFC). He knew as far as the commander was concerned, if they held a popularity contest and Private Wood was the only one who entered, he would still come in second. Private Wood possessed very good qualities that no one could deny, not even Captain Hicks. He was very honest, treated everyone fairly, American and Korean alike, and he performed his duties in a superior manner to his peers, including being the best basketball player on the unit's basketball team. It had to be because of those qualities that he was promoted, as well as because of the respect shown him by his peers and immediate supervisors. Even Staff Sergeant Pearson forgave him for running off at the mouth and not letting his yobo take his food through his gate. Several of the guys in his squad became pretty close friends, but he wouldn't allow them to become too close because it would be the same as with the guys he had come to know too well while in basic training and AIT. They would eventually go their separate ways. He and Johnny were still good friends and kept in touch with each other and that was the only close friend he needed. Even that friendship was slowly fading because they were headed in difference directions.

Private Wood started going to the ville with the guys on the unit basketball team every now and then after games. He was amazed at the number of clubs and tiny shops crowded together in the small spaces in the village in Itaewon. Private Wood was also surprised at how good the street vendors' chicken was. His mom would never believe he was eating chicken cooked on the streets. He was further surprised at how cheaply the Korean tailors could make suits and other clothing. All you had to do was give them a design or picture and several days later you had the finished product. It amazed him how the local people used almost everything they threw away as trash. It was nothing to buy a bag of peanuts from a street vendor and the bag is constructed from the centerfold of a playboy magazine. Or see c-ration cans used as small dry food containers, or to store crushed up medical plants.

The girls were pretty and accommodating. They went out of their way to try and make the man they were with happy. Private Wood could understand why his peers went ape shit over them, and spent their entire paycheck within the first two weeks after getting paid. On top of being cheap, Private Wood couldn't see why a man would pay for something God put on earth for man to conquer and enjoy. However, he would be a liar if he said he wasn't tempted on quite a few occasions to throw a few dollars in their direction. But the letters he received from Gina were what kept him from letting loose and tasting the nectar of those pretty Oriental flowers. His fellow soldiers didn't understand how the letters from Gina enabled him to keep his built-up passion in check. Private Wood chalked it up to them never having been in love.

As the army has a tendency to do, they over compensated for the shortage of personnel at the time Private Wood and his fellow arrivals were assigned to the unit. Within three months of their arrival in the unit, it had gotten enough replacements in so that they no longer had to work twelve-hour shifts. They went to 9 days on and 3 days off rotating shift. Under this system they worked 3 midnight shifts, 3 swing shifts, 3 days shifts, and had 3 days off. This allowed for a lot of time off. Private Wood spent the majority of his time at the gym playing basketball or going on sightseeing tours with Mr. Kim every chance he got. To Private Wood, Korea was a very beautiful and exciting country. He couldn't understand why the veterans back home who had been to Korea could say the country was so screwed up. Sure the customs and food were different, but you could find that without even leaving the United States.

Almost every comment Private Wood ever heard made about Korea was how bad the people stunk, that they all lived in mud huts reinforced with straw, and that they were all thieves out to rip off American servicemen. Whenever his daddy overheard him repeating negative gossip about Korea prior to his leaving, he would sit him down and tell him that as long as he lived, he should never believe everything he heard. Now that he was getting a first-hand look at the country, and getting to know the people, he came to the conclusion that what he had heard about Korea was plain lies. Private Wood could understand why those who fought in the Korean War didn't like the country, but Korea had changed a hell of a lot since then. The current soldiers who served in Korea didn't like it because they were either racists, hermits who never went anywhere, had one bad experience, or didn't like anywhere other than America.

    Private Wood had to admit it took a while to get accustomed to the smell of the countryside and some of the food, especially kimchi. It also took him a while to get use to doorways built for people less than six feet tall. On more than one occasion while visiting First Sergeant Tucker or Mr. Kim at their hooches, Private Wood would bump his head going in and out the doors. Another matter it took some getting used to were the outhouses. Being Private Wood was born and raised on a farm he was no stranger to outhouses, but the outhouses in America had seats to sit on while you were taking a crap. The outhouses in Korea were designed the same as a soldier's latrine was when they were playing war games in the woods, a trench. The difference was, in the bush there was no protection from the elements of nature, ie rain, wind, or cold, etc. And when the soldiers finished their training they just covered the trench and were on their way. The Korean toilets gave protection from the elements of nature, but they had to be cleaned out by dipping the waste out with big buckets and hauling it away in what the American soldiers called a honey wagon. Private Wood never made the connection between feces and honey, but agreed it stunk to high heaven if you happened to be in the vicinity when one passed your way during the summer months. The waste haulers would haul the waste out to the countryside to be use as fertilizer in the rice paddies. As gross as it sounds, Private Wood never ate a grain of rice that smelled like crap. And as far as stealing was concerned, his fellow servicemen did most of the stealing. Of course there were times when Private Wood himself would lose his temper and say something stupid about the Korean people or their country. Normally, though, he ended up admitting to himself that there were undesirables all over the world, including America.

One of the things Private Wood found extremely difficult to adjust to was the name calling. The Korean people he knew as Mr. Kim, Mr. Park, Miss Kim, or Mrs. Park, to most of the American GI's, they were slant-eyed gooks. It was upsetting to Private Wood to hear his fellow American soldiers talk like that because to him it was the same as him being called a nigger back in the good old U.S. of A. The other thing that upset him was hearing the white soldiers tell the Korean people they should learn to speak English. They acted as if the Korean people were visitors in their own country.

Private Wood wondered what it would take for the Korean people to rebel against white soldiers acting as if they owned the country, and disrespecting them on a daily basis. One hot summer night he got his answer. All hell broke loose in Itaewon after several white soldiers raped an eleven-year-old Korean girl.

Private Wood was lying on his bunk reading when the CQ came running into the barracks telling everyone to get dressed, there was a riot in Itaewon and the locals was beating the hell out of American GIs. Every off duty MP in the barracks was dressed and on their way to the ville in Itaewon in a matter of minutes. Although the American MPs knew the Korean drivers paid no attention to an MP jeep siren on the main roadway, they used the emergency equipment anyway, fussing and cussing all the way to the riot scene. When Private Wood and the rest of Company C 728th MP back-ups reached the ville, there were beat-up GI's lying in the streets groaning, moaning, and begging for someone to help them. A large number of Korean locals were on top of the buildings throwing anything they could get their hands on.

There were sticks, bricks, chairs, desks, bottles, shot glasses, bar glasses, tea cups, and regular water glasses strewed up and down the streets, and alleyways. Korean police officers and Korean Army MPs were standing around not making any attempt to stop what was going on, or attempting to help the down soldiers. They said they were tired of ducking and dodging the crap being thrown at them when they tried to help the white soldiers.

Private Wood was surprised to learn the Korean people were only beating the hell out of white American GIs. Each American MP patrol was augmented with a KATUSA (Korean Auxiliary to The United States Army) MP. The KATUSA were used as interpreters. The KATUSAs were from well to do families who did not want their sons serving in the ROK (Republic of Korea) Army whose leadership was known for their unwavering discipline of its soldiers. This caused a lot of animosity between the ROK soldiers and the KATUSAs. The KATUSAs slept on U.S. Army cots, ate American food, wore American type uniforms, and were required to do very little physical exercise. Therefore in the eyes of the ROK soldiers, the KATUSAs were weak individuals and not real Korean soldiers because they had it too easy. The real ROK army soldier slept on the floor. They ate unappetizing food, and were pushed to the limit of their physical endurance almost daily.

To get even with the KATUSAs, the ROK MPs would beat the hell out of them every chance they got, and there were no retaliation or recourse for the KATUSAs to demand justice. The American soldier could understand why the KATUSAs joined the Ameri-

PATRIOTISM

can army. In the ROK army it was common to see ROK enlisted soldiers being disciplined with some type of object because physical punishment was standard policy. Disobeying an order could be deadly, like the incident related to Private Wood by Specialist Thomas.

Private Wood was enjoying a relaxing day off watching television in the dayroom when Specialist Thomas came in to report the highlight of his duty day. The story he told confirmed their belief that an American soldier wouldn't survive in the ROK army because the American soldiers had a habit of disrespecting lower ranking officers.

"Man, those ROK army officers are brutal. I mean hard core brother," Specialist Thomas said.

"Yeah I know," Private Wood said before he could continue.

"No man, you don't know. Check this out. The KNP and KSG at gate #10 goes ape shit when this ROK general, and three ROK MP jeeps come roaring up to the gate and tell the guards they don't have time to explain everything because they had a soldier with a gunshot wound on the back seat that needed a doctor, and they were transporting him to the 121 Evac Hospital. Specialist Schultz notifies the desk and we get the call to check it out, right? So we cruise up to the hospital thinking a soldier got shot accidentally at the firing range or something. Sergeant Davis didn't sound excited or anything when he told us to check it out, so we knew there were no shootout or anything like that going down. We were told to make contact with the general and he would explain what happened. Anyway, we pull up in front of the hospital and there are these three ROK MP jeeps. Check this shit out man. There is a four star ROK army general's jeep parked in front of the hospital. They didn't tell us it was a damn four star general. How the hell were we supposed to deal with a fucking four star general? We notify the desk of the ROK general's jeep and they're freaking out, and tell us not to do anything stupid, that Colonel Heath, Captain Gardner, and Master Sergeant Snoop were already en-route to our location. Private Jung sees the general's jeep, and the ROK MP jeeps and he freaks out. He's scared shitless because he knows the ROK MPs and general are going to jump knee deep in his ass if he asks the wrong questions.

We get out of the jeep and go into the hospital to see what happened. I go up to the front desk and ask to speak with the doctor who was treating the dude, but they say he's still in surgery. So I tell Jung to ask the ROK MPs what happened. He said maybe we should wait until the colonel and captain got there. I said to hell with that, so I went up to the ROK MPs and asked what happened. The ROK MPs couldn't speak English but the general could. He asked me what was it I needed to know. I said, like what happened to the dude, sir? He tells me one of his lieutenants drove up to the entrance gate to their compound and the private refused to salute him, and when the soldier disobeyed an order to salute him, the lieutenant took out his 45 cal pistol and shot him. The general said he was there because he knew the soldier's family. I freak out, right. I didn't know what to say. Luckily by this time the colonel and captain show up and took control of the situation. We heard later that the dude died on the operating table. I didn't notice it, but Jung said the ROK MPs called him a flunky and gave him a hard time. I tell you man, that general sounded like if the dude didn't die he was going to shoot him again," Specialist Thomas finished his story.

"So what did the colonel say to the general?" Private Wood asked.

PATRIOTISM

"I don't know. When Master Sergeant Snoop told us to bail, we bailed. I wanted to see where the dude was shot, but they didn't let us in the operating room. This was one hell of a day. Hey, lets go to the club and have a few before I go to the ville," Specialist Thomas offered.

"Naw man, you go ahead. I'm going to finish watching this old movie," Private Wood said.

Private Wood asked Sergeant Chang, his KATUSA partner, what was happening after he had talked to several individuals hanging around in the streets.

"They say some tissue GIs raped a young girl. Since they don't know who it was, they're beating up all white GIs."

"Do they have any idea who the GIs are?" Private Wood asked.

Sergeant Chang talked to the individuals briefly again and said, "They say they don't know. So if they beat up all the white GIs in the village tonight they'll get the right ones."

Ambulances from 121st Evacuation Hospital were dispatched to recover the hurt soldiers. The white ambulance drivers were assaulted with thrown objects as they attempted to load the hurt soldiers into the ambulances. The MPs ended up loading the hurt soldiers because the Korean locals knew they would be in serious trouble for assaulting American Military Policemen. The situation wasn't brought under control until the midnight curfew when the bars and shops were required to closed. A total of 25 white GI's ended up getting hurt, two seriously. Supposedly there was no way to prove who was responsible for injuring the GIs, so no one in the local community was held responsible for what happened. Everyone knew the Korean Policemen could have found out who the ringleaders were if they wanted to, but swore they couldn't.

The white soldiers who raped the little girl were eventually apprehended and sent to a Korean jail in Suwon to serve seven years each under the SOFA (Status of Forces Agreement) between Korea and the United States that gave Korea jurisdiction of GIs committing crimes on Korean on their soil.

Private Wood learned the following day that black soldiers had pointed out the hiding places of any white soldier they could find. They said if it were black soldiers getting the hell beat out of them, white soldiers wouldn't have given a damn about them either. Private Wood wondered what it was going to take for America's soldiers to put aside that racist crap and realize they were all on the same team, and that they were in Korea to help the Korean people secure their country and not disrespect them. That wasn't necessarily what happened because the majority of the GIs disrespected the Korean people on a daily basis, especially the women.

Private Wood thought back to his first night on the town with the guys and wondered how the women put up with the abuse and disrespect shown them by the American GIs. The guys talked about how they treated the whores in the ville, but hearing about it and seeing it first hand was as different as day and night. He had been raised to respect people, especially women, regardless of their downfall, excluding drugs. The MP hangout was the Seven Club in Itaewon. As soon as the guys got out of the taxi, they started grabbing the butts and breasts of every girl within their reach. The girls who spoke English cussed them in English, the girls who couldn't speak English cussed them in their native tongue. Some cussed them in both languages. This seemed to amuse his fellow soldiers instead of pissing them off.

"They ain't nothing but whores, hell, they used to shit like that," Specialist Thomas explained, when Private Wood asked why they did stupid stuff like that.

Fourteen of Private Wood's fellow MPs ended up at the Seven Club that night. He was having a really good time for the first time since he had been in the country that is until later that night when the guys said they had all chipped in and paid for a cherry girl for him, meaning she was a virgin. The girl was so beautiful she looked like a fragile doll, labeled 'do not touch,' as momma-san led her to the center of the dance floor for all to see. Momma-san swore up and down she was telling the truth about the girl still being a virgin.

"A cherry girl for the cherry boy," they all sang in a chorus.

"She got big tits too. I show you," Momma-san said, grabbing the girl's blouse and opening it in front, exposing her bare breasts.

The guys all howled and cheered. The poor girl burst into tears and ran out of the club clutching her blouse as if by doing so she could hide her shame.

"She be okay when you go hoochie," he was assured by Momma-san.

Private Wood had been so repulsed by the humiliation the girl had suffered he had to get out of there. "Hey, fellows, I really appreciate what you guys have done for me, but I can do my own shopping. I need a bit of fresh air," he managed to say without showing his true feelings.

"Her hooch is right around the corner, man. Go for it," Specialist Thomas encouraged him.

Private Wood left the club and went to the girl's hooch and knocked on the door. He could hear her still crying. After a long hesitation she finally opened the door and told him to come in. She spoke very little English, so communication with her was difficult. As soon as he was inside, she turned off the light and started to undress.

"No, don't do that," he stopped her and turned the light back on.

"You no likey me?" she asked perplexed.

"It's not that. I don't even know you. I just don't like what Momma-san did to you there in the club. And I came to see if you're okay."

"You no wanna makey love?"

"No. I see you don't know what I'm trying to say, so I'm going back to the compound."

"Why no wanna me? I looka no good?"

"No, you're not ugly. You're very, very pretty. Look, I don't know what or how to tell you what I'm trying to say, so I'm going to leave." He stood up to leave and she burst into tears again. He sat back down beside her until her sobs subsided.

"Me wanna go home. Me wanna go home," she managed to say.

"Why don't you? Why you no go home?" he asked using sign language to stress what he was trying to say.

"Me oma sell Momma-san. Now me hava stay. No home cango," she explained in broken English and started crying again.

Private Wood imagined this must have been how his ancestors in America felt as slaves. It really pissed him off, but as he knew he could not change the history of blacks in America, he couldn't prevent or stop what was happening in Korea. So he stayed with her until she fell asleep in his arms. She had also managed to tell him she was only eighteen. He covered her with a blanket, left $20.00 for her on the small table in the room and made his way back to the compound. It was 2:30 a.m., long after the midnight curfew. Since he allowed this courtesy to his fellow MPs and other solders kicked out of their hooches, he didn't have to worry about getting into trouble for breaking it.

The next day everyone wanted to know if Miss Lee was any good in bed. Private Wood told them she was a lousy lay. Maybe it was because she was a virgin. They let it go at that, and they no longer called him a cherry boy. The Korean women on the other hand knew better. Therefore, his cherry-boy status with them remained unchanged. *Damn twentieth century slavery*, he said to himself whenever he thought of Miss Lee.

Private Wood saw Miss Lee off and on after that night, but he didn't have the heart too mess with her, knowing what she was going through. She told him he didn't have to pay momma-san, or her, anything in the future if she didn't have anyone to take home with her at the end of the night, she liked him. He told her he had a girlfriend stateside and wouldn't want her to get attached to him because he had no intentions of breaking up with Gina. They could be friends, but that was as far as it would go.

The other thing that pissed Private Wood off was the drug abuse among his fellow black soldiers. White soldiers were just as guilty, but he looked at being in Korea as an opportunity to show another part of the world that Black Americans wanted more than just drugs and a woman to have a good time with, but sometime he felt it was a lost cause. Night after night the same scenario played itself out on the streets of Itaewon, and other villages throughout Korea in one form or another.

Private Wood would meet brothers from other units he played basketball with on a daily basis on the streets of Itaewon and they would be stoned out of their minds. One of the best basketball players in Korea was Specialist Graham; he was also one of the biggest drug abusers in Korea. Every time Private Wood met him on the streets of Itaewon or at the club on post, the conversation was always the same.

"Hey, Wood, what's up brother. I'm so high. I don't feel a thang. I'm on cloud nine baby, and everything's groovy," he slurred.

"Graham, man, don't you know you're killing yourself with that crap. Those pills, the grass, and booze is doing terrible things to your body, man," Private Wood told him.

"Hey, I can still take your ass on the basketball court, huh?" he laughed.

"Yeah, when your mind ain't fucked up with drugs," Private Wood said.

"It's my way of dealing with the shit that's going on in my life, and this fucked up racist world man. When I'm high none of that shit matters, man. I'm in a world where nothing can hurt me. If I have to go through life sober, I'm going to kill someone man. Every day I want to take a white boy out. Naw, Wood, I can't survive without this shit man. I wished I was like you, but I'm not. Very few brothers are capable of dealing with this racist shit like you can. That's why so many of us are strung out man, its a means of escape," Specialist Graham said.

"How're you going to escape once you get back to the world and they bust your ass for using that shit?" Private Wood asked.

"I don't think about it brother. I'll deal with it when I have to. But here in Korea, I have my yobo, my drugs, and nothing else matters. Peace brother." He would stagger off lost in the fog enshroud world of his mind.

PATRIOTISM

The next day at the gym, Specialist Graham wouldn't even remember the conversations they had the previous night. If it had just been Specialist Graham destroying his brain, Private Wood wouldn't have been so concerned about his brothers in arms, but there were too many to count. It didn't help that in Korea anyone could go to a corner drugstore and get whatever your heart desired. The army knew about the drug trade, but it didn't matter because the bodies may be needed in Vietnam.

Drug abuse aside, the one thing Private Wood was most proud of was the unity shared by almost every black soldier in Korea. Of course the degree of discord shown depended on how far up the chain of command the black soldier was. They didn't have much of a choice because racism in Korea was almost as bad as it was back in the United States. As unreal as it sounds, white soldiers established Jim Crow clubs in Korea, and the Korean bar owners refused to serve black soldiers. White commanders routinely refused to promote black soldiers and constantly put them on the worst details. When they complained, the black soldiers were threatened with disciplinary action for being disobedient or lazy. Complaints about the injustice suffered by Black American Soldiers went unheard and ignored until drastic measures were taken by the black soldiers to correct the problems.

Private Wood got a lot of his information of what was going on in Korea, racially, from the guys he played basketball with from the different units throughout Korea, and those who complained to him when he had to apprehend them for some minor infraction in their unit or in the ville. It didn't take a genius to see that black soldiers were punished unfairly for minor infractions; because the same infractions committed by white soldiers on many occasions was handled by NCOs or the platoon leaders, which was usually a second lieutenant. When the rumor of a countrywide sit-in started among the black soldiers in Private Wood's unit, he asked First Sergeant Tucker about it one day at the gym, unknowingly the day before the actual sit-in occurred.

"First Sergeant, I know you've heard the rumor that a lot of black soldiers are planning on having a sit in on the 8th Army Headquarters parade field. If they do, what're we going to do, shoot them?" Private Wood asked.

First Sergeant Tucker rubbed his chin and said, "Yeah, I've heard the rumor, but I don't believe it. Do you really think the majority of the black soldiers in Korea are going to risk being busted or thrown in jail for something they can't change? I know the situation for black soldiers here in Korea is not how it should be right now, but me and other senior NCOs are working our asses off to try and do something about this racist crap. As long as we don't give them a reason to screw us anymore than they're screwing us already, we should be able to change things over time."

"How much time does the army establishment need to do the right thing, First Sergeant? You know I'm not going to be a part of no sit-in, but I won't shoot the black soldiers that do," Private Wood said.

"You don't have to worry about that. We wouldn't come out with guns blazing against our own troops. Bust a few heads maybe, but I'm sure we won't be ordered to shoot them," First Sergeant Tucker said, unsure of what he had said.

Private Wood hoped what the First Sergeant had said was true because he would refuse an order to shoot black soldiers who were tired of being treated unfairly. He was well aware that most of the flack he was catching for being patriotic, and not going along with the unit's unwritten policies about allowing each other to break the laws they had sworn to enforce was because he was black. Private Wood also knew when the black soldiers finally reached their breaking point, the repercussions would be felt throughout the country. He entertained the thought of joining the demonstration if it did happened, but knew he wouldn't because it was against the law for any group of soldiers to hold a demonstration against the United States Army, especially on foreign soil. The belief among the white officers and NCOs throughout the 8th U.S. Army Command was black soldiers weren't capable of organizing to the point that it would make a difference in 8th Army policies or regulations.

History tells us that people can be suppressed for only a period of time before they rebel against their suppressors, or the system that allows that suppression. This is the point the black soldiers of the 8th United States Army Korea had reached in 1971. For years the army establishment had ignored the complaints of its black soldiers, of all ranks, about the unfair treatment of their commanding officers and the local Korean bar and shop owners. Many of the black soldiers helping to put the demonstration together were members of black power groups prior to being drafted into the army. At least one was a card-carrying member of the Black Panther Party. So in the hooches of yobos, smoke filled bars, and over orderly room telephones throughout Korea, the black soldiers decided they had had enough; it was time to act. Their slogan was *"what the hell can they to us, send us to Vietnam."* The 8th Army parade field was chosen by the black leaders of the group because of the impact it would make on public perception. Two weeks later the plan was executed with unfathomable results.

The week leading up to the demonstration, the word was passed along by mail clerks, fuel truck drivers, dispatchers, orderly room clerks, and even Korean villagers for everyone who was tired of their treatment to be at the parade field in front of the 8th U.S. Army Headquarters' building at 0600 hours that Saturday morning. They converged on the headquarter building in groups of five and ten until their numbers swelled to at least a hundred to demand equal treatment. The leaders of the demonstration had stressed the point that no weapons were allowed among the demonstrators.

The only staff personnel on duty at the time were the post duty officer and his runner. The leaders of the group moved quickly to prevent them from sounding the alarm of their presence. The white duty officer and his white runner didn't know what to make of the six to seven black soldiers, in civilian clothing, who entered the duty office and told him to chill-out, they were taking over the command for a while.

"What the hell is going here, troops?" the duty officer asked.

"Don't do anything stupid and everything will be okay, sir. We want to talk to General Iron Mike McMichaels about the treatment of his black soldiers."

"You can't just come in here and demand to see the general. Who the hell do you people think you are?" the duty officer demanded weakly.

"Since the general wouldn't come to us, we decided to come to him. What's the number to his quarters?" the leader of the group asked.

"I don't know who you are, but I'll be damned if I'm going wake the general this time of morning," the duty officer said.

"Hey, what about you, Specialist?" the black soldier asked the runner.

PATRIOTISM

"Shit, you crazy if you think I'm gonna call the general," the specialist said.

"Okay, I guess I'll have to call him myself. Give me your notification roster," the black soldier said. After getting the notification roster, he dialed the general's quarters and waited for an answer. The general answered the phone himself.

"Hello, this has better be good," the general answered the phone.

"General McMichaels, this is one of your black soldiers who you don't give a damn about. We came here to your headquarters to give you a list of our grievances. Can you come down to your headquarters and talk to us, sir?"

"Talk to who? Who the hell are you?" the general asked perplexed.

"Like I said general, one of your black soldiers who would like to take advantage of your open door policy, " the soldier answered.

"You have to use the chain of command to talk to your commander, you know that soldier," the general remained calm.

"Tried that already, sir. Black soldiers can't even use the chain of command to talk to their unit commanders. So as you can see, sir, the chain of command, when it comes to your black soldiers don't work," the black soldier said.

"Just how many of my black soldiers are there to see me, soldier?" the general asked.

"I would say about two hundred sir," the black soldier answered, slightly inflating the number.

"Jesus. Are you soldiers armed?" the general wanted to know.

"No, sir. The only thing we're armed with is a list of grievances we want you to address, that's all. By the way sir, we wrote a letter to the NAACP in Washington, D.C. a week ago informing them of our intentions so they'll be able to tell the American people what happened in the event we're gunned down by our fellow soldiers. I'm sure they have the letter by now," the black soldier said.

"Okay, I'll see what I can do. Let me talk to the duty officer," the general requested.

The black soldier handed the phone to the duty officer and laughed when the duty officer tried to explain how black soldiers had walked into the office and taken over. He told the general that the black soldiers were not armed. He didn't know how many there were because he hadn't been outside since they showed up. No, sir, he hadn't called the MP Station because they had control of the phones. No, sir, he didn't get a chance to notify the post commander. Loud enough for everyone present to hear, the general shouted into the phone that the duty officer was an incompetence piece of shit. After hanging up, the duty officer ask them if he could notify the post commander, maybe he would come down and talk to them.

The black soldier in charge said, "Sure, you can call the post commander. But just in case you call the MPs instead, we have notified them already."

"What do you mean?" the duty officer asked.

"You'll find out soon enough," the duty officer was advised.

A group of black soldiers, approximately 20, went over to the MP Station to let the MPs know they were holding a peaceful demonstration on the parade ground in front of the headquarters building to air their grievances, and they weren't going to leave until they were heard. If they wanted to lock them up in the detention cells, that was ok, but pictures were being taken to send to the NAACP in Washington, D.C. to show how the army deals with its black soldiers who are being discriminated against in Korea.

PATRIOTISM

Lieutenant Colonel Heath, the Provost Marshall, was notified of what was going on by the MP Duty officer. Colonel Heath in turn called the post commander, Colonel Archer, to inform him of what was going on. Colonel Archer informed Colonel Heath that he had already been informed by the post duty officer. He told Colonel Heath to do whatever he thought appropriate to break up the demonstration, but he was not to apprehend, nor physically hurt, any of the demonstrators.

Every officer and noncommissioned officer in positions or authority, every MP, and off duty MP that could be reached was dispatched to headquarters. The PM decided that the black soldiers at the MP Station posed no threat, so he left a skeleton crew of MPs to handle that situation. There were no black officers on the staff at 8th U.S. Army Headquarters, so they sent in every black NCO they could get their hands on to try and get the black soldiers to disband and go back to their units. The black NCOs advised their fellow black soldiers that their voices had been heard and they were sure something would be done about the racism and discrimination they were experiencing, which of course the black soldiers didn't believe and refused to disband.

Private Wood was on duty when the demonstration went down. He and Specialist Thomas were dispatched to the parade ground in reference to a disturbance. When they arrived at the scene and saw all the black faces, he was completely blown away. He didn't even know there were that many black soldiers in Korea. Private Wood thought it was creative on their part to lower the Stars and Stripes and raise the African red, green, and black flag in its place. Although Private Wood knew it was illegal to demonstrate against your government on foreign soil, he couldn't help but sympathize with them because he was faced with white racist attitude on a daily basis also. The difference was, he at least got a chance to get back at some of the white racists when he was locking them up for illegal conduct.

Caught unprepared for such a large gathering of disgruntled black soldiers, the Post Commander, Colonel Archer, was forced to listen to their grievances. When he arrived at the headquarters building, Colonel Archer surveyed the situation and asked who was in charge of the demonstration. He was told the leaders of the demonstration were in the duty officer's office. The colonel walked into the building with confidence that he would be able to tell the black soldiers what they wanted to hear and put an end to the disturbance. He walked into the office and asked who was in charge.

Although there were several leaders, only one did the talking so far, so he spoke up. "I am sir." The designated leader said. No one had identified themselves by name or rank throughout the demonstration.

"Okay soldier, talk to me," Colonel Archer said.

"Sir, we have been complaining to our commanders throughout Korea about how we're discriminated against by them and the Korean local bar and shop owners for some time now. We're given article 15s for the same offenses white soldiers are given counseling statements. There are local Korean bar owners right here in Itaewon who won't serve a black soldier at the request of white soldiers. In many cases we have time in rank over our white counterparts, but they're the ones who get promoted. An example of what I'm talking about sir is an incident that occurred in my unit. I won't say what unit it is though you'll probably find out later. Anyway, I was given an article 15 for possession of a joint that was found under my bed. A white specialist, same unit, was busted with a two pound bag of grass in his wall locker and was given a counseling statement because he said he didn't know how it got in there. We requested black reading material such as Jet and Ebony magazines be put in the dayroom, only to be told it would be a waste of money because black soldiers don't or can't read anyway.

We can no longer put up with this racist bullshit, sir. We'd rather be court-marshaled and kicked out of the army rather than to continue being subjected to this racist shit," the black soldier said angrily.

"Is that it?" Colonel Archer asked.

"That's it for now, sir. But if we continue to be treated like dirt and discriminated against, we'll be back again and again. As a matter of fact, we'll be back tomorrow to insure you're doing something about our grievances," the black soldier finished.

"I'll make sure your grievances are addressed with General McMichaels, but you all have to disband and go back to your units and let us handle this," the colonel said.

"We'll return to our units after we talk to you tomorrow at noon here at headquarters," the black soldier said.

"I'll talk to you and the other leaders of this demonstration, but we can't have this mob mentality that is taking place right now."

"Mob mentality? What mob mentality, sir? Not one black soldier has committed a crime, or threatened anyone with physical harm. All we want is equality, sir, and we won't be satisfied until we get it," the black soldier explained to Colonel Archer.

"I promise you, things will change but it's going to take time. But I promise you things will change in time," Colonel Archer promised.

"We'll be back tomorrow to make sure our message got out, sir," the designated spokesman for the black soldier said and walked out with the other black soldiers at his heels. When he got outside and said their message had been delivered, the black soldiers on the parade field lowered the African flag and re-raised Old Glory. As word spread that the demonstration was ending, the black soldiers disappeared into the villages of Itaewon, Sam-gotchee, Yong-dong-po, and the villages adjoining their compounds upon returning to their units that night. The demonstration lasted a total of five hours, but it seemed much longer.

After the demonstration ended, Colonel Heath was on the horn trying to gather support to crush the rebellion should they keep their promise to return the following day. He had been pissed because there weren't enough MPs to control the situation. He and his staff had run around like individuals with diarrhea looking for a toilet. Colonel Heath knew the lack of control would look bad on his Officer Evaluation Report (OER).

The following day, in addition to PFC Wood's company, Company C 728th MP, Colonel Heath brought in MPs from Company A & B 728th MPs from Deagu and Peongtaek, and MPs from the 2nd and 7th Infantry Division stationed at the DMZ. The MPs were decked out in full battle gear, to include the long black bayonets at the end of their M-16 rifles. Private Wood and the other black MPs sat around and laughed at the spectacle, because they knew none of the black soldiers were going to return that day. They had been told by the black members of their unit who were involved in the demonstration that no one would be back because the demonstration had served its purpose. The several black MPs who had been involved in the demonstration avoided punishment because they had blended into the crowd on the parade field. When asked later why they hadn't responded to the alert and returned to the unit, they said they were asleep in their yobos hooches and no one notified them as to what was going on.

When the black soldiers didn't show up to get beaten or locked up, the MPs were told to stand down at seven o'clock that Sunday evening. The only incident that happened that day was an MP cut himself while playing with his bayonet and had to be taken to the 121st Evacuation Hospital for stitches.

Not wanting the U.S. Army to be embarrassed by the bad publicity it would receive if wholesale punishment was handed out to all of the demonstrators, only the leaders of the demonstration were given Article 15s, reduced in rank, and given dishonorable discharges because the NAACP had notified General McMichaels in writing that they were aware of what was going on in his command in Korea. The 8th U.S. Army Commanding General put out a directive informing the Korean bar and shop owners countrywide, if they didn't serve all of his soldiers he would put the whole village off limit to everyone in the command. And to go a step further, he ordered all clubs to play both soul and country music upon request. Money talks, you know what walks.

Race relations classes were started throughout the 8th United States Army Command, and commanders had to justify why black soldiers in their commands were not being promoted or explain why the perception existed. It would be a false analogy to say, *'they lived happily ever after'*, but changes were made that were more favorable to the black soldiers serving their country in Korea.

Private Wood thought it was ironic that black soldiers had to fight the military for equality in Korea, while black soldiers were fighting and dying in the war in Vietnam to insure the South Vietnamese people could have the freedom black soldiers themselves didn't have in the military or the United States. He wasn't bitter, but he knew something had to give if America was to convince the world that it was a country that treated all its citizens equally.

Private Wood was with the first group of soldiers to attend a race relations class when the policy was implemented by 8th U.S. Army Headquarters. Ironically the Sergeant they chose to lead the race relations classes on the installation in Yongsan was Sergeant First Class Rodney Black, a black NCO. They chose him because of his unique story about how he was able to deal with the race issue. A story people from all walks of life said may be true, but took with a grain of salt.

Sergeant First Class Black was born and raised in the Mississippi Delta where Klu Klux Klan members wore their attire in public as a symbol of pride. At the age of 12, he and his family were awakened in the middle of the night by Klan members who dragged his daddy out of the house and hung him from a tree in the front yard. They told his momma it was because he had bumped into a white woman on purpose while coming out of the local grocery store, and had the balls to tell her she should watch where she was going. His momma told him and his nine brothers and sister their daddy said he bumped into the white woman by accident, and that he apologized to the white lady for bumping into her.

When his momma screamed at the lynchers that they knew that the white lady was lying, they laughed and said it didn't matter, he should've waited until the white woman was inside the store before coming out the door. When his momma reported the murder to the local sheriff she was told since there were no witnesses to the crime, there were nothing he could do about it. And since she was the wife of the so-called murder victim her testimony wouldn't hold up in a court of law. The class participants were in awe that he wasn't bitter about the incident until he advised them that wasn't the most unique part of his story, because lynching of black men in 1930s and 1940s was common. It was what occurred later in his life that made his story unique.

During Sergeant First Class Black's senior year in high school, he started seeing the daughter of one of the Klan members who hung his daddy, Judy Mae. Every other day after school they would meet in a secret location in a wooded area behind the levee and make plans for after they graduated. Their plans were for him to join the army after graduating and he would send for her when he reached his first permanent duty station, unless his first duty station was overseas. In that situation they would hook up upon his return stateside. On one of those secret meetings, Judy Mae's brother followed her, without her knowing it, to see where she went on these excursions after school.

Luckily for Sergeant First Class Black, on this particular day he was in a hurry so the meeting was very brief. Lucky because if he hadn't been in a hurry her brother would have seen the parting kiss they always shared at the end of these meetings. When her brother told her pa what he had witnessed, Judy Mae said the nigger just happened across her path. She only went there to clear her head when she was feeling the pressures of upcoming tests and her pending graduation. Still, her pa stopped by Sergeant First Class Black's house and told him if he even thought he was trying to mess with his daughter he would receive the same treatment that his daddy did. Of course he told his momma he wasn't stupid enough to mess with white girls. Undeterred, they resumed their secret rendezvous until he graduated. They just made sure no one was following them.

As planned, after Sergeant First Class Black graduated from high school he joined the army and was sent to France. They wrote each other regularly, but she had to get a post office box in town because she couldn't risk her ma or pa intercepting his letters to her. At the end of his tour in France he was assigned to a unit at Fort Carson, Colorado. Prior to reporting to Fort Carson he was given a thirty-day furlough. While home on leave he and Judy Mae made arrangements for her to join him in Colorado. Somehow their plan was uncovered several days before they were to leave and Sergeant First Class Black had to get out of Mississippi in a hurry. Sergeant First Class Black stayed with relatives in Arkansas until it was time for him to report for duty at Fort Carson. Judy Mae was forbidden to leave the house until her pa was certain that army nigger was gone. But love found a way. They simply met in their secret location and slipped away in the middle of the night. That was fifteen years ago Sergeant First Class Black said proudly, and we're still together.

The white soldiers wanted to know how his wife was treated by the white dependents wives in their neighborhood on post, by the white people in the town, and did her family ever accept her marriage to a black man. Sergeant First Class Black explained that it was hard at first, but times were changing and people were becoming more tolerant of interracial marriages. And no her family never did accept her marriage to him, but it was their loss because they were missing out on seeing their three grandchildren grow up.

PATRIOTISM

The black soldiers wanted to know why he wanted to marry Judy Mae knowing her daddy had a hand in the hanging his daddy, or why he wanted to marry a white woman period knowing what the white men had done to his daddy. He explained that his wife was not guilty for the sins of her daddy. They were two young people who happened to fall in love and got married. Everyone wanted to know if it was his way of getting back at Judy Mae's pa because he had participated in the hanging of his daddy. After all, what better way was there to get even with a racist than to marry his daughter? He assured them it wasn't his motivation for marrying his wife.

To give white soldiers a feeling of what it was like to be a black soldier in the United States Army, Sergeant First Class Black had them play roles whereby they switch who was the dominant race in power. The first scenario played were two soldiers of equal rank, Sergeant E-5, one black the other one white, and both are receiving article 15's for possession of marijuana. The commander is black and decides their punishment. While receiving his punishment, the white soldier tells the commander he knew he made a mistake and how much he regret embarrassing the unit and himself. He pleaded with the commander for leniency because he had a wife and two kids. If he were given another chance he wouldn't be caught in that position again. The commander tells him there is no excuse for what he did and bust him to private, gives him fifteen days confinement to the barracks, and fifteen days extra duty. The white soldier leaves the commander office feeling the punishment is too severe for a first time offense. The black soldier tells the same commander that he was sorry about what happened and would make sure he never got caught with marijuana again. The commander tells him that since this is his first offense he would receive fifteen days confinement to the barracks, fifteen days extra duty, and fined one month pay. The black soldier was pissed because the commander was taking a month's pay from him. The two soldiers ends up in the dayroom (recreation room) comparing notes on their punishment.

"Man, the commander is a hard bastard. He busted me down to private and didn't bat an eye. I beg him not to take my stripes because I have a wife and two kids back in the states. Does he give a damn, hell no, I don't know how I'm going to explain this to my wife," the white soldier said.

"I don't think he's all that bad, although the bastard took a full month's pay away from me. Hell, everybody in Korea smokes grass or worse. Why do you think he busted you and not me?" the black soldier asked.

"Hell, you know why," the white soldier responded.

"What do you mean, I know?" the black soldier asked, genuinely ignorant of the fact that racism exists in the military.

"It's because you're black. You're one of them, the dominant black race," the white soldier answered.

"Aw, come on man. I get so sick and tired of you white guys bellyaching when you get caught screwing up and the punishment is handed out. You got what you deserve," the black soldier said.

"Oh, yeah? Then explain to me why your punishment was less severe than mine even though we got busted for the same crime," the white soldier said.

"I don't know. Maybe it's because you guys are always getting high and he wanted to send a message to the rest of you white guys that if you mess up he'll have no mercy," the black soldier said.

"That is so not right, man. You black people are always taking up for each other, even when you know you're wrong," the white soldier said.

"Okay, you're right. You got screwed, so what am I supposed to do about it? I'm sure as hell not going to give you my stripes," the black soldier said and walked off.

Some of the white soldiers in the class took exception to the scenario saying white commanders were not that unfair, until Sergeant First Class Black showed them the data he had compiled of the article 15's handed out throughout the command. It showed the unequal punishment handed out by white commanders when it came to black and white soldiers committing the same offenses. The figures didn't lie.

The second scenario was the same two soldiers had been recommended for promotion to Specialist E-4 this time by their respective platoon sergeants. The white soldier was an outstanding young troop and showed promise of being an outstanding leader in the future. He had never been counseled for anything other than for doing good work. The black soldier was average, had several counseling statement for being late to work, but he worked in the orderly room and interacted with the commander. The dilemma was, the commander only had one set of stripes to hand out. He calls them both into his office to let them know who was being promoted.

"Private White, I've heard some good things about you, but since I only have one set of stripes I'm going to promote Private Black. I made this decision because I work with Private Black on a daily basis and I know he is a good soldier. I only see you at formations or guard mounts. Don't get me wrong. I believe what your platoon sergeant said about you being a good soldier and all, so the very next set of E-4 stripes I get you'll be the first one promoted," the commander said.

"But sir, everyone knows Private Black has been written up on several occasions for being late to work, so how can you say he is a better soldier than I am?" Private White asked.

"Are you questioning my judgment private?" the commander asked.

"No sir, I just thought the best soldier was supposed to be promoted first," Private White said.

"And so he is. Now both of you, get out of my office," the commander said. Private Black was promoted at the next formation held.

When Private White asked his platoon sergeant why Private Black was promoted over him his platoon sergeant, who was black, said "Hey that's way the cookie crumbles."

There wasn't too much opposition to this scenario because it was common knowledge that the white soldiers were promoted over the black soldiers. Other scenarios on confinement, Military Police brutality, and the off post pass policies were played out during the course of the class. At the end of the day, most of the white soldiers were stunned to find out what their fellow black soldiers had to endure on a daily basis. Most agreed that the sit-in was the right thing since it brought attention to the problems they faced. Private Wood believed the race relation classes were good, but knew it would take more than classes to rid the military of the deep-seated racism that existed throughout the establishment. After all, the commanders and white soldiers were representative of white America as a whole, and they weren't ready to relinquish any of that power yet. It had to be demanded or taken away.

During his whole tour of duty in Korea, Private Wood was considered an odd black soldier because he didn't fit the mold

PATRIOTISM

established by a racist society. Even the Korean people constantly asked him why he didn't act like the other soul brothers. When he asked them how he was supposed to act, they'd say they didn't know. Mr. Kim was the first Korean individual he had this conversation with after several months in country. One day after returning from the gym, he was in the dayroom reading a library book.

Mr. Kim looked at him curiously and asked, "Why you no like other soul brother GIs?"

"How am I supposed to act, Mr. Kim?" Private Wood asked in return.

"You no likey go village, you no likey girls, you no likey happy smoke [marijuana], you no likey get hay-lay-lay [drunk], and you no giv-a me hard time," he said.

Private Wood laughed and asked "Would that make you happy if I did all those things?"

"Why you no likey Korean girl, and you no talkey soul brother talk?" Mr. Kim asked.

"You don't understand what I'm saying when I talk to you, Mr. Kim? And as far as the girls goes, I do like girls but I have a yobo stateside waiting on me." he explained.

"Other GI have wifa, still hav-a yobo. Why you no same?" Mr. Kim persisted.

"Because I don't want a yobo, ok?" Private Wood answered.

"All you do is workey, workey, workey, go gym, and read books. I think you wanna be sargie, huh?" he asked.

"Yeah, I want to be a sergeant as soon as possible," Private Wood said.

"Why tissue soldier no likey you?" Mr. Kim asked.

Private Wood had heard white soldiers whispering behind his

back that he thought he was tough shit because he talked proper and kissed the lifers asses. Private Wood laughed because that was what Captain Hicks wanted him to do, but he wouldn't have any of it. They also disliked the fact he didn't believe in going along with the yobo rules of their unit. To make it simple, he just didn't care what they said or how they felt about him. The only thing that mattered to him was his job performance.

"White soldiers don't like me because I don't care if they don't like me. I like the army," Private Wood answered.

"I think you be number one GI. I likey you," he said patting Private Wood on the back.

Private Wood laughed and said "Yeah, I be number one soul brother."

Other than spending his first Christmas away from home, everything was going well for Private Wood until his sixth month in the country. He received a letter from Gina saying she was in love with another man. It probably wouldn't have been so upsetting if the other man hadn't been his old friend Johnny Tongas.

Gina explained that whenever she felt lonely and depressed while she was at the Job Corps center she could always call Johnny on the phone to cheer her up. And he'd come up to the Job Corps Center every other weekend to comfort her through those lonely times. She said if he could come home for a little while, a weekend or so, it would make all the difference in the world as far as their relationship was concerned. She swore they hadn't gone to bed yet, but her resistance to his advances was getting weaker every time she was with him.

Private Wood was tempted to write and tell her life is a bitch that cares for no one's feelings. If she wanted to screw the whole world to go ahead and do it, but don't expect him to be waiting in that line. Visions of her and Johnny doing the things they'd done together before he left ran through his mind. He could still taste the sweetness of her lips, and smell her intoxicating perfume. God, he hated Johnny at that moment, even though he knew a man could go no further than a woman let him.

Most of the guys stationed in Korea went home on a mid tour leave after six months. Private Wood started to put in for his leave to see what the hell was going on between Gina and Johnny, but instead he wrote and told her he understood what she was going through, because he was going through lonely times even as she read his letter. He missed her terribly, but couldn't come home until his tour was up. He still loved her very much and regardless of the outcome of their romance, he would always love her. After mailing the letter, he became angry again.

The lying wench, I bet she has given it up to half the horny bastards in Texas and all the bastards back home. Well screw her. I'm going to start sleeping with every Korean broad I get my hands on, Private Wood swore, knowing full well he wouldn't go to that extreme. He knew he would not screw every Korean girl who took her panties off for him, but he was serious about losing his cherry-boy status. Private Wood started to write Johnny and cuss him out, but he already knew Johnny would put all the blame on Gina.

Although he was pissed, Private Wood didn't run down to the ville and start screwing anything that moved. Actually he waited a couple weeks in hope that Gina would come to her senses and realized she would be making a mistake to dump him for Johnny. When he received no answer from her, he figured Johnny had gotten what he wanted. His girl. Private Wood tried hard to convince himself that it didn't really matter, that he was probably better off having only himself to worry about. But it wasn't that simple. The love formed between a soldier and his girl when the soldier is going off to war is a different kind of love than that of two people that live across town from each other. The lovers that live across town from each other can assume that they can see each other whenever they want. But for the soldier going off to war their last encounter may be just that, their last encounter. For the first time in his life, he knew what it felt like to lose someone he loved. He read that last letter he received from her several times, as if what she had said would change if he read it one more time.

Private Wood tried hard to hide his hurt feelings from his squad members but to no avail. They knew something was wrong because he became more outgoing and hung-out with them more. He'd been somewhat of a loner, now he started joining them in the day room to have a few after getting off duty, which was a daily ritual. They viewed this change as a good thing, not realizing the agony Private Wood felt internally. Duty wise nothing changed, it was easy to keep his personal problems separated from his duties. There were times he wanted to take his frustrations out on the public, but he was too proud of the reputation he had established to do something that stupid. Besides, they didn't send screw-ups to Vietnam; they sent them to Leavenworth.

After several weeks and still no letter, Private Wood accepted the fact that he had lost Gina. He went back to his normal routine, except he started drinking a little more. He had always heard that Dear John letters were blunt and to the point. *'I don't want you anymore.'* Gina had left a small ray of hope that she may somehow be able to fight Johnny off and get herself together. He swore on his live mother's grave, he would never be hurt like that again. Mr. Kim assured Private Wood Gina was dinky, dinky (crazy) for not waiting for him. And predicted she would be sorry for doing it.

After six months in country, Private First Class Wood and several of his fellow Privates, were promoted to Specialist (E-4) by Captain Hicks. As was customary during that time, the newly promoted personnel were to supply the booze on their next day off for the entire squad. Being their unit was semi-isolated from the main compound, the government allowed the unit to have their own club. The club extended credit to unit personnel for occasions such as promotions and going away parties. He was looking forward to his next day off because he'd made up his mind to go all the way. Drink, fuck, and if necessary, fight.

The girl Specialist Wood had chosen to indulge himself with was named Kwak, Sun Hui. She was the most beautiful girl he'd ever seen in his life. She was only eighteen years old and not yet turned out to the dogs. The most impressive thing about her was, she was the first Korean woman he'd met who didn't speak broken English. The only thing noticeable about her English was her accent. He liked her a lot, but as long as Gina was waiting for him back home, he had been able to control his desires. Now there was nothing holding him back. He talked to her several times while attending get-togethers with First Sergeant Tucker and his friends. Although he was only a Private, First Sergeant Tucker invited him to several of his gathering because he wanted to mold him into the type soldier he felt would benefit both the army and himself.

Private Wood knew Miss Kwak was involved with an Air Force Master Sergeant stationed at Osan AFB. He treated her more like his daughter than anything else. She carried herself with such dignity and pride Private Wood knew right off she was not a whore. He'd also learned that before she met Master Sergeant Singleton, she was a tour guide with one of the biggest tour guide associations in South, Korea. The tour guide company she worked for sent her to an English-speaking school as part of her tour guide training, and that was how she learned to speak English so well. They had long conversations while the senior NCOs played spades or poker until daybreak most of times they got together. The last time he had talked to her, he knew something was wrong and had tried to cheer her up.

"What's wrong with you, Miss Kwak? How can a beautiful lady like you have any problems?" Private Wood asked.

"Maybe someday I'll tell you why I'm not feeling too happy these days. However, right now I don't want to talk about it," she said.

"Hey, if your yobo won't treat you right, you let me know and we'll DX his ass, and trade him in for you a new boyfriend."

"I like you, Private Wood. The times we've laughed and talked to each other, you have never shown anything other than respect toward me. And you've always been honest with me whenever I got nosey and asked you questions about your personal life. I think I'm beginning to get jealous of your yobo stateside, knowing how committed you are to her."

"I like you also, but you're taken," Private Wood said.

"I don't know for how much longer. If things don't work out

for me, can I cry on your shoulder? You can always lean on me if things don't work out for you," she said.

"If things go wrong with me and my girl back home, believe me, you'll be the first one to know." That last conversation occurred a couple of days after he received Gina's Dear John letter. He had managed to keep his hurt feelings concealed from her.

The day before he was promoted to specialist, he ran into Miss Kwak accidentally while window-shopping in downtown Seoul. "Hello, pretty lady. What brings you downtown this beautiful afternoon?" he asked.

"The same thing that brought you down here, I guess--shopping for something to wear."

"Naw, I'm just window shopping. And freaking your people out, because I know they're wondering what this big black GI is doing downtown," Private Wood laughed.

"And freaking my people out amuses you? Can't you find something better to do with your time?" she asked.

"Yeah, you're right. Hey, how would you like to come to my promotion party tomorrow night? That's if Master Sergeant Singleton won't appear in the picture," Private Wood said.

"I'd love to come to your promotion party. But this is something new coming from you. What'll your girl back in the states say, knowing you're wining and dining a Korean lady?" she asked smiling.

"My lady back in the states is in the same boat as Master Sergeant Singleton," he said.

"And what is that supposed to mean?" she asked, surprised he knew Master Sergeant Singleton was no longer in the picture.

"Would you like to come to my promotion party tomorrow night?" he asked again ignoring her question.

"I'd be honored to attend your promotion party, Specialist Wood," she accepted, and congratulated him on his promotion.

"Hey, are you finished shopping? If not, how about me tagging along with you?" he asked.

"Sure, why not? I'll show you how to bargain with the shop owners," she said.

Inside one of the stores they were followed by a bunch of little schoolgirls in their customary black and white school uniforms. They looked at him and laughed. Each time he and Miss Kwak stopped to look at something the girls came a little closer. Finally they came up to Miss Kwak and asked her something, which resulted in her trying to shoo them off.

"What did they ask you?" Private Wood asked.

She laughed and said, "They want to know if the black on your skin will rub off."

"Tell them to see for themselves," he said, holding out his arms for them to touch.

Miss Kwak told them why he was holding his arms out and they rubbed his arms and looked at their hands. They looked surprised when they looked at their hands and found no black stains. One little girl wasn't satisfied with seeing if his blackness would rub off, she asked Miss Kwak if she could feel his hair. They had never felt curly hair before. When she told him what the little girl had asked, Private Wood bent over and let them feel his hair. They laughed and squealed as they ran their fingers through his hair. They thanked him for his cooperation and ran away comparing notes.

"That was a nice thing you did for those little girls, you

PATRIOTISM

know," Miss Kwak said after they had left the store.

"I rather they know for sure that our blackness won't rub off and our hair is real, than listen to people who don't know what the hell they're talking about," he explained his reasoning for allowing the probing by the kids.

A couple hours later Miss Kwak was worn out. "I'll see you tomorrow night, I gotta go," she said.

Specialist Wood and his compadres were true to tradition. They ran their bar tabs as high as the bartender would allow, which supplied more than enough booze for all those in attendance.

Specialist Wood couldn't drink another drop of alcohol when he asked Miss Kwak to take him home with her, she agreed. He expected her to take him to one of the regular, dingy little hooches he was used to going to when visiting the guys from his squad. But to his surprise they went to an apartment-type complex.

Upon their arrival to her hooch, they sat down and opened a large bottle of OB beer. He asked, "Now that Master Sergeant Singleton's out of the picture, where is your Momma-san?"

"I don't have a Momma-san. As you know, I lived with Master Sergeant Singleton for the past year and a half. He rented this place for me, but he's been back in the states for two months now. He gave me enough money to eat and pay the rent for a couple of months before he left, but that's just about gone. So I have to pay the rent myself now, or get a momma-san. I don't want a momma-san. They get the girls in debt and they can never leave unless their yobos pay momma-san off, they run away, or they are sold to another momma-san. I don't want that to happen to me. I've never had a momma-san and I don't want one. Pimp is a better name for them. I hope I can get my job back as a tour guide. Our people don't want much to do with us after we have fooled around with an American GI. We're automatically considered whores, especially if the GI is black. How did you know Master Sergeant Singleton was gone?"

"That's all well and good, but how much longer can you make it on your own?" he asked, more interested in her than her question.

"Oh, I don't know. I still have a little money, but it's running out fast," Miss Kwak said.

"Well, I'll tell you what, why don't you be my yobo and we'll play house for the remainder of the time I have left in Korea," he offered with a big smile on his face.

"On one condition," she answered.

"And what condition is that?" he asked suspiciously.

"That you'll never say you love me or want to marry me."

"Who said anything about getting married? Hell, I'm not looking for a wife, especially after what I just went through with my yobo stateside," he exclaimed.

"That's what I like about you, Specialist Wood. You're a very honest man. Master Sergeant Singleton lied to me for nine months that he was going to marry me because he didn't want to see me end up on the street whoring. And I believed him. When he told me two days before he left that he was already married and had five kids, it broke my heart. I felt so stupid. I can never let that happen to me again. So if we decide to play house, it'll be for mutual comfort only because I don't think I could ever trust another American GI," she said close to tears.

His heart went out to that beautiful, young girl because he knew what she was going through. He started to tell her about the Dear John letter he had received from Gina but decided against it.

"I'll tell you what, Miss Kwak; if you promise to never tell me you love me, I'll never ask you to marry me. I believe love is a game in which the one who believes in it the most is the one who ends up hurt. Deal?" he asked, extending his hand.

"You got it, Specialist Wood. I could never fall in love again anyway," she said with a sigh of relief.

"Is that why you were so unhappy the last time I talked to you at First Sergeant Tucker's little get-together?" he asked with a smile.

"So, First Sergeant Tucker told you Master Sergeant Singleton was gone."

"Yeah," he admitted and continued. "I think I'm the only one who noticed how sad you were. Don't worry, I won't make any promises I won't be able to keep," he promised.

"Well, guess what First Sergeant Tucker told me? It has something to do with a "Dear John" letter a certain Specialist received," she laughed.

""First Sergeant Tucker talks too much," Specialist Wood said, laughing.

That night he lost his cherry-boy status and became a member of the yobo community. Everyone teased him, saying now that he had a yobo, he wouldn't be so hard when working the gates if someone's yobo came through with food from the commissary. But to their disappointment, nothing changed duty-wise. Specialist Wood took all the food and other articles he purchased at the PX and commissary to their hooch himself. Never once did he ask her to break the law by carrying American goods off the installation. The most important decision he had to make in joining in this union was giving up sleeping in his semi-comfortable bed in the barracks for a pallet on the floor. He figured if he could sleep on the ground at an ambush site while playing war games, the floor should not be too much of a problem; especially when he would have a warm body beside him.

Specialist Wood hadn't sampled much of the Korean food since he'd been in the country, but after hooking up with his lovely little Korean roommate, he learned what he had been missing. Miss Kwak was a wonderful human being and a damned good cook. She waited on him hand and foot. She even got a job as a bartender at one of the local bars because she didn't want to be totally dependent on him. She was a complete 180 degree turn around from the girls he had known back in the United States, Gina included. Miss Kwak slowly began to develop a special place in his heart, but he felt because of the promises he'd made to her and her to him, love was out of the question. Specialist Wood felt he would be wasting his time telling her how much she was beginning to mean to him. He enjoyed the picnics in the countryside and when they embarked on sightseeing tours, because she would take the time to answer his every question. On previous tours the guides had to try and answer everyone's questions at the same time.

Although Miss Kwak spoke English well, she had trouble reading it. Therefore, Specialist Wood enjoyed teaching her to read, using his poetry writing skills as a study guide. Miss Kwak enjoyed reading his poems and listening to him read them, probably because most of them were about her. She always said someday he would be a very famous poet, or maybe a famous songwriter. He doubted it, but it was nice to hear.

Time passed and before he realized it, he had only two months left in Korea before he was due to rotate back to the states, or be transferred to Vietnam. Along with the realization of time being short, he also realized he could no longer fool himself about how he felt about Miss Kwak. Their conversations when talking about each other constantly came to a sudden halt. Neither of them wanted to admit to the obvious. There was a strong bond between them, which could no longer be denied. And one of the things that had made it even easier for him to fall for her was his entire family had written and told him how pretty she was and if she was half the person he had been describing in his letters, by all means bring her home with him. He had sent his momma at least a dozen pictures of him and Miss Kwak together.

Specialist Wood sat down one afternoon in their hooch with pen and paper and wrote down every reason he could think of why he shouldn't let the thought of marrying Miss Kwak enter his mind:

1. With all the red tape the guys who had gotten married had gone through, they didn't have enough time;

2. He had promised her he would never ask her to marry him;

3. He couldn't take her with him to America and then leave her in a foreign country while he went off to Vietnam;

4. Lastly, but no way least, he was afraid of being hurt again. All he needed was for Miss Kwak to tell him she didn't feel the same as he did. He was certain it would push him over the deep end. Specialist Wood tried to convince himself it would be for the best if they went their separate ways. He'd have enough to worry about in Vietnam without taking personal problems with

him. On the other hand, Specialist Wood knew they had to reveal their true feelings before he left. Not once did he waste his time thinking of the problems they might encounter in America because theirs would be an interracial marriage. It wasn't like she was a white klansman's daughter like Sergeant First Class Black's wife. He sure wished his father were there at that moment. He needed advice badly and didn't know where to turn.

During this time of no confrontations and personal bliss, Specialist Wood was promoted to sergeant, E-5. It was truly one of the happiest days of his life. Now the initial circle was complete. He was now ready to be the true life Sergeant Rock. He wrote his family and bragged about making sergeant in only fifteen months. He knew for sure now that he could walk through hell with gasoline drawers without a care in the world. First Sergeant Tucker had personally requested that he be allowed to promote Specialist Wood to the rank of non-commissioned officer. After pinning on his stripes, he was informed by First Sergeant Tucker it was his last official act as the First Sergeant of Company C, 728th MP Battalion, in Korea. His replacement had reported in that morning and he would be leaving in seven days. Sergeant Wood asked him if he would honor him by attending his promotion party the following night.

"Wouldn't miss it for the world," he winked.

Sergeant Wood knew First Sergeant Tucker was short, but the time still snuck up on him. Sergeant Wood needed some meaningful advice about his relationship with Miss Kwak, and First Sergeant Tucker was the only person he felt would give him some sound advice, whether he agreed with it or not. The promotion and subsequent planned party would give him the perfect opportunity to talk to the First Sergeant. And he wasn't

PATRIOTISM

about to let it pass. He also invited every other NCO and officer in the unit to his party. But he knew only a handful, other than the ones he worked with, would attend.

It had been a very busy year so far. Captain Hicks and Staff Sergeant Pearson had extended their tours in Korea; Sergeant Davis had rotated back to the States and left him as the assistant squad leader; and he had somehow managed to stay out of Captain Hicks' way. But most importantly of all, he was promoted and ready to lead his own squad of men. The day of the party while he was at work, Miss Kwak insured his promotion party would be a huge success on the home front. She even went out and had a plaque made welcoming him to the Non-Commissioned Officer Corps, First Sergeant Tucker's idea of course, and without Sergeant Wood's knowledge. Just prior to his getting off duty that afternoon, Staff Sergeant Pearson told him that Master Sergeant Snoop, the operations NCO, Provost Marshall's office, wanted to see him before he departed the area.

"Aw, shit, what the hell have I done now?" he asked.

"I haven't the faintest idea. But he did seem to be in a pissed-off mood," Sergeant Pearson said, sounding serious.

Sergeant Wood couldn't think of anything he had done within the last few days that would piss anyone off in the back office. Well he was sure whatever it was, he could defend himself. Master Sergeant Snoop was the only NCO who worked in operations he felt he could trust. Since tearing up the ticket he gave General Hutchison's wife, Master Sergeant Snoop had nothing but praise for him. However, he was soon to learn he was mistaken about the trusting part. Master Sergeant Snoop was almost always serious, but every once in a while you would catch him in a humorous mood and he was very funny.

As Sergeant Wood entered Master Sergeant Snoop's office, he could tell he wasn't in any trouble because Sergeant Snoop was smiling.

"Well, good afternoon, Sergeant Wood. I'm very happy to see you got my message. I know you're anxious to find out why I called you in."

"Yes, Master Sergeant Snoop, I am," he interjected before he could continue.

"Have a seat. Now that you're officially an NCO, I guess it's all right for you to sit back and relax. As you know, the only reason Staff Sergeant Pearson extended his tour of duty in Korea was because he was promised a job here in the back office, and we're ready to make that move. And Sergeant Davis is long gone." Master Sergeant Snoop hesitated for a while as if trying to find the right words for what he wanted to say next. "Let me ask you a question," he finally continued. "Do you think you can handle your squad as their leader until we get another Staff Sergeant in the unit?"

"Sure I can, Sergeant Snoop," Sergeant Wood answered without any hesitation.

"Want to tell me why you think you're ready to be a squad leader? You just got promoted this morning you know," Master Sergeant Snoop reminded him.

Sergeant Wood smiled and said, "Well, as you know, Master Sergeant Snoop, I've been working hard so I would be prepared when this day finally arrived. I've been Staff Sergeant Pearson's assistant squad leader since Sergeant Davis left and my whole squad respects me because they know I'm a fair and honest person," Sergeant Wood said.

"As simple as that, is it?" Master Sergeant Snoop asked,

amused.

"Not really, since Captain Hicks also extended, I'm sure he'll find something wrong with my leadership ability; probably before I even get started. But it doesn't matter, because it won't be the first time I've been criticized about something, and I'm sure it won't be the last. Therefore, I'm willing to give it my best shot," Sergeant Wood said, sounding over confident.

"That's where you're wrong, young buck sergeant. Being a non-commissioned officer and a specialist-four is as different as day and night. But I see you'll have to learn the hard way. I know First Sergeant Tucker has had you under his wing since you've been here and kept them off your back. What happens now that he's leaving?" Master Sergeant Snoop asked.

"Well, what can I say, Sergeant? I've always believed you were on my side when you knew I was right. Can I still come to you if I get my butt in a sling?" Sergeant Wood asked hopefully.

"I suppose so, but you'd better keep your shit together, young buck sergeant. Now get the hell out of my office before I'm the first one to kick off in your young buck sergeant ass. Oh, by the way, if you don't have enough Johnny Walker Red tonight, I want to see you first thing Monday morning," he said with a wink.

"You got it, Master Sergeant Snoop. See you tonight. And if I don't have enough JWR for you, you won't have to worry about me because I'll be AWOL," he assured him as he was going out the door. *Hot damn! Finally a leader of men,* he thought to himself.

As Sergeant Wood went about his daily duties, the Army establishment had ways of reminding him that he was a Black

NCO, not just a non-commissioned officer. Namely, you are Black, we are White, and you do whatever you're told, nothing more nothing less. And because he wasn't yet a seasoned politician, it would make for some very rough times during the remaining couple of months he had left in Korea.

Sergeant Wood got off duty at 1500 hours and spent the remainder of the day helping Miss Kwak insure his party would be a success. He had planned on really tying one on that night because it was his first true weekend he'd had off in a month of Sundays. Although he had invited all the overhead personnel to his party, he knew only a few would show. He wasn't disappointed. A couple of senior NCO's other than Master Sergeant Snoop and First Sergeant Tucker attended, but no officers. The majority of his peers did attend the party and they all had a very good time. Sergeant Wood didn't get a chance to talk to First Sergeant Tucker until all of his guests had arrived, the plaque was presented, and the party was in full swing. He didn't know how to begin because he didn't particularly like exposing his deepest feelings to anyone other than his daddy. So he began by asking a question.

"First Sergeant Tucker, if you cared for someone very much but you made that person a promise you'll never tell her how you truly felt, what would you do?"

"Look, young buck sergeant, if you want my advice on something, you had better tell me what the hell you're talking about," First Sergeant Tucker said, annoyed at him for beating around the bush.

"Alright, I think I'm in love with Miss Kwak but I promised never to tell her that," he confessed. "And now I'm afraid to let her know it."

"Why did you make such a dumb ass promise like that in the first place?" First Sergeant Tucker asked.

Sergeant Wood explained the circumstances surrounding the promise they had made to each other.

'Well, I can certainly understand why neither one of you want to get hurt again," he sympathized. "However, what are you going to do now that you realize you care a lot more for her than you intended to?" First Sergeant Tucker asked, but went on before Sergeant Wood could answer. "I guess that's where I come in. If I were you, the first thing I would do is find out if she cares as much for me as I do for her. And if she does, I would then talk to the First Sergeant about extending my tour of duty in my present assignment. That would give you plenty of time to marry her. On the other hand, what if you did marry Miss Kwak and took her home with you just to find out you still love Gina and she still loves you? What if you discovered you only used Miss Kwak as a crutch because you were a long way from home and needed someone to lean on? Do you think that would be fair to Miss Kwak for you to take her 16,000 miles from home, not knowing if she is really the girl you want to spend the rest of your life with?"

"But I didn't say anything about still being in love with Gina," Sergeant Wood protested.

"Do you think you're the first slime ball that got a Dear John letter when he was overseas? As you said yourself, she did leave a ray of hope that somehow you two would get back together when you got back home. It does happen you know."

Sergeant Wood was now totally confused. First Sergeant Tucker had told him what he needed to do in order to marry Miss Kwak and at the same time discouraged him from doing

213

so. "I really don't know what the hell you're trying to get me to see, First Sergeant," he confessed.

"What I'm trying to tell you is if you really love Miss Kwak and she loves you, it wouldn't hurt anything if the two of you were separated for a while. Go home and make sure you left no home fires burning. It's better to be lonely for a little while than to be miserable for the rest of your life. The separation would also give you the chance to find out if it's true love or just an infatuation. Lonely GIs have a habit of falling in love with every female that puts out to them. I know you're not the average, run-of-the-mill GI, but this is your first time away from home. Then again, let's say Miss Kwak is serious about the promises you two made to each other and doesn't want to marry you. What then?" Sergeant Tucker asked, throwing the ball into Sergeant Wood's court.

"I don't really know," he answered honestly. "I guess that's what I'm afraid of finding out," Sergeant Wood admitted.

"Well, I've given you all the advice I can give you. The final decision is yours. I wish you the best of luck, regardless of the outcome," he said and rejoined the party.

Knowing what he had to do, he resumed playing host to his party guests. After a few more drinks, he felt he was king of the hill. He felt so good he challenged First Sergeant Tucker and Master Sergeant Snoop to a JWR drinking contest. It turned out to be one of the biggest mistake of his entire life. The last thing he remembered before passing out was that he and Miss Kwak had to have a talk regardless of the outcome.

The next morning when he awakened, Sergeant Wood was afraid to open his eyes. He was sure he had died and gone to hell. *Why else would I feel so bad?* he asked himself. When he finally built up enough courage to open his eyes, he shut them again quickly because the whole world was spinning like crazy. He'd never felt so sick in his life. Sergeant Wood thought the previous times he'd gotten drunk were bad, but compared to this hangover, he'd only had a stomach ache.

While lying there trying to decide whether to just stay in bed for the rest of his life, or get up and let the chips fall where they may, the decision was made for him. The booze and food he had consumed at the party were having a hell of a war inside his stomach and wanted out. He barely made it to the toilet before he was puking his guts out. After what seemed an eternity, the nausea passed. He dragged himself back to bed, determined never to get up again, at least not in this lifetime. Once he was back in bed, he realized Miss Kwak was nowhere to be found. But it didn't really matter because he was sure no one could save his life at that point.

Several hours later he was awakened by a voice that sounded far, far away, asking if he was all right. When his eyes finally came into focus, he saw it was Miss Kwak trying to wake him up.

Sergeant Wood said, "Yeah, I'm fine. Just call the undertaker and tell them you have a dead man at your hooch you'd like picked up."

Miss Kwak laughed, kissed him on the cheek and said, "Come on and get up, my dear macho man. You showed First Sergeant Tucker and Master Sergeant Snoop you can drink with the best of them and still hold your own." He might have believed her if she hadn't burst out laughing.

"Don't shit me, Miss Kwak. What the hell happened after I got drunk? Did I make a fool of myself?" he asked embarrassed.

"No, not really. But you did look funny staggering around the hooch trying to play host until everyone left. You would've made it if you hadn't let First Sergeant Tucker and Master Sergeant Snoop talk you into having one for the road."

"And then what happened?"

"You passed out half way through the drink and they had to help me put you to bed."

"Oh man. How many people were still here?" Sergeant Wood asked, hoping not too many of his peers were still there.

"Only First Sergeant Tucker and Master Sergeant Snoop. I guess they wanted to make sure they drank your young ass under the table before they left," she theorized. "Here, First Sergeant Tucker left you a note," she handed him a folded piece of paper.

As he took the note, Sergeant Wood figured the First Sergeant just wanted to rub in the fact that he had drank him under the table. To his surprise, the note was a serious one.

Thank you for an outstanding night. I was glad to see you went to the extent you did to insure the White members of the unit would have just as good a time as the Blacks. If you need any more advice in reference to your predicament with Miss Kwak, stop by my hooch today. Oh, by the way, rookie, in a few more years you may be able to drink with senior NCOs.

ISG Tucker

"What did he have to say?" Miss Kwak asked after seeing he had finished reading the note.

"Nothing much," Sergeant Wood lied trying to avoid having

to explain the contents of the note.

"If you don't want me to know what he had to say, just say so. Don't give me a half-assed answer," she snapped. From the way she had reacted, it led him to believe she had already read it.

"OK, miss smart ass. Why don't you tell me what the hell he had to say?" he challenged her to admit she had read the note.

"How the hell can I tell you what the note said if I didn't read it?" she asked, trying to sound innocent.

"If you didn't read it, why are you getting so upset?" he answered her question with a question.

"Well, if you want me to admit I read the note, I did. So what did he mean about giving you more advice about you and me? What've I done to you that require advice from someone else? We've always been able to say what we felt in the past. Why not now?" Miss Kwak asked, sounding hurt.

He decided it was now or never. "Miss Kwak," he began, "do you remember the promises we made to each other when we first agreed to play house?" Sergeant Wood asked as if the possibility existed she had forgotten.

"Of course I remember," she answered. "But what're you getting at?"

"Aw, what the hell," he said and proceeded to confess to her his true feelings towards her. "Miss Kwak, I've wanted to tell you for some time now how I really feel about you, but I was afraid of being hurt again. I promised you I would never ask you to marry me, which in reality meant I would never fall in love with you. At the time I said it I meant it. I didn't think I was capable of loving another woman as long as I lived. But I guess fate has a way of playing with a person's heart. I thought

217

I loved Gina, but now I realize it was only a physical thing. She never made me feel the way you do. I was also afraid you'd keep your part of the bargain. And where in the hell would that leave me? So I asked First Sergeant Tucker what would he do if he was in my shoes. There, you have it in a nut shell," Sergeant Wood finished.

"So what did he advise you to do?" she asked.

"He gave me some good advice, but said the final decision was mine alone."

"Well for your information, Sergeant Wood, I asked First Sergeant Tucker the same question a week ago and he told me the decision was up to us to work out together. Not just up to you and you alone," Miss Kwak smiled and threw her arms around him.

"What're you saying?" he asked dumbfounded.

"Well, if you haven't figured it out yet, I'm trying to tell you that I'm in love with you and would like nothing more than to become Mrs. Sergeant Bob Wood."

"Outstanding," he replied forgetting his hangover. "But you know there is more to our situation than that. I only have two months remaining in Korea, which doesn't give us enough time to get married. And on top of that I want to go to Vietnam and win some medals. What'll you do while I'm away?" he asked.

"I'll be right here waiting for you to return to Korea. I'll continue working my bartending job until you get back. Upon your return we'll get married and have a beautiful honeymoon. What do you have to say to that, Sergeant Wood?" she asked excitedly.

"I couldn't ask for anything more," Sergeant Wood said, taking her into his arms and kissing her.

PATRIOTISM

Considering how everything had turned out, Sergeant Wood hadn't needed the First Sergeant's advice after all. But he knew it was sometimes helpful to get the advice of a friend, whether you agree with what they had to say or not. Sergeant Wood thought nothing could spoil his happiness. He'd been promoted to sergeant, the girl of his dreams loved him and was willing to wait for him until he won his medals before she made any demands on him. And Master Sergeant Snoop would take him under his wings now that First Sergeant Tucker was leaving. But again, as they say, all good things must come to an end.

Chapter 6
SERGEANT

Still patting himself on the back because he had pulled off his promotion party to sergeant without a hitch, he showed up for duty that Monday afternoon for his first day of swing shift without a care in the world. Sergeant Wood knew as an acting squad leader, the leadership didn't expect too much of him. However, now that the stripes and the position were legit, he would be in the bull's eye of every target of those who wanted to see him fail. Sergeant Wood knew this from the acting platoon sergeant position he held while in basic training. It seemed most of the white trainees were constantly telling Drill Sergeant McCoy they could do a better job than he was doing in the position and should be replaced by one of them. He survived in basic training, he would survive in the real position. However, it wasn't going to be easy because he had reached the starting point of political bull crap 101 that comes with being a non-commissioned officer. Sergeant Wood didn't know how much the command expected him to give up to keep his stripes, but he knew it wouldn't be at the expense of giving up his manhood. The first shot at his ability to lead came before the stripes stitches had settled on his sleeve.

Upon reporting for duty Monday afternoon, Sergeant Wood was advised by Master Sergeant Snoop that he was to report to Captain Hicks after guard mount. Master Sergeant Snoop explained that over the weekend a member of his squad was caught by Captain Hicks smoking grass in the barracks while on duty. Captain Hicks had some work in his office he wanted to complete before Monday morning and decided to take a walk through the barracks. While doing so he observed Specialist Coleman in full MP gear sitting on his bunk smoking marijuana. Therefore, he was to report to Captain Hicks' office along with Specialist Coleman the following morning.

"What in the hell was Specialist Coleman doing on duty anyway? He was supposed to be on break along with the rest of the squad," Sergeant Wood said, not wanting to believe what he was hearing.

"The story I got from First Sergeant Green," the new first sergeant, "is Specialist Coleman was working for Specialist Wright, third squad, who in turn was going to work for him next Saturday," Master Sergeant Snoop explained.

"Well, I didn't approve it. As far as I'm concerned, his ass is grass," Sergeant Wood said as he stomped out of Master Sergeant Snoop's office. He stopped by the barracks after assigning his patrol their areas of assignments and briefing the gate guards.

Since Specialist Coleman had been relieved of duty, which was standard procedure, Sergeant Wood had to go to the barracks to find him. This was the first time Specialist Coleman had been in any serious trouble since he'd been a member of the squad. He did have a couple of counseling statements for being late to guard-mount, but nothing as serious as this. Sergeant Wood was steaming after going to his room and not finding Specialist Coleman there. He asked a couple of soldiers in the barracks if they had seen him. One of the soldiers said he heard him say something about going to the supply room to talk to Specialist Gibbs. Sergeant Wood located him in the supply

PATRIOTISM

room shooting the bull with Specialist Gibbs.

When he got Specialist Coleman outside, Sergeant Wood asked him, "What the hell were you doing on duty yesterday?"

"I was working for Specialist Wright because he had something he wanted to do yesterday. And next Sunday he is supposed to work for me," he explained.

"And who, pray tell, authorized the switching of these days, not to mention squads?"

"Staff Sergeant Stone said it would be ok with him," Specialist Coleman said nervously.

"Who do you work for, me or Sergeant Stone?" Sergeant Wood asked, pissed because he liked Staff Sergeant Stone about as much as he did Captain Hicks.

Staff Sergeant Stone was black, but he was whiter than any white soldier in the unit. He said Dr. King and Malcolm X were both communist and deserved to die. Sergeant Wood wondered how Staff Sergeant Stone made it out of Vietnam alive knowing he had to have served with a number of black militants soldiers during his tour over there. Rumor had it that it was common for officers and NCOs like Stone to be fragged in Nam.

Staff Sergeant Stone called Sergeant Wood a black loud mouth troublemaker who would probably get kicked out of the army before his tour in Korea was over. However, he never said anything to Sergeant Wood face to face. Sergeant Wood shook his head every time he interacted with Staff Sergeant Stone because he was the only black man Sergeant Wood ever met that he could kill and not feel bad about it. Sergeant Wood didn't like the feeling. Needless to say, Staff Sergeant Stone wouldn't be caught dead hanging with the brothers.

"I work for you, sarge, but I couldn't get a hold of you. And when I told Sergeant Stone, he said not to worry about it; he would explain everything to you later."

"I'll deal with Sergeant Stone later. I guess Sergeant Stone also fired up that joint you got caught smoking in the barracks," Sergeant Wood said sarcastically.

"No, sergeant, it was my own stupid fault. I stopped by the barracks to get my camera and I thought it would be ok to fire one up. I didn't even know Captain Hicks was in the company area. As far as the bag of grass he got out of my wall locker, it wasn't mine. I was holding it for someone else."

"I didn't hear anything about a bag of grass being taken out of your wall locker. Who does it belong to?" Sergeant Wood asked.

"I can't tell you that, Sergeant Wood, it would make me a stoolie."

"So you're willing to take the rap for him?"

"I figured if I hadn't gotten caught smoking the shit, the bag wouldn't have been found. It was my screw-up, so I'm willing to take the fall," Specialist Coleman said sickly.

"And fall you will, my friend," Sergeant Wood assured him. And added, "I don't want to have to look for you in the morning."

"You won't Sergeant. I'll be in my room," Specialist Coleman assured him.

The following morning when Sergeant Wood and Specialist Coleman entered the orderly room, First Sergeant Green was waiting for them. "You and Specialist Coleman wait here until I call you into the commander's office," he instructed. First Sergeant Green knocked on the commander's door and entered.

Specialist Coleman was visibly shaking as he asked, "What

do you think the commander is going to do to me?"

"I can't say, but since this is your first major screw up, he shouldn't be too hard on you. Hell, he knows how tempting it is to mess with that crap."

Sergeant Wood was still explaining the Commander's options when First Sergeant Green stuck his head out of the commander's office door and said, "Report to the commander, Specialist Coleman. And you come on in too, Sergeant Wood."

After reporting to the commander and having the charges read, Specialist Coleman was asked what punishment he thought he should receive.

"I don't know, sir. I have never been in trouble before," Specialist Coleman answered.

"Do you realize the seriousness of this offense, Specialist Coleman?" the commander asked.

"Yes, sir, I do. And I guess I deserve whatever punishment you decide to give me," Specialist Coleman said.

"What punishment would you impose on Specialist Coleman, Sergeant Wood, if you were in my position?" Captain Hicks asked, turning to him. He figured because Sergeant Wood was a newly promoted sergeant, he wouldn't know what to recommend.

Sergeant Wood on the other hand had listened to First Sergeant Tucker and his First Sergeant friends talk about handing out non-judicial punishment on numerous occasions, when he was allowed to sit in on their weekly spade or poker games. He knew from their conversations a soldier's first Article 15 for an offense was usually the most lenient. And as in every other potential situation, he had rehearsed what he would say in any given situation regarding non-judicial punishment procedures that may arise once he became an NCO. He had also practiced religiously at presenting himself as his leaders presented themselves. Both in the way they acted and the way they talked.

Therefore, without any hesitation Sergeant Wood answered, "Well, sir, taking into consideration this is Specialist Coleman's first major screw up, I recommend taking some money away from him, fourteen days extra duty, and fourteen days restriction to the barracks. After all, we want him to learn from this mistake, not feel that we as his superiors are out to burn him without taking into consideration his past duty performance."

First Sergeant Green looked as if he had swallowed something nasty and it was choking the hell out him. His eyes were bulging and his mouth was open as if he was trying to catch his breath.

Captain Hicks didn't seem impressed with what Sergeant Wood had recommended, or how well he had presented it to him. "Are you condoning the use of marijuana within your squad, Sergeant Wood?" he had the audacity to ask.

"Sir, I know we have our differences, but I would like to think you know me better than that," Sergeant Wood answered, knowing the way he had answered the question would irritate the good captain.

"I'll talk to you after I've finished with Specialist Coleman," Captain Hicks said nonchalantly. He turned his attention back to Specialist Coleman. "I'll get with First Sergeant Green and we'll decide what should be done to you."

"Yes, sir, I understand."

"Dismissed, Specialist," Captain Hicks said.

Specialist Coleman saluted, did an about face and exited the office. Captain Hicks then turned his full attention to Sergeant

Wood.

"Do you know what conclusions I've drawn from this incident, Sergeant Wood?" Captain Hicks asked.

"No, sir, I haven't the faintest idea," Sergeant Wood answered, getting himself ready for a verbal war with the commander.

"Well, I'll tell you. You've been a squad leader for one weekend and already your people are getting caught using drugs. I personally don't think you have what it takes to be a squad leader. As far as I know, you may even be smoking dope with them. That would explain why Specialist Coleman had no fear of being caught smoking marijuana in the barracks. Do you smoke marijuana, Sergeant Wood?"

Sergeant Wood smiled involuntarily. "Sir, I know why you're saying these things. You want me to get upset, say something stupid in front of First Sergeant Green so you can burn my ass. Isn't that what's supposed to happen?" he asked. Then continued before the captain could answer. "And as far as my leadership ability is concerned, sir, it hasn't been tested yet. Also, it's common knowledge that quite a few individuals in this unit smoke grass. However, it happens that I'm not one of them. Correct me if I'm wrong, sir, but if there is a drug problem within a unit, doesn't that mean there is a lack of leadership within that unit? Usually that means from the commander on down? I'll say this, sir, if I do catch anyone smoking dope, you'll be the first one in the unit to know about it."

The captain looked as if he was about to explode when First Sergeant Green decided he'd heard enough. "By gawd, sir, you weren't bullshitting about this one being a smart ass," he began. "I don't know you, Sergeant Wood, but I have a feeling we're not going to get along too well. In my army, subordinates do what they are told, when they are told, whether they like it or not. No questions asked. I can tell you're not that type of soldier. But let me enlighten you, son; either you play by my rules or you don't play at all. The captain has told me how Sergeant Tucker has protected your young ass since you've been here. Well, now that he's out of the picture, either you play ball with us or you're heading for a fall. Do you understand what I'm saying to you, buck sergeant?" First Sergeant Green snarled.

Sergeant Wood smiled knowing First Sergeant Green had broken one of the basic teachings of military leadership and said, "First Sergeant Green, it sounds as if you've prejudged me. Not only do you not know me, it seems you have no intentions of doing so. In the army leadership manual, FM 22-100, it says a good leader will take the time to learn everything about his subordinates before casting judgment upon them. Those subordinates in turn are supposed to want to be like their leader, a person to be looked up to. Right now, First Sergeant Green, from my first impression of you I don't know if I'll be able to look up to you if you're going to condemn me before you get a chance to know me. I know you have to support your commander, but you also have a commitment to your troops.

And as far as you're concerned, sir," Sergeant Wood turned to face Captain Hicks, "you know where we stand in the likes and dislikes department. There's no doubt in my mind that between the two of you, you can and probably will get me sooner or later. However, when that day comes, I'll have the satisfaction of knowing it took two of the highest-ranking people in my chain of command to trump up the charge. I guess I'm somewhat of a pain in the ass, but I only insist when I know

I'm right. Even you have to admit that fact, sir. First Sergeant Green, I'll tell you the same thing I told Captain Hicks and every other officer and NCO since I've been in the army; I'll do my job to the best of my ability at all times, but it doesn't mean I'm afraid of your rank or your position. However, I'll always show you the proper respect due you because of that rank and position," Sergeant Wood said. He was trembling he was so mad at what they were attempting to do to him.

"Are you quite finished, buck sergeant?" Captain Hicks asked.

"Yes, sir. I'm now at the mercy of my superiors," Sergeant Wood answered, giving them the impression he knew he was fighting a losing battle.

"Since you know we can and will have your ass if you don't play ball with us, are you willing to reconsider your position and join the team?" Captain Hicks asked, thinking Sergeant Wood had finally realized his days were numbered if he didn't change his attitude.

"I need some time to think, sir, if you don't mind," Sergeant Wood said humbly, trying to get them to let him get the hell out of the captain's office to plan his defense against the difficult times ahead.

"Take all the time you need. The Provost Marshal tells me you have great potential as a non-commissioned officer. He is very impressed with all the good things you've done since you've been in the command. I would hate to see you take a fall for being stubborn," Captain Hicks said, letting him off the hook.

First Sergeant Green, however, was not as diplomatic as Captain Hicks. He said, "Just in case you didn't get the Captain's message, I'll say it on a level where there'll be no doubt in your mind as to what we're saying. If you don't cut out this I'm-holier-than-thou bullshit and do what the fuck you're told, you won't be an NCO for very long. Furthermore, for your information, there isn't a colored soldier in the United States Army as good a soldier as I am. Therefore, it would benefit you a lot if you did try to be like me. As far as your looking up to me, I could give a fuck less. I don't play games, son, when it comes to buck sergeants questioning my authority. Playing politics is the commander's role, not mine. And as far as giving you the time to think about it, I strongly suggest you make up your mind before you leave this office. Because the next time you're called into this office it'll be for an Article 15. Now give us an answer right now, or your ass is ours," First Sergeant Green threatened.

Sergeant Wood stared First Sergeant Green straight in the face and said, "First Sergeant Green, when I was drafted into the army I wanted nothing more than to serve my country to the best of my ability. I wanted to do that in Vietnam, not Korea. That's still my ultimate goal. One thing I've learned since I've been in the U.S. Army so far is I have enemies wearing the same uniform as I do. And they're more dangerous to me than any soldier in the Vietnamese Army. Just as I would never give in to the Vietnamese, I'll not give in to individuals within the army's establishment, no matter what you do to me. Thank you, First Sergeant Green, without your honesty I would probably have gone along with the program. The Mutt and Jeff charade you and the commander just performed on my behalf was very impressive. You had me totally confused for a little while, but thanks to you, First Sergeant, I see no matter what I do as long as I'm in this unit, my ass is grass and I'm staring the lawnmowers in the face. Get me if you can," he said.

"I'm going to enjoy getting you, boy," First Sergeant Green said smiling.

Captain Hicks said, "Sergeant Wood, you have now entered the world of basic political bullshit. Unless you learn diplomacy now as an E-5, you won't make it, son. Things would be a lot smoother for you if you go ahead and cooperate with us."

"You mean grovel at your feet and do whatever you say even when I know it's wrong. No way sir, I swore to uphold the law and that's what I intend to do. Get me if you can, sir," Sergeant Wood repeated.

"It's your career. Get the fuck out of my office," Captain Hicks dismissed him.

Specialist Coleman was waiting for Sergeant Wood as he exited the commander's office. "Sergeant Wood, I want to thank you for standing up for me in there. I thought you were pissed off and were going to suggest the commander throw the book at me."

"You can bet your sweet ass I was pissed off, and I'm still mad as hell at you. However, I feel that throwing the book at you for your first major mistake isn't the answer. It's not like you killed anyone. Now don't get me wrong. You have a lot to prove to me, mister, before I trust you again."

"I understand, Sarge. But since you had the balls to stand up for me after getting caught red-handed screwing up, you can bet your life I won't do anything stupid again," Specialist Coleman promised.

"Don't forget, you're not out of the frying pan yet," Sergeant Wood reminded him.

"At least because of you, sergeant, I'm out of the fire. The logic you used in making your suggestion will make the commander decide whether he wants to be viewed as an a-hole or an understanding commander. I think he wants to be viewed as an understanding commander."

"Let's hope for your sake you're right," Sergeant Wood said, walking away, not wanting to pursue the conversation any further.

When Sergeant Wood returned to the MP station, he was told to see Master Sergeant Snoop.

"Did you want to see me, Sergeant Snoop?" he asked as he walked into Master Sergeant Snoop's office.

"I just wanted to find out how things went with you and Specialist Coleman."

"OK, I guess. I gave the commander my suggestion as far as what punishment I thought Specialist Coleman deserves. And other than that, I would say everything went pretty well," Sergeant Wood informed Master Sergeant Snoop, omitting the conversation he had with Captain Hicks and First Sergeant Green after Specialist Coleman had been dismissed.

"If I were you, I'd stay on my toes. From what information I can gather, First Sergeant Green is one tough hombre. A red neck from Alabama, but still one tough hombre," Master Sergeant Snoop warned.

"You know I keep my stuff together, Sergeant Snoop," Sergeant Wood reminded him.

"Just the same, you watch your step, buck sergeant," he said seriously.

From that day forward Sergeant Wood took notes of everything said to him that could have an adverse effect on his short career. He also kept notes from every squad leader's meeting so he would have documented evidence of what they were instructed to do. Any adverse information on himself or anyone in his squad could be found in his little "black" book, which was actually army green.

The night after the episode with Captain Hicks and First Sergeant Green, Sergeant Wood was in a pretty foul mood when he got to his hooch. It seemed everything Miss Kwak said or did got on his nerves. Every time she asked him what was bothering him, he said nothing. He felt there was no reason to get her involved in his personal state of affairs. To try and make up for the way he was acting, he offered to take her to see a movie and afterward to the NCO club for lunch and a couple of drinks before reporting for duty at 1500 hours the following day. The movie theaters off post started at 10 am in the morning. So he had plenty of time to uphold his promise. Just because he couldn't have a drink didn't mean she couldn't have a couple of drinks herself.

Miss Kwak stopped him. "I won't let you take me anywhere until you tell me what's bothering you. Do you realize this is the first time you've ever been this down since I've known you?"

"I know. It's just that I don't want to get you involved in my personal problems. That's all," he said, hoping she wouldn't persist.

"If you don't trust me enough to tell me when you have a problem, maybe we don't have as good a thing going as I thought," she said with a pained expression on her face.

Sergeant Wood explained to her what had transpired that day. "I just don't know whether I should fight them anymore. Hell, if it wasn't for the Provost Marshall and First Sergeant Tucker, they'd probably have busted my butt a long time ago."

"Yobo, if you ever stop believing in yourself, you might as well give up and do whatever they tell you to do. There's always going to be someone in authority who's not going to like you," Miss Kwak assured him.

"Hell, baby, we're not talking about just anyone. We're talking about two people who can mess me up if I want to stay in the army for twenty years. We're talking about two people who probably won't hesitate to scare the hell out of the other squad leaders and get them to say anything against me they want them to say. I can deal with Captain Hicks and First Sergeant Green, but the scared ass NCOs I work with are another matter. The commander and First Sergeant Green will need them to set me up for my downfall, because they work with me on a daily basis. I know at least two squad leaders who would go along with whatever the commander told them to say because they don't like me, especially Sergeant Stone. You know something, Yobo? There've been times when I wanted to say to hell with it and just go along with the program. I get so tired of being looked upon as just another hard ass that's bound to screw up sooner or later. And half the unit can hardly wait for that day to come."

"Would that make you happy, just going along with the program?" Miss Kwak asked, knowing the answer.

"Hell, no, and you know it wouldn't."

"Well, to hell with them. Why spend your whole life worrying about what people are going to say about you?" Miss Kwak advised.

"You're right. Let's go to the movies tomorrow morning

and later a burger at the snack bar," Sergeant Wood said, feeling better.

"That's better. Wine and dine me, Yobo-ya. But at the NCO club, not the snack bar. I feel likey havin steaky dinner," she laughed, imitating how the majority of her countrywomen often spoke.

Sergeant Wood didn't sleep well that night. Every time he dozed off to sleep, there standing over him was Captain Hicks and First Sergeant Green holding a set of slave bracelets saying they were going to get his ass because he was now their slave. The following morning he took Miss Kwak to a movie and to the NCO Club for a steak dinner as promised.

Throughout the movie and the meal he kept remembering what First Sergeant Tucker had told him. *Young men like you can change the army establishment; however, it's going to take time. You have to sometimes give up a mile just to gain an inch. I believe you have what it takes to hang in there and fight for those changes which have to be made if we, as Black soldiers, are to get our just dues.* Sergeant Wood had to talk to First Sergeant Tucker at least one more time before he left Korea.

Things smoothed out for him over the next couple of days. But he still needed to talk to First Sergeant Tucker so he could get some tips on how to keep his behind out of a sling now that he was an NCO.

Specialist Coleman was given an article 15, fined $150.00 a month for two months, 14 days extra duty, and 14 days restriction to the unit. Captain Hicks told Sergeant Wood his mind was already made up as far as what punishment he was going to impose on Specialist Coleman before asking for his input, so he needn't think his decision had anything to do with what he suggested. They both knew better, and Specialist Coleman thanked him again. From that day forward Specialist Coleman was one of his best soldiers. After talking to Staff Sergeant Stone, he had no more problems with him concerning his squad, but Sergeant Wood never forgot the conversation.

Staff Sergeant Stone's squad was Sergeant Wood's relief. After he had his squad on the road and Sergeant Wood had his squad officially off duty, Sergeant Wood asked if he could talk to him for minute before he left. When they entered the briefing room Staff Sergeant Stone looked at Sergeant Wood suspiciously

"What's this about, Malcolm X," Staff Sergeant Stone asked

Sergeant Wood laughed and said, "Look man, the next time one of your troops want to switch a day with one of mine you make sure I'm notified before a decision is made for me."

"Since I out rank you, I made a command decision," Staff Sergeant Stone said.

"You made a command decision my ass! What you did was show disrespect for me as a fellow squad leader and NCO. I may not be a Staff Sergeant yet, but I'm the squad leader until a Staff Sergeant is assigned to the unit. So I demand the respect of my position," Sergeant Wood said.

"You really get on my nerves trying to talk white with your black-country ass. You're nothing but a country nigger pretending to be something that you ain't. So get off your high horse and let the real NCO's run things around here," Staff Sergeant Stone said.

Sergeant Wood smiled and said through clenched teeth, "Damn if that ain't the skillet calling the kettle black. The only so called nigger around here pretending to be someone they're not is you. You running around with these white boys singing country and western songs, hollering hee-haw, and acting like you're one of them is pathetic. The first time something goes down between black and white soldiers they're going to turn on your black ass like you're a dreaded disease, and you're too damn stupid to see it. The only thing I want from you is for you to leave my squad the hell alone. And don't dare use my people without my permission. You got that, Sergeant Stone?"

"You live your life and don't worry about mine. You won't last the remainder of your tour. Captain Hicks and First Sergeant Green are going to get your ass, and I'm going to be there cheering them on," Staff Sergeant Stone said and walked off.

Sergeant Wood got his chance to talk to First Sergeant Tucker the day before he was supposed to leave. He and Miss Kwak were invited over to First Sergeant Tucker's hooch for a short timer's party, just the four of them. First Sergeant Tucker had already been given a going away party by his fellow senior NCO's and the unit. Sergeant Wood had never heard so much sugar coated bull crap in his entire life, especially from First Sergeant Green.

"By gawd, from what the captain's been telling me about First Sergeant Tucker, it is going to be mighty hard for me to fill his shoes. Not only the captain, but everyone from the provost marshal to the lowest private in this unit has told me how much they respect and admire this man. I just hope everyone in the unit gives me the support you've given First Sergeant Tucker during his tour of duty here. First Sergeant Tucker, I'm mighty proud to be chosen to replace such an outstanding individual as yourself." So on and so on--three bags full.

"First Sergeant Tucker, you've been around for quite a while. How did you manage to keep your stripes?" Sergeant Wood asked him that evening at his short timer's party.

"Let me tell you something. Equality and justice for everyone in the army does not exist right now, especially where black soldiers are concerned. Sometimes I want to say to hell with these damn rules and regulations. But I always remember there's just as many screwed up rules and regulations out there in the civilian world as there are here in the army. The only difference is you can tell your civilian boss to screw off and get another job without having to worry about the humiliation of going through a court martial or getting an article 15. The main reason I've been able to keep my stripes is I love the army. There is nothing on the face of this earth I'd rather be. It's something about this uniform that makes me feel important. People see me in uniform and they know I stand for something."

"I like being a soldier too, First Sergeant, but how are you supposed to react when you know you're doing your job well and still people are out to get you, the same damn people I'm supposed to be fighting alongside of to insure America protects her interests and way of life? Aren't we supposed to be fighting for the same thing?" Sergeant Wood asked, hoping Sergeant Tucker could somehow explain it in terms that he could understand.

"The only thing I can tell you is if you truly believe in yourself and what you're doing, no one will be able to get to you. As long as you keep doing everything the army requires, you should have no problems keeping the ass holes off your back. And it's no big secret how to accomplish this. It's called tact. You have more tact than half the senior NCO's and officers in the United States Army combined. Captain Hicks has told me time and time again if you weren't so damn tactful, he would have had your ass a long time ago. And he doesn't care

PATRIOTISM

that you're one of the best soldiers he has ever had in this command. I guess what I'm trying to say is if you continue doing the things you're doing now and don't let them get you in the position they want you in, hell, you'll be gone before any type of plan can be put into action."

"I doubt that, First Sergeant, but I'll do my best to stay out of their way," Sergeant Wood said sounding dejected.

"I know you can, and will. Let me show you something," First Sergeant Tucker got up and went over to his night stand and brought back a laminated copy of a newspaper clipping of Dr. King's assassination. "I idolized that man. I guess it's because I never had the guts to stand up and be counted. I had no problems facing the Viet Cong, but when it comes to dealing with the white man, that slavery mentality kicks in and I accept everything that is going on in the world. Sometimes I want to make a stand and put everything on the line, but I always convince myself I have worked too hard to get to where I'm at today to lose it for a moment of glory. Besides, we have to work the system from within as well as from without. It may take longer working the system from within, but I feel it's necessary. It hurts to be truthful about yourself sometimes.

You remind me so much of Dr. King. I guess that's why I made sure I was in on everything that concerned you. Here you are, a young, I can't say militant, determined young man, who pulls no punches. White people, white men especially, in America and the army fear you and every other young black man like you. I know you and a lot of other young black soldiers say if you had my rank, you'd be able to change something within the system. Maybe you could, but I believe it's going to take black soldiers as a whole to change the establishment's way of thinking, not one man.

Take the sit-in this past summer. I knew when and where it was going to take place. A First Sergeant from 2nd ID gave me the heads up. I didn't feel you had a need to know about it, so that is why I didn't say anything to you about it. I almost told Colonel Heath what those soldiers had planned because I disagreed with the tactic. Thank God I didn't. That sit-in at 8th Army Headquarters was a good thing because it bought about some much needed changes. It was too bad those eight leaders of the sit-in were court-marshaled. I hope there's an easier way to get the system to change other than mass protest in the future. If there is, we have to find out how so our leaders who fights for these changes won't end up being kicked out of the army. Still, as long as these commanders see that black soldiers are willing to sacrifice their standing with the military and risk their lives for change, they'll be willing to compromise to save their asses from the glare of the news media. As I said earlier, sometimes I wished I didn't have anything to lose so I could join a protest, but I can't afford to lose everything I have worked so long and hard to achieve. To some of my fellow soldiers I use my rank and status as an excuse to wimp out, that at heart I'm a coward. Sometimes I wonder if it's true," First Sergeant Tucker said, putting the newspaper clipping back in the desk drawer.

"First Sergeant Tucker, you have more guts than any NCO I know. I'm well aware that it takes internal fortitude to be able to beat these white officers and NCOs at their own game. Not to mention taking the heat for taking me under your wing. I'm not as intelligent as you are yet, so I have to do things as best I can. I don't mind putting my butt on the line every day because I want to show my fellow black soldiers that we can succeed in the military without having to stab each other in the back, or give up our manhood to make the white man happy. That maybe, just maybe, if some of the other young black NCOs see me not backing down from the threats of my white superiors, and still take care of business, they won't either. I was also a follower of Dr. King's teaching, but I also listened to Malcolm X. Either way, we as Black people in America are being killed every day by an unjust system. My biggest question has always been, should we die in peaceful protest or should we go down in a blaze of glory? As you know, First Sergeant, I've never threatened anyone with bodily harm, although I'm sure it would not bother me in the least to do so. First Sergeant, I want your honest opinion. Do you think I'm wrong for standing up for what I believe in? For standing up for what I believe to be right?" Sergeant Wood asked.

"No, I can't say you're wrong. However, here in the military, sometimes being right doesn't mean a damn thing to the establishment. Now that you're an NCO, they're going to expect some type of loyalty from you. That means they'll expect you to support the commander's policies, both written and implied, whether you agree with them or not."

"In other words, they'll expect me to do whatever it takes to keep the overhead personnel from looking bad, even if I have to be the fall guy," Sergeant Wood said.

"That's about it," First Sergeant Tucker affirmed.

"That would be a hard pill to swallow because we both know if I mess up, I might as well grease my behind, bend over and grab my ankles; because the big green weenie won't hesitate to screw me over," Sergeant Wood understated.

"Unfortunately, that's true. But you're good at keeping yourself covered at all times. And as long as you continue doing so, they won't be able to screw you. I've already cleared everything with Snoop for you to take me to the airport at Osan, AFB tomorrow. There's something else I want to tell you, but it'll have to wait until then. It's 2330 hours, buck sergeant. Y'all better get going before the taxis stop running. I don't want you and Miss Kwak to get into trouble for violating curfew," First Sergeant Tucker joked, knowing the Korean Police took care of the MP's as far as the curfew was concerned. Every MP in Korea carried an MP brassard in his pocket to show the KNP's on such occasions.

Sergeant Wood didn't sleep well that night either knowing the only person he trusted was leaving that morning. He picked First Sergeant Tucker up early the following morning. They rode in silence until they were almost at Osan, AFB.

Out of the clear blue-sky First Sergeant Tucker said, "Let me tell you one thing I don't want you to ever forget. No matter how well you think you know someone, never tell anyone in that company everything you do or plan to do. Do you understand what I'm saying?"

"First Sergeant, I hear you talking, but to be honest with you, I don't know what you're talking about," Sergeant Wood said puzzled.

"I'm talking about you telling Master Sergeant Snoop that now that I'm leaving, you'll have to confide in him. You trust that fucker too much. Don't you realize that no white person of rank appreciates hearing a black sergeant call one of their commanders unjust? Don't tell him I told you, but the next time you see him, you ask him why Captain Hicks really decided to walk through the barracks that day he caught Specialist Coleman smoking the grass. Also, ask him who found the bag of grass in

Specialist Coleman's wall locker. I just found this out yesterday. I overheard Snoop talking to First Sergeant Green about it. But the biggest question you have to ask him is why he felt you shouldn't take over your squad even though everyone knew you were the most qualified after Sergeant Pearson was moved to the back office. If not for me, they would've given your squad to that white boy Sergeant Pickett." (Sergeant Wood and Sergeant Pickett had been promoted the same day.) "I wish you all the luck in the world, son. I started to extend just to make sure you made it through this tour without getting screwed over. But I have some business I have to attend to back in the States. Besides, I know you have the qualities to accomplish anything you want. It's all on your shoulders now. So keep a cool head and you'll make it through the two months you have left with no problems. Hopefully, we'll meet again," First Sergeant Tucker finished, looking saddened because he was leaving Sergeant Wood to fend for himself.

"Good luck, First Sergeant," was all Sergeant Wood could manage to say after helping First Sergeant Tucker take his bags into the terminal. They shook hands for the last time, because it wasn't in the stars that they should meet again. On his way back to the compound Sergeant Wood felt so young and so dumb.

The day after First Sergeant Tucker left, Sergeant Wood went to Master Sergeant Snoop's office to have a talk with him. He had to find out for himself if what First Sergeant Tucker had said was true. Since it was 1800 hours, he thought no one other than Master Sergeant Snoop would be in his office as usual. He thought he'd made sure everyone was gone, but as he started to knock on Master Sergeant Snoop's office door, he heard voices from inside the office.

"Dammit Jim, Sergeant Wood is a real pain in the ass. Part of the reason I extended in this damn country is to burn his smart black ass. I've never had a nigger talk to me the way he has and gotten away with it. I wish I had his black ass back in Mississippi. I would've had him locked up a long time ago. I just knew you had something I could use against him. Now that that nigger Tucker is no longer around to protect him, we should be able to burn his ass," Sergeant Wood recognized Captain Hicks' voice.

"No, sir, not yet," Sergeant Wood heard Master Sergeant Snoop respond. And then he added, "But he does trust me. He doesn't even know I'm the one who reported Specialist Coleman. He tells me everything he does since Tucker got short. As soon as I get something good on him, I'll let you know, sir. I sure wish he wasn't black because he's a damn good soldier."

"Good soldier or not, we can't have a black ass nigger, regardless of rank, walking around here acting as if he owns the place," Captain Hicks spat.

"I fully agree, sir," Master Sergeant Snoop agreed.

Sergeant Wood stepped into the latrine across the hall after hearing Captain Hicks say he would be checking back with him later. He watched through the crack of the latrine door as Captain Hicks exited Master Sergeant Snoop's office and left.

I'll be a son of a bitch. First Sergeant Tucker was right about that backstabbing bastard, he said to himself aloud. Sergeant Wood waited until he had given Captain Hicks enough time to leave the building before he knocked on Master Sergeant Snoop's office door. He was told to enter.

Master Sergeant Snoop greeted him with a big smile. "Well,

hello, if it isn't my favorite buck sergeant. What can I do for you this evening?" he asked, shaking his hand.

It was hard to believe this was the same man who just a minute ago told Captain Hicks he would help set him up for a fall. So cool, and nothing in his face gave any indication that he was a backstabbing bastard.

"I had to ask you something, if that's all right with you," Sergeant Wood said.

"Sure, why not? What's on your mind sergeant?" he asked.

"Well, ever since Specialist Coleman got busted, there has been a rumor going around that you were the one who dimed him out just to make me look bad. But I find that hard to believe. I wanted to hear what you had to say about the matter," Sergeant Wood said, as if he wasn't really concerned with what his answer might be.

Master Sergeant Snoop turned red and lost that cool composure he had a second ago. He tried to keep the anger he felt out of his voice, but to no avail. "I don't know where you get off asking me a question like that. Why the hell would I get one of your troops busted if it was you I was after? Hell, you're only a mere damn buck sergeant," he hissed.

"You don't have to sound so pissed off, Master Sergeant Snoop. I just wanted to reinforce my belief that you're not that type of person, that's all," Sergeant Wood lied.

"I'm sorry, buck sergeant. I had a bad day. How is life treating you?" he asked, changing the subject and at the same time not answering his question.

"I'm doing just fine, but I'm sure going to miss First Sergeant Tucker," Sergeant Wood said truthfully.

"We all will. He's such a damn good man," Master Sergeant

Snoop agreed.

"Well, I know you're on your own time and would like to finish up whatever it is you're doing, so I guess I'd better get out of here and back on the road," Sergeant Wood said standing. He left Master Sergeant Snoop's office with more hate in his heart than he knew what to do with.

From that day forward Sergeant Wood trusted no one in the unit, Black or White. He did his job and went home to Miss Kwak. However, being an NCO, he couldn't shut himself completely off from unit functions. Other than those functions and work, Sergeant Wood was very seldom seen around the unit. Earlier in the year, after realizing he wouldn't be allowed to transfer from Korea to Vietnam, Sergeant Wood had submitted for an ITT (InterTheater Transfer) to Vietnam upon PCSing from Korea.

His momma had been highly upset upon hearing what he had done. He explained to her that he could get killed just as easily there in Korea as he could in Vietnam. Sergeant Wood's momma knew it was a lie, but said what the hell. He was no longer a kid and had to live his own life and make his own decisions, regardless of how messed up they were.

"Sergeant Wood, the First Sergeant wants to see you after you get off duty today," Staff Sergeant Edwards, the unit chemical training NCO, informed him during a day shift.

"Do you know what it's about?" Sergeant Wood asked.

"Something about an ITT to Vietnam you put in for," Sergeant Edwards informed him.

Sergeant Wood knew First Sergeant Green would probably fix it so he wouldn't get the ITT approved, but nonetheless he decided to go into his office with an open mind. Sergeant Wood

PATRIOTISM

hoped that maybe, just maybe, they hated him enough to help him get to Vietnam in hopes that he would get his head blown off. He knocked on the First Sergeant's office door and was told to enter.

After being seated, First Sergeant Green smiled and said, "Sergeant Wood, I have here in my hands an approved ITT request for you to be assigned in Vietnam. However, all I have to do is make a call to personnel and tell them the commander and I don't think it would be in the best interest of the army to send you over there. That although you show no outward sign of having a mental problem, we feel one does exist. Now if you can give me a good reason why I shouldn't do that, I might decide to let you go to Vietnam and get your butt blown off," the First Sergeant smiled, leaning back in his chair.

I'll be damned. I might get my wish after all, Sergeant Wood whispered to himself. "I don't know what you expect me to say, First Sergeant. The truth of the matter is I'd hoped to go to Vietnam since the day I was drafted. Believe it or not, and so far no one has, I want to do my part to help put an end to the war being fought over there," Sergeant Wood said.

First Sergeant Green broke into a roarous laugh. When he finally regained his composure, he said, "I'll be gawd damned. When Captain Hicks told me that was why you wanted to go to Vietnam, I thought he was pulling my leg. If you think I believe that crap, you're not as smart as I gave you credit for. If that's the best you can do, you'd better hope you get a good assignment stateside because this ITT is history."

"Fine, First Sergeant. If I'd known the only way an American serviceman could serve his country where he is needed most is to lie, I would've told that lie a long time ago," Sergeant

Wood said.

First Sergeant Green became angry and growled, "That patriotism bullshit you're telling me sergeant, is about as believable as a man on the damn moon. So get off that shit and tell the truth about why you want to go to Nam," he said, now leaning forward.

"First Sergeant, if you can't accept the fact that a young black man believes in America, I have nothing else to say. Sure we as Black Americans are catching hell back home and in the military right now, but things are changing and getting better all the time. And probably the best thing about the whole situation is equality is going to happen whether the majority of White America wants it to happen or not," Sergeant Wood said, staring Sergeant Green in the face, hoping what he had said would awaken his deepest fears. And so it had.

"By gawd. I hope I never live to see the day when a black man is allowed to be equal to a White man," First Sergeant Green sputtered.

"Whether you live to see it or not, First Sergeant, it doesn't really matter because if not you, your sons and daughters will see it," Sergeant Wood smiled, irritating him further.

"You know something, boy, even though I hate your guts, you're one of the best damned young ass soldiers I've ever run across. Too bad you're stepping on your superiors' toes to get your point across. Otherwise, you would stand a chance to go a long way in this man's army. I'm going to ignore that little remark you made about me probably being dead when this vision of yours comes to light, because you're pissing against the winds of a hurricane. The White power structure of America will never let the likes of you gain power--only token *"yes"*

PATRIOTISM

blacks. So forget Vietnam. And as I said earlier, hope you get a good assignment stateside," he said.

When Sergeant Wood didn't answer he was dismissed. He found himself becoming more and more disgruntled with the military system, not actually the military system but the individuals who ran it. Not a day passed without an officer or senior NCO, in certain ways or speech, reminding him he was a Black NCO. Not just an NCO in the United States Army, but a Black NCO. Therefore, he constantly found himself on the defense.

It seemed whenever he made a mistake, which was always minor, it was blown out of proportion to make it sound as if he had made a major screw up. For example, one day he instructed his radio operator to call ETD (end tour of duty) before the oncoming patrols were put on the road, a common practice among the squads. The patrol didn't actually come into the station until they were relieved, but they returned to the station and stayed in their jeeps parked outside the station until the other squad got on the road. It meant his soldiers on guard duty at the gates would be relieved at least 30 to 45 minutes late. They couldn't leave the gates until they were physically relieved by the oncoming shift. The oncoming squad was already fifteen minutes late and showed no signs of being ready to relieve them. This had been going on for at least four consecutive shift changes and Sergeant Wood was tired of it. He had complained to Master Sergeant Snoop to no avail.

The next day after guard mount, Sergeant Wood was told he had to see Master Sergeant Snoop. Since he had found out about the two-faced bastard, their relationship had deteriorated to the point of no return.

"Master Sergeant Snoop, you wanted to see me?" Sergeant

Wood asked as he entered his office.

"Yeah, I did. What's this shit I hear about you pulling your squad off the road before Staff Sergeant Johnson, a new white sergeant in the unit, relieved your people last night? You're lucky as hell I wasn't the duty officer when you pulled that little stunt. I would've had your ass, buck sergeant," Master Sergeant Snoop said.

"I'm tired of Sergeant Johnson relieving my people fifteen and twenty minutes late every damn day. I've complained to you about him relieving my troops late, but still nothing's been said to him. But the minute I decide to do something about it on my own, I have to come and see you as if I screwed up. What's the deal, Sergeant Snoop?" he asked, losing his military bearing. "Besides, everyone pulls their people off the road when the relieving squad is late, and everyone knows that," Sergeant Wood added to let Sergeant Snoop know that he knew having his patrol return to the station early wasn't the real reason Master Sergeant Snoop was on his ass.

Master Sergeant Snoop looked him straight in the eye and said, "If you ever pull your people off the road again before being properly relieved, your ass is mine. And I don't care if the on-coming shift is two minutes or two hours late. Do you understand what I'm saying, buck sergeant?" Master Sergeant Snoop hissed.

"Yeah, Master Sergeant Snoop. I understand you perfectly. If I mess up again, it'll make Captain Hicks a very happy man," Sergeant Wood said, catching him off guard.

Sergeant Snoop blushed and told him to get out of his office.

Upon being relieved by Staff Sergeant Johnson the following day, on time for a change, Sergeant Johnson asked Sergeant

PATRIOTISM

Wood if he would stick around for a while, he wanted to talk to him. Sergeant Wood gathered the patrol reports and gate logs from his people and put them in the PM's box for review. He waited in the report writing room while Sergeant Johnson insured all of his people were where they were supposed to be. After his squad was on the road, Sergeant Johnson entered the room and stood there saying nothing, as if he didn't know where to start. Sergeant Wood figured it was because Sergeant Johnson was afraid he was pissed at him for relieving his people late four consecutive days.

Sergeant Wood didn't want to get into a pissing contest, but he did want to get this confrontation over with as soon as possible, so he asked, "What did you want to talk to me about, Sergeant Johnson?"

Staff Sergeant Johnson looked relieved to hear from the sound of Sergeant Wood's voice that he was not pissed off or in a hostile mood. "As you know, I've only been here a little over a month and don't know everything that's going on in the unit. What I wanted to know is what does Captain Hicks and Sergeant Snoop have against you?" he asked.

Sergeant Wood resisted the temptation to go into details because he no longer trusted his fellow NCOs in that particular unit. "I guess I've been on the wrong foot with them for some time now. Why do you ask?" Sergeant Wood asked suspiciously.

"Because Master Sergeant Snoop instructed me to relieve you late, hoping you would get pissed off enough to hit me or something so they could burn you. They know how it pisses you off for your troops to get screwed over. If you had fallen for their trap and shown disrespect to me as a senior NCO or hit me, they were going to bust you all the way down to private E-1," Sergeant Johnson enlightened him to what was going on.

"Why are you just now telling me this?" Sergeant Wood asked, but continued before Sergeant Johnson could answer. "This has been going on for almost a week now. And you know I've been going to the back office complaining about you. What is your reason for not telling me sooner?"

"I know this is going to sound fucked up to you, but when they told me you were a smart-ass troublemaker, I believed them. I thought if I got you to do what they wanted you to do, the better off I'd be," Staff Sergeant Johnson confessed.

"So what changed your mind?" Sergeant Wood asked.

"Hell, I know a good NCO when I see one. There are very few E-5's who have the respect of their entire squad as you do. Your people will do anything you ask them to without asking questions as to why they have to do it. And because the majority of them are White, that pisses Captain Hicks and Sergeant Snoop off more than anything else. Did you know they have been trying to get several of the people in your squad to say you smoke pot? Hell, if not for the PM, Master Sergeant Snoop would have given me your squad. Colonel Wells, the new PM who replaced Colonel Heath, likes you for some reason. I tell you man, they want you bad," Staff Sergeant Johnson said.

Sergeant Wood smiled and said, "Thank you for that bit of information, Sergeant Johnson, but the only thing you have told me that I didn't already know was about them trying to use you to get to me. In the meantime, I've had my people check you out. For instance, I know you're from the hills of Kentucky and ain't too fond of black people in America. Don't deny it," Sergeant Wood said, cutting off his attempt to protest. "I also know you and Master Sergeant Snoop were stationed together at Fort Hood, Texas, but didn't get along too well. But the most upsetting thing I've heard about you, from your own people, is you don't know which you hate the most, niggers or Koreans. So I say to you, Sergeant Johnson, as I've told Captain Hicks and First Sergeant Green, don't let the color of my skin fool you. I'm not easy to deceive, and I'm no one's fool. If you're sincere in what you're saying, I'm glad to see you have your own set of standards. But if you think you can snow me with kind praise, forget it. Because in time you're bound to show your true colors sooner or later," Sergeant Wood finished, staring Sergeant Johnson down. Staff Sergeant Johnson was blushing the whole time Sergeant Wood was talking.

"Goddamn, I really under estimated you, Sergeant Wood. It's true, early in my military career, before Vietnam, I didn't care much for colored people...."

"Black," Sergeant Wood corrected him.

"OK, black people," Staff Sergeant Johnson said, sounding upset at being corrected. "I didn't think much of Black people, but as time went on and I had to work closely along side of black NCOs, I finally realized the only real difference between us is the color of our skin. We have the same ambitions, to make things better for ourselves and our kids, whenever we have some, so they won't have to struggle in life as we did. I'm not saying I want to be your closest friend, or a friend at all for that matter. I'm only trying to say I want to have a good working relationship with you for the short time you have left before going back to the world. As I said earlier, I know a good NCO when I see one."

"Thanks for the compliment. And as you'll soon learn, I'm

very easy to work with. But please, if you ever have any questions as to why I said or did something, ask me why. Don't guess or try to read my mind. And for God's sake, don't ask anyone at the unit or in the back office," Sergeant Wood instructed him.

"You got it," Staff Sergeant Johnson said, offering his hand.

Sergeant Wood shook his hand, but something in the back of his mind kept saying, *'A snake is a snake and always will be a snake.'* He made a mental note to stay away from Staff Sergeant Johnson as much as possible because if push came to shove, he would end up with the end of the stick that was covered with thorns.

Time passed and Sergeant Wood's PCS date got closer and closer. Since he wasn't going to Vietnam upon PCSing from Korea, he and Miss Kwak had to make different plans. He would PCS back to the states and re-enlist for Vietnam, and after his tour of duty there he would return to Korea and they would get married. However, if the gaining command felt the same as the other commands that he had been assigned to, he would be back in Korea within seven months. Miss Kwak was very happy with this change of events. She was thrilled at the possibility of becoming Mrs. Sergeant Bob Wood a lot sooner than expected.

Master Sergeant Snoop left Korea three weeks prior to Bob's departure. He was given an Army Commendation Medal (ACM) and a bigger send-off than First Sergeant Tucker had been given. It pissed Sergeant Wood off after seeing what had been planned for him. He had no intention of attending this function, but he had been told by Master Sergeant Greenspace, Snoop's replacement, in no uncertain terms to attend or else.

When it came to the hand-shaking part of the function, he said to Master Sergeant Snoop (so no one else could hear), "I heard you and Captain Hicks talking about burning me the day after First Sergeant Tucker left. Maybe at your next duty station, you'll be able to accomplish that underhanded deed with someone not as smart as I am."

Before Master Sergeant Snoop could respond, Sergeant Wood walked off. *Maybe the bastard will think next time before he makes such a stupid ass promise to another commander*, Sergeant Wood said to himself as he departed the area.

Master Sergeant Greenspace made it obvious he didn't like Sergeant Wood, so it was easy for Sergeant Wood to stay out of his way for his remaining three weeks. Despite the distrust Sergeant Wood felt toward Sergeant Johnson, they ended up having a good working relationship during the short period of time he had left in country. Although he didn't want to admit it, Sergeant Wood had enjoyed the mind games so much, before he realized it, it was his turn to return to the world.

"Yobo, do you realize that I only have two weeks left before I have to go back to the world?" Sergeant Wood asked. When she didn't answer he asked her what was wrong.

"I don't know how to tell you this, yobo," Miss Kwak said and started crying.

"Tell me what? It can't be that bad. I love you. You can tell me anything, you know that," he said hugging her.

"I know, but I don't want you worrying about me while you're away," she said.

"Come on Yobo, tell me what's wrong," Sergeant Wood pleaded.

"I wasn't going to tell you, but I knew it would be wrong

not to. I'm four month pregnant, and don't know what to do about it. I could take care of the baby until you got back, but you know how they treat women who have babies out of wedlock, especially women with black half-breed babies. The baby would be treated worse than most because it'll be half black. As I said, I don't know what to do," Miss Kwak finished.

All the wind had been knocked out his sails. The last thing he expected her to tell him was she was pregnant. He held her at arm's length and said, " I want to do whatever's best for you. The last thing I want is for you to suffer because of me. What do you want to do about the baby? You know I don't have a choice. I have to leave," Sergeant Wood said.

"I don't know. I'll talk to mama-san, the old lady next door, tonight and see what she says I should do. The final decision is still going to be up to us you know," Miss Kwak said with a sigh.

"Yeah I know," Sergeant Wood said, dreading what he knew the outcome would probably be.

The last thing he wanted was for Miss Kwak to get an abortion. This was un-chartered water for him. He didn't even know a girl who had an abortion. It was a subject that never came up in his community. When a girl got pregnant, she and the boy got married and she had the baby. He didn't have time to marry Miss Kwak, and she was going to catch hell while he was away if she had to raise the baby alone. He knew once the deed was done, the word abortion would forever remind him of what he and Miss Kwak did to their child. But he had to think of what was best for her.

After consulting with mama-san, Miss Kwak confirmed his fear. She decided that it would be for the best if they got rid of the baby. Reluctantly, he agreed. Two days later he found himself in a dinghy little hospital to witness the destruction of his unborn child. He stayed at Miss Kwak's side because he felt it was partly his fault she was suffering this pain and humiliation.

Sergeant Wood wanted to know the sex of his child because his daddy had told him the Wood's men first baby was always a boy. And that first boy was the one who became the head of the house in the event something happened to the daddy. That first boy was the one who set the standards for the other kids to follow. He had to fight back tears when the doctor told him it was indeed a baby boy, a baby boy that would never live to continue the tradition of previous generations. The only satisfaction he gained from the destruction of his child was the knowledge that he had kept the Wood men tradition alive, as far as the their first child being a boy. After Miss Kwak was taken to her room to recover from the procedure, Sergeant Wood went outside and cried for the child whose life they had allowed to be taken.

Sergeant Wood had listened to Vietnam Veterans talk about how they had to shoot little kids that had tried to blow them and their fellow soldiers up. He found himself wondering if he could kill a child after what he had allowed to happen to his own. He would have to cross that bridge when he came to it, because his desire to go to Vietnam didn't change. Sergeant Wood put his life in God's hand and swore to follow whatever road he was lead down.

After asking God for forgiveness one last time, Sergeant Wood went back into the hospital to check on Miss Kwak. Seeing her lying there in that hospital bed dressed in white, looking so vulnerable, so angelic, he had never loved her more. He knew at that moment he could never be happy with any woman other than her. It was like they had made a blood covenant with each other that neither of them could ever break, least they both would end up in hell. He would return to her in time. There was no doubt they were meant to be lifelong mates. For the remainder of his stay he treated her like a precious stone that the world was trying to steal from him. Leaving her was like when he left home for basic training, but knowing he would be back for Miss Kwak made it a little easier to do what he had to do.

Sergeant Wood knew it was customary for all NCOs departing the command to receive an Army Commendation Medal (ACM) or a higher award. He figured if Captain Hicks and First Sergeant Green had their way he would receive a burning cross with KKK stamped all over it. As it turned out, that probably would have been better. He was given a letter of commendation. The same award they gave all E-4's and below who departed the unit. Sergeant Wood knew he deserved nothing less than an ACM. Captain Hicks knew it also because of the number of award and certificates he had to present to him during his tour in the command. This was the only way Captain Hicks could get back at him for having stood his ground. Sergeant Wood only accepted the letter because he had to. But he knew exactly what he was going to do with it before he left. Captain Hicks got away with his underhandedness because Colonel Heath had completed his tour of duty in Korea a couple months earlier, and Colonel Wells didn't feel he should interfere in unit matters such as the awarding of awards.

The parting with Miss Kwak was sad, but they knew they shared a love that was meant to be. "Yobo, I love you more anything in this world, but you know this is something I have to do. But you can rest assured there's nothing in this world that can keep me from coming back to you," Sergeant Wood said.

"I know that. Still, it don't ease the pain I feel at the thought of you not being with me for a whole year or more. I'll be waiting patiently for your return," Miss Kwak said with tears running down face.

"Only God can keep me from coming back to Korea to marry you," he said, trying to kiss away her tears. Sergeant Wood left her standing in the doorway of their hooch, crying her heart out. He refused to say good-bye because there was no doubt in his mind that he would be back. He caught a taxi to his unit to pick up his duffle bag and suitcases for the long trip home, and from home to Fort Leavenworth, Kansas.

Sergeant Wood had packed everything except the Letter of Commendation he had received from Captain Hicks. That he took to the latrine with him. After taking a healthy dump, he wiped his butt with it, placed it in an envelope and just before leaving the unit, he placed it in the unit distribution box addressed to Captain Hicks, Commander. Even though he tore out his name and social security number, Sergeant Wood was sure the captain would know who had left it for him, although he wasn't the only one leaving that day that was pissed off because of receiving a lowly letter of commendation. Sergeant Wood knew the distribution paperwork would not be opened until the following day. He would be long gone by then. Sergeant Wood had stood his ground and walked away with his head held high because of the rank he had earned. The down side of his tour was, he had been in the army over a year and the only person he had killed was his own son. He didn't dare tell his momma about the abortion because she would never forgive him for agreeing to the taking of a life that wasn't his to take, because

259

he hadn't given it in the first place.

Chapter 7
BACK IN THE WORLD

It was a beautiful but cold winter day when Bob stepped off the bus in Helena, Arkansas. The flight back to the States didn't seem as long as the one that took him to Korea. His whole family was waiting for him at the bus station. They were so happy to see him after a year plus absence. Bob's momma smothered him with hugs and kisses. His daddy, this time, shook his hand and commented on how well he looked. Little Harvey was disappointed he had not killed any of them VC's. Ronda looked as if she had grown two feet since he last saw her. It was amazing how much difference a year and a sneeze made. They asked him a million questions about Miss Kwak, Korea, and the Army. He tried his best to answer everyone's question. Although nothing had changed physically in his hometown, Bob felt he no longer belonged. Mentally, he had outgrown the small town he had once loved so dear. His momma no longer said, "My baby," but "My son." It felt good to be with his family again.

That night after Bob's momma, Ronda and Little Harvey had gone to bed, he asked his daddy what had happened between Gina and Johnny.

"Well, after Gina finished the Job Corps, she graduated as a nurse's assistant, she came back home and got herself a job working at the hospital in town. She was doing well, that is until Johnny supposedly swept her off of her feet. He then, again supposedly, convinced her to quit her job and move in with him at his daddy's house. Needles to say, Mrs. Samson was pissed big time. That girl changed a lot while she was in Texas. Anyway, they stayed together several months. Then something went wrong and she moved back in with her mother, but not before she got herself pregnant. That's where she is staying now. She asked me yesterday if you were coming home today. I told her yeah. She said she had to talk to you," his daddy said.

"I want to talk to her to, but I'm not the same kid who stepped on that bus a year ago," Bob said.

"Hell, boy, she'll know that right off. The same as we did when you stepped off the bus. Gina said she knows you'll never forgive her and Johnny for hurting you the way they did, but she wants an opportunity to explain what was going through her mind at the time she was making those bad decisions."

"She doesn't have to explain anything to me. I kept every letter she wrote me explaining how she was gradually giving up on us. I even kept the Dear John letter," Bob said bitterly.

"Just the same, I think you should listen to what she has to say," his daddy reasoned.

"Yassuh. I will, the first chance I get. I'll listen to my good buddy Johnny too," Bob said, getting slightly pissed because the old Johnny would've been at the bus station along with his family when they picked him up. "Is she still pregnant?"

"Naw, she had an abortion. Well, it's time for me to go to bed. I'll talk to you in the morning," his Daddy said and left him with his thoughts.

After his daddy went to bed, Bob sat in front of the television thinking of how things had changed in such a short period time. He had been drafted, left home for the first time, flew on an airplane for the first time, survived basic combat train-

PATRIOTISM

ing and AIT, was sent across the Pacific Ocean to Korea, lost Gina, found Miss Kwak, reached the rank of noncommissioned officer, learned that race relations in the military and America was awful, was accused of being a liar because he was patriotic and wanted to help win the war in Vietnam, and now he had returned home to a hero's welcome by his family. Life was good.

While stationed in Korea, Bob's unit, through his efforts mostly, had won several basketball tournaments. This meant several additional trophies for his trophy case, which was not a case at all. Harvey had designated the top of the bookcase in the living room as the official Bob Wood trophy case. That made up for Bob not killing any of them VC's. Little Harvey was thrilled to death as Bob handed him the trophies to set on top of the living room bookcase. Harvey felt with all those trophies, sixteen total now counting his high school trophies, Bob was ready for the NBA. Bob could hardly wait to show off his new additions to the trophy case to his high school buddies. He didn't realize how good he had become while stationed in Korea until that first day back on the school ground. He was so dominant it was no longer fun playing against the guys in his hometown.

First Sergeant Tucker never told Bob his basketball playing ability played a part in keeping Captain Hicks off his back. The unit basketball team won two tournaments and the 8th U.S. Army championship. Sergeant Wood was named MVP in one of the tournament, and in the 8th U.S. Army championship. Colonel Heath told Captain Hicks to lay-off of him because he made the command look good, on and off the basketball court. So he spent his tour in Korea convinced it was First Sergeant Tucker's protection alone that had gotten him through his tour.

To Sergeant Wood, his exploits on the basketball court were just a past time for him without any significant meaning. He received the praise bestowed on him with distrust and skepticism. Sergeant Wood didn't know it at the time, but basketball would become a very important factor in his life while stationed at Fort Leavenworth, Kansas. This time there would be no doubt that basketball would help keep him from getting busted.

    The day after his arrival home Bob called all of the guys and girls who had run in his circle of friends prior to his leaving for Korea, the ones that were still there anyway. As expected, he was challenged to a pick-up game that afternoon. The only two people he didn't call were Gina and Johnny. That afternoon he brought along his five new trophies to the playground to show them off. Everyone said he probably bought the trophies at a trophy shop on his way home from Korea. But after a couple of games on the concrete court, he erased all the doubts as to why he had received them. Seeing how good he had become, no one wanted to play against him anymore. They all wanted to be on his team. The competition in Helena, Arkansas, was non-existent as far as Bob was concerned. The only two people nowhere to be found were Gina and Johnny. He figured they were trying to avoid him, but Helena was too small a town to avoid anyone for any length of time. Bob figured he wouldn't see them until that Saturday night at the Hangout Club. It was where the young people in the community hung out on weekends. After leaving the playground, he spent the remainder of the afternoon visiting friends who were not at the playground, with Harvey and Ronda in tow.

    While getting dressed Saturday evening to go to the Hangout Club, Johnny called. "Hey, Bob, will you be at the Hangout later on tonight?" he asked, sounding guilty as hell.

"Yeah, I'm getting dressed now. I'll be out there in an hour or so. Why?" Bob asked, playing with his mind.

"I want to talk to you. To explain what happened between Gina and me."

"Sure, no problem. I'll see you there. Hey, will Gina be there?" Bob asked before Johnny could hang up.

"I don't know, but she usually is," Johnny answered.

"Well, I'll see you there, good buddy," Bob said hanging up the phone.

As Bob was hanging up the phone, his momma walked in. "Don't you go out there getting into a fight," she warned, which sounded more like a plea.

"Don't worry, momma. The only woman I would fight over is 16,000 miles across the ocean," Bob assured her.

"Let's hope so," his momma said, sounding concerned about his health.

Bob had no intention of fighting anyone, especially Johnny. However, on his way to the club his mind flashed back to how pissed he'd been when Gina told him how she was slowly giving in to Johnny's advances.

When Bob pulled into the parking lot of the Hangout, he saw Johnny waiting in front of the club. Johnny was pacing back and forth like a caged cat.

"Well, hello, stranger," Bob spoke, catching Johnny by surprise. It was apparent Johnny hadn't seen him approaching because he jumped back as if he had been swung at.

"You look good, man. The army must be good to you," Johnny said nervously.

"Hey, dick head, you going to give me five or what?" he

asked, trying to put Johnny at ease.

Johnny gave Bob five and said, "I would've called when you first got home, but I thought you were pissed at me for what happened between Gina and me."

"Look, man, I was mad as hell six months ago. But things changed for the better. I met a woman who loves the hell out of me, and I love her. And believe me, it goes deeper than anything me and Gina ever had going. I may still like her, but there's no longer any room in my heart for her as far as love is concerned. By the way, is Gina here yet?" Bob asked, looking around.

"I ain't seen her, but then again, I ain't been inside. I just got here a little bit before you did. I wanted to talk to you before I got my head bad. I wanted you to know I didn't take advantage of Gina's loneliness. What happened was perfectly innocent at first. I never expected anything to happen between us. It just did," Johnny attempted an explanation.

"Well, I hope you two get back together again because from what I hear you two make a good couple," Bob lied.

"I still love her," Johnny said hesitantly and continued. "But that bitch of a momma of hers is something else. Mrs. Samson was the main reason we broke up. She said I'd never be anything other than a dirt farmer like my daddy. She even told Gina she should've waited for you to come home from Korea, not that it wasn't a good idea, but hell we were living together at the time" he groaned.

Bob couldn't help from laughing at that. "Come on, good buddy, I'm thirsty. Let's go in and have a drink. The first one's on me," Bob offered. He could see a flood of relief come over Johnny's face.

PATRIOTISM

Talking to Johnny was a lot easier than he had thought it was going to be, considering his old friend had stabbed him in the back. Bob thought he would feel at least a little hostility toward Johnny for what he had done, but to his surprise he didn't. Bob knew he had left no home fires burning. In the very near future Gina would only be a pleasant memory.

A couple of drinks later Johnny was his old self again. He appeared to be genuinely happy that his truest friend was still his friend after the pain he had caused him. They were feeling pretty good when Gina walked through the door around midnight. She looked devastating.

Gina was dressed in a white mini skirt with a white ruffled matching blouse and knee high black leather boots. For a moment Bob's mind raced with the memories of the passionate times they had shared together. Although she appeared confident in herself and knocked the socks off every man in the club, Bob noticed the hesitancy in her walk as she headed over to where he and Johnny were sitting. It seemed every man in the club was watching with mouths agape as she swayed over to their table. Bob pretended not to notice, but the way she looked, a dead man would have sat up and took notice.

"Hi, Bob, I heard you were back in town. Could I talk to you alone please?" Gina asked with a concerned look on her face.

"Sure, lets go out to the car. Want a drink before we go outside?" Bob asked her, his eyes roaming over that splendid body.

"Sure, Hennessy and coke."

"Since when?" Bob asked, remembering she didn't drink at all when he left.

"Oh, about a year ago. Anything wrong with it?" she asked.

"No, I like your style, that's all," he smiled and ordered their drinks.

As they walked out to the car with drinks in hand, Bob tried hard to keep his eyes off that hot, tempting body, but to no avail. *Hell, I'm only human*, he thought. Every movement of her body oozed sex appeal. He opened the door for her and went around the car as fast as he could without making it too obvious that she had gotten his attention.

Bob got in on his side of the car. He sat sipping his drink waiting for her to start the conversation, but when she said nothing, he said, "You're more beautiful than I remember."

"You're a sight for sore eyes yourself. They told me you were a hunk, but they didn't give you the credit you deserve," Gina countered.

"Enough of the small talk; daddy told me you said you wanted to explain why you, how should I say it, dumped me," Bob said.

Gina took a sip of her drink. "That's a very cruel way of putting it," she protested.

"Well, how would you put it?" Bob asked, somewhat sarcastically.

"In my last letter I told you how lonesome I was at that Job Corps Center. I just wanted someone to lean on until you got back home. I never intended for anything to happen between Johnny and me. It just happened," Gina explained.

"Johnny said the same thing. So I guess it was destiny that brought you two together. Did you ever take the time to think that I was lonely too? Do you really think I didn't need someone to lean on? Believe it or not, because I cared so much for you, I was able to resist the women over there. And believe me, it was not easy," Bob said, stressing the not easy part.

"I guess deep down I thought you was messing around. I hear there are a lot of pretty girls over there," Gina said.

"That's true. But up until I received your Dear John letter, there were none as pretty as you."

"You know how to make a girl feel guilty, don't you?" Gina asked defensively.

"That's not my intention, but I'm being honest with you," Bob said.

"So how long have you known Miss Kwak?" she asked accusingly.

"I don't know, about a year at least, but not on a personal basis. And not once did I attempt to take her to bed. Not until a couple of weeks after I received your letter," Bob answered.

"That means you hadn't fooled around when you received my last letter?" Gina asked incredulously.

"You got it. Even after receiving your letter I didn't start talking to Miss Kwak seriously for a couple of weeks. I was hoping you'd write and tell me all was right with the world. But I guess it wasn't meant to be."

"What's so special about this Miss Kwak?" Gina asked.

"I like her because she was the only Korean girl I'd met that didn't speak broken English. Still, I resisted her because I thought you still loved me enough to wait for me. But I don't hate you. You're still one of the prettiest girls in the world," Bob complimented her.

"Are you saying what we had is over?" Gina asked sounding hurt.

"As much as I hate to say it, I'm afraid so," he answered.

"I bet if you gave me a chance, I could make you forget about Miss Kwak," Gina challenged him.

"Maybe you could for a little while, but not forever," Bob responded.

"Do you dare?" Gina asked, a wicked smile crossing her lips.

Bob could tell by the way she talked she was now used to getting her way. He tried to think of a reason, other than revenge, why he should try and bring this cocky bitch back down to earth when she provided the answer for him.

"What's wrong, Bob? Afraid you can no longer handle a real woman?" Gina teased.

"Lady, I hope you know what you're doing. I can see you're no longer the innocent little girl I left behind. By the same token, I'm not the same immature little boy who rode off that day with tears running down his face," Bob said, staring her down.

So the battle of wits began. They sat in the car talking for a long time. Instead of going back into the club, other than to return the bar drink glasses, he took her home. He would let Johnny know what happened later.

"Aren't you coming in?" Gina asked, surprised he made no attempt to seduce her after such an open invitation.

"Not tonight. I'm not up to playing games," Bob said as he walked Gina to her door.

"What do you mean you're not up to playing games? I ain't playing," she assured him.

"You know damn well your momma and daddy aren't going to stand for any hanky panky in their house," he reminded her.

"Well, let's go to your house," she countered.

"I'll have to take a rain check until tomorrow night."

"You don't know what you're missing, soldier boy," Gina said pressing that gorgeous body of hers against his.

Bob took Gina into his arms and kissed her, his hands gently stroking her back, buttocks, and long, slender thighs. A soft moan escaped her lips as she pressed herself harder against him. The sweet taste of her luscious lips, combined with the softness of her body pressed against his, almost pushed him to the point of no return.

"Hey, this shit is getting heavy," Bob said letting go of her. "If we keep this up much longer, I'll have to take you up on your offer," he breathed heavily.

"The offer still stands, soldier boy, if you dare," Gina said swaying her hips from side to side.

"I'm tempted, but I really have to get going. I've got an early date with the family in the morning."

"Bob, it's only one o'clock. We used to stay out until three and four in the morning before you left for the army, and you never had any problems getting up," she reminded him.

"And we will again, but not tonight. I've only been home a couple of days, so I thought I would chill out for a while before hitting the streets hot and heavy," Bob said.

"Hopefully I'll be free tomorrow night," Gina said disappointed but hoping he would change his mind and stay a while longer.

"Let's hope so," Bob said and turned and walked back to the car. Gina was still standing at her door with her hands on her hips as he drove off.

Although Bob knew he could never love Gina again, that animal magnetism between them was very much alive. He felt he'd won round one. He hoped he would be able to maintain control of the situation for the remainder of the time he had left at home.

Because of an incident with the chaplain in Korea, Bob

no longer believed in the church, the preachers really, but he attended Sunday services with his family at the request of his mother. He figured she wanted to show him off to her friends. All of the old brothers and sisters raved about how well the army must be treating him because he looked so well. While at church Gina told him she would not be able to see him that night because of a previous engagement.

"I guess I'll have to check with you at a later time," was all Bob said.

After leaving church, he, Ronda and Harvey went to the school playground and stayed there the remainder of the afternoon. Johnny tried to get someone, anyone, to bet they could beat Bob one on one. He would pay them double their bet. There were no takers because they knew how good Bob was.

The weekend passed and the workweek began. It was boring as hell at home with everyone either at work or school. Gina didn't work, but they were still not on speaking terms. So Bob spent the first three days just lying around the house, which he was no longer used to doing. He drove down to the shop where his daddy worked a couple of times, but his daddy was always too busy to talk to him for any length of time. He wrote Miss Kwak almost every day telling her how much he loved and missed her. He had received a couple of letters from her saying the same thing.

As the days dragged, Bob found himself thinking of Gina. He thought maybe she had honestly tried to wait for him, but was too weak. If that was the case and she still cared for him, what he had planned for her would not be justifiable. But the only way he could find that out was to continue with the game plan. He called her on Wednesday to see if she would be busy the following day; if not, would she like to take a ride around the countryside? She thought that was an excellent idea. She could hardly wait. The following afternoon he picked her up at 1 p.m.

As they rode, Gina talked about the things she had experienced while he was in Korea. While at the Job Corps Center in Texas, she had learned she possessed all the attributes it takes to make men eat out of the palms of her hands. At first she didn't like playing with people's minds. However, over a period of time, and after coaching from other girls doing the same thing, she learned to like it. When she returned home, the games continued. When she hooked up with Johnny, she never really intended to marry him. She couldn't stand her mother telling her what to do all the time. Always telling her where she could go, who with, and what time she had to be home at night. So she manipulated Johnny into believing she was in love with him to have a place to stay once she could no longer stand her momma's bitching. And to her satisfaction everything had worked to perfection.

She said the only part of her scheme that was unplanned was her getting pregnant. She had tried in vain to convince Johnny they were not ready for children. That they should wait until after they were married and had a house of their own. Therefore, the only solution was for her to get an abortion. When he wouldn't go along with her way of thinking, she made up lies that her mother would disown her for getting pregnant out of wedlock. When that particular lie didn't work, she started telling her momma that Johnny was constantly telling her he didn't know whether he wanted the baby or to marry her. And he had threatened to beat her when she told him she wanted to move back home. This was all it took to bring her family around to her way of thinking. They even paid for her abortion, although her parents and the older generation didn't believe in taking the life of an unborn child, regardless of the stage of life the baby was at. However, believing the lies Gina had told her about Johnny, her momma said she would never allow her daughter to give birth to the child of an ungrateful ass hole like Johnny Tongas. So things had worked out well for her, even though she was still living at home. She was now doing anything she wanted to do without having to answer to anyone. As far as Johnny trying to explain his side of the story, Mrs. Samson wouldn't even listen to anything he had to say.

When Gina asked Bob what he had done while stationed in Korea, he told her he had spent the majority of his time trying to fight the injustice black soldiers had to face on a daily basis. That black soldiers in the army were being screwed over the same as the brothers on the streets. The only difference was the method being used. They ended up on Lover's Levee where their relationship had begun, which seemed like a century ago.

"Do you remember that first night we shared up here together?" Gina asked as they strode along the levee in the brisk winter wind.

"How can I forget? But, God, that seems so long ago," Bob reminisced.

"I know what you mean, but in my mind it's as clear as if it was yesterday. I never wanted what we had to ever end," she sighed.

"Neither did I, but I guess life has a way of testing young love. And we failed the test miserably," Bob said.

"Yeah. The test we had to face was very cruel if you ask

me," Gina said with a heavy sigh.

They walked on in silence until Bob noticed she had started to shiver. "We'd better head on back. It's getting chilly out here."

"It sure is," she agreed, putting her arm around his waist and leaning against him for warmth.

It was late afternoon when he dropped her off at her house.

"Will I see you tonight?" Gina asked in a hopeful voice.

"Sure, I'll give you a call later on," Bob promised.

Upon his return home his momma was waiting for him. "Bob, I don't want to meddle in your affairs, but Gina ain't the same girl you left here in Arkansas. She have changed so much. It seems she cares for no one other than herself anymore. Almost every man, and boy for that matter, around here would give anything to marry her. But she just uses them up and then casts them aside," she warned him.

"Momma, you don't have to worry about me falling in love with her again. But I'm going to give her a dose of her own medicine. She told me how much she enjoys using people. I saw through her little game before she even told me," he assured his momma.

"I hope you know what you're doing," she said, unconvinced that he knew what he was doing.

"Don't worry, Momma, there's no one who could ever take the place of Miss Kwak in my heart," he assured her.

Bob's momma was still not convinced he knew what he was doing, but dropped the subject.

It was the truth about him not falling in love with Gina again because he felt nothing for her, other than the desire to screw her brains out. Bob also realized that Gina's only mission in their new found relationship was to see if he was as weak as the rest of the poor slobs she was used to screwing over. She wanted to prove to herself that no man could resist her womanly charms. And Bob wanted to prove he could.

Bob's daddy on the other hand was all for it. After telling him what he had planned for Gina, his daddy said, "If anyone can do it, you can. It's about time someone brought her down off that high horse she's been riding on since she brought her pretty black ass back home."

"Who's supposed to be her boyfriend now?" Bob asked.

"One of those damn fools around the lake. His name's Sam Shepard," his daddy frowned. The lake separated the farm his family lived on and the farm from which his daddy was talking about. "Gives her damn near his whole paycheck every Friday and hasn't even been to bed with her as far as I know. Gina keeps telling him they should wait until after they're married. That's the oldest damn lie in the world. And the damn fool falls for it," his daddy said, shaking his head as if he felt sorry for any boy dumb enough to fall for simple bull crap like that from a girl who had recently had an abortion.

"I guess that means he's jealous," Bob surmised.

"You'd better believe it. He gets in a fight almost every Saturday night because someone tries to talk to her. But he's nothing but a runt. You could stomp a mud hole in his bony little butt with no problem," his daddy assured him.

"I'm not planning on fighting anyone over her. I just wanted to know what type of person I'll have to deal with eventually."

"He's a real nut. That you can believe," Bob's daddy laughed.

"Daddy, did you know Gina was playing Johnny for a fool?

PATRIOTISM

That she never really cared about him?" Bob asked.

"Hell, boy, everybody in Helena knew that girl didn't give a damn about Johnny. Hell, he knew it himself, but said he loved her too much to give her up. Damn fool," his daddy spat.

"Well, at least it's not Johnny I'm going to screw over," Bob said, his mind off in left field.

Bob was remembering the fights he'd had to break up because of jealous lovers while stationed in Korea. And he was planning on doing something stupid that he knew would probably make Sam want to fight him, but hoped he could pull it off without having to fight. Bob felt with the right plan he should be able to handle her boyfriend without even an argument. Under no circumstances, other than being punched or shot at, was he going to give Gina the satisfaction of seeing him fighting because of her. That evening Bob and Gina went to see a movie, and later they stop for a burger at Dairy Queen.

"So who's your main man right now?" Bob asked her in between bites of his burger.

"You are, or did I forget to tell you?" Gina said, wrinkling her nose at him.

"You know what I mean," he said, giving her a stern look.

"Oh, all right. His name is Sam and he lives around the lake. But it's nothing serious going on between us," she lied.

"What do you call serious? The man gives you the majority of his money each week, doesn't he?" Bob asked roughly.

"I see you've been talking to your daddy about me. What else did he tell you about me?" Gina asked as if annoyed that anyone would dare spread gossip about her.

"That's my only concern at this particular moment. I don't want to accidentally run into someone's fist without knowing why," he said.

"He wouldn't dare fight you. He's nothing but a runt," Gina confirmed his daddy's assessment of her current boyfriend.

"Jealous men have been known to do some foolish things," he reminded her.

"Well, I won't let him mess with you."

"Great! That's what I always wanted. A female body guard," Bob pretended he was fond of the idea.

"I always protect what interests me," Gina said, playing footsy with him under the table. "I have a girlfriend who said we could use her house until midnight. And we don't have to worry about being interrupted because she lives alone," Gina informed him with a knowing smile.

"By all means, let's go. I didn't have anything planned anyway," Bob said, putting aside his half-eaten burger.

Upon reaching her friend's house, he reached over and touched her face ever so gently and said, "You owe me nothing, Gina. I don't want you doing this if it's because you feel guilty or feel you owe me something. Our relationship just didn't work out. Maybe we were too young to handle such a relationship in the first place," he said getting cold feet. He hadn't slept with another woman since he and Miss Kwak had hooked up.

"I appreciate that, but I'm doing this because I want to. Whether you want to admit it or not, the physical attraction between us is just as strong now as it ever was. Right or wrong?" she asked, squeezing his hand and placing it in her lap.

"You're absolutely right. What're we waiting for then?" he asked, opening the door for her.

The house was small. It had one bedroom, a living room, a dining room, a bathroom and a kitchen. Once they were inside, they wasted no time getting undressed and doing what they came there for. The sex between them was good, very good in fact. The only thing missing was the total trust they once shared. Bob knew they were playing a game in which only one of them could win. He intended to be the winner. Afterward they rode all the way to her house in silence.

"I'll see you tomorrow night. That's if you aren't busy," Bob said as he pulled into her driveway.

"You bet you will, even if I have to come over to your house and get you," Gina laughed.

"What happens when Sam shows up at the Hang-out tomorrow night while we're there having a ball?" He wanted to see how she would react to the question.

"I'm sure you know how to handle yourself," Gina winked.

"Right. Well, I'll pick you up at eight. And please be ready to go. You know I hate to wait on anyone."

"See you then, you naughty boy," she smiled as she exited the car.

Damn, that girl knows how to please a man. I had forgotten just how good she is. I'd better be careful or she's going to turn the game around and take over the controls, Bob thought to himself after leaving her house.

Saturday is always a shopping day in the country, so he took his momma shopping and they stayed most of the day. He had forgotten it took his momma a century to find what she was looking for, which ended up being socks for Ronda and Harvey. They were very disappointed at getting nothing but socks because they'd put in their orders for a new pair of jeans and a new pair of tennis shoes before they left to go shopping that morning. After taking her home, he drove to the shop to shoot the bull with his daddy until it was time for him to get off work. Saturday for his daddy was just another workday. Usually his daddy hitched a ride home with the foreman when he didn't have his car, but Bob picked him up because he wanted to talk to him. On the way home he told his daddy what had happened between him and Gina the previous evening.

"What you should do tonight is stand her up. That'd show her she don't have you by the balls after just one roll in the hay," his daddy advised.

"I thought about that, but I think I'll wait for Sam to show up at the Hang-out and dump her on him. She actually thinks I'm ready to fight over her."

"That should get your point across," his daddy agreed. "Just make sure you don't mess around and piss the crazy bastard off. Or you'll end up fighting him anyway," his daddy warned.

"Don't worry, I won't. I have everything figured out," Bob assured his daddy.

"You should wear your uniform, just to piss him off," Bob's daddy laughed.

"Good idea, Daddy. I think I will," Bob agreed.

That evening Bob was fifteen minutes late arriving at Gina's house for their date. She was ready and waiting outside for him when he arrived, but he decided to go in and say hello to Mr. and Mrs. Samson.

"Hello, Mr. Samson, Mrs. Samson, I thought I'd stop by and pay my regards since I haven't been over since I've been home."

Mrs. Samson was the first to speak. "Well, hello, Sergeant Wood. I heard you looked good in your uniform, but I never thought you looked this good. My, but the army must be treating you well. I guess I was wrong about you. So how do you like being a military policeman?" Mrs. Samson asked, smiling the friendliest smile he'd ever seen on her face.

"It's great. I get a chance to meet all kinds of people. I also like the authority that goes with the job," Bob answered.

"Do you get to mess with the White officers?" Mr. Samson asked, remembering that when he served the army was still segregated, but they had White officers who did whatever the hell they wanted to while commanding colored troops.

"I sure do. I think I enjoy that more than anything. And I don't cut them any slack either. It gets me into hot water sometimes, but nothing I haven't been able to handle so far."

"Just don't get too comfortable and get yourself screwed over. You know how sneaky these damn White people are," Mr. Samson cautioned him.

"I'm glad to see you and Gina back together again, Bob," Mrs. Samson interjected. "That girl hasn't been the same since you left. Now that you're back in the States, I hope you two will stay together this time," she said hopefully.

"I'm planning on it, ma'am," Bob lied. After saying good night and promising to see them again soon, he and Gina departed.

As soon as they were in the car she said, "Eight o'clock sharp and you'd better be ready. And who shows up late?" Gina asked.

"I apologized, ok?" Bob said, spreading his hands.

"Apology accepted. Let's go boogie," she laughed.

When they arrived at the Hang-out, Sam was already there.

Gina pointed out his car to Bob and said, "I hate to tell you this but Sam carries a .32 caliber pistol."

"So, does that mean he's going to start blasting away the moment we walk into the club?" Bob asked unafraid.

"I certainly hope not," Gina said, taking hold of his arm and leading the way to the club.

When they entered the club, Bob felt as if he had watched this same scene on television. The good guy (him) finally gets his girl, but the bad guy (Sam) wants her back. So when they step into the saloon, everyone looks at the bad guy to see what his reaction is going to be. As if on cue, everyone looked over to where Sam was sitting when Bob and Gina entered the club and made their way over to an empty table. Bob could feel the icy stare Sam gave them running up and down his spine. Sam was sitting with three other guys who looked just as pissed as Sam was. They were drinking heavily. He could tell by their actions and their loud, slurred speech as they spoke loud enough to be heard.

"Hey, Sam, ain't that your gal with that tall sum-bitch that just walked in?" one of them asked.

"Yeah, I guess that means it's ass whuppin time," another one added.

Sam only mumbled something unintelligible under his breath. Bob knew it would only be a matter of time before Sam built up enough courage to say something to either him or Gina. He waited intentionally for a slow song to play before he asked her to dance. Bob knew if Sam didn't make his move after seeing his woman being held by another man, he wasn't going to say anything at all. The whole time they were dancing, Sam sat there looking as if he was going to kill Bob at any moment. As expected, he intercepted them as they were leaving the dance floor.

"Hi, Gina. I thought you were coming to the club with one of your girlfriends?" Sam said, trying to maintain control of his anger.

"Can't a girl change her mind?" Gina asked in a huff.

"It looks like you lied to me on purpose so you could come out here with your ex-boyfriend," he said, giving Bob an icy stare out of the corner of his eyes. He then turned and faced Bob. "Look, man, let me tell you sumthin right now. Befo tonite is over yo ass is mine," he said trying to stare Bob down.

Bob smiled and said, "Look, brother, I don't know what you're getting upset about. But just in case you decide to get stupid, let me hip you to something." Bob moved the left side of his uniform jacket back so Sam could see the 38 cal. special he had nestled at his side. He had borrowed it from Johnny, but the pistol belonged to Johnny's daddy. Johnny also knew Sam carried a gun. He then said, "Don't forget, my man, I shoot these things all the time as a cop in the army. And to be truthful with you, I hit whatever it is I'm shooting at. Oh, one other thing. You have to bring ass to get ass. So if you'll excuse us, we would like to finish our drinks before all the ice melts," Bob said, taking hold of Gina's arm and leading her back to their table.

Sam looked as if he had seen a ghost as he made his way back over to his table. Bob had spoken low enough so Gina couldn't hear what was being said, nor was she aware he had a gun. Bob wanted her to think he was willing to face Sam with nothing but his bare hands. After returning to their seats, Bob figured it was now or never; he had to dump her on Sam.

"Gina, since Sam has been so good to you, don't you think you owe him an explanation as to why you're doing him like this?" Bob tried to reason with her.

"Doing what to him?" Gina asked, playing dumb.

"Look, you're not going to use me as you've used half the guys in Helena. So what I want you to do is go over to his table, sit down with him, tell him your true feelings, and I'll see you tomorrow," Bob said and stood to leave.

"You bastard," she hissed. "You're not afraid of him, I could see that when you two were talking. So why are you doing this to me?" Gina asked, pissed.

"I want to be with you, but not if I have to watch my back all the time. So get rid of Sam and I'll see you tomorrow."

"You think I'm not worth fighting over, is that it?" she asked, jumping to her feet. "Well, if you walk out of here tonight, you can forget we ever met," Gina threatened.

"Have it your way. I thought you'd grown up, but I guess I was wrong. You know my number if you change your mind," Bob said and left her standing at the table with her mouth wide open.

Before Bob was out the door, Sam was making his way over to where she was standing. Bob left the club and went looking for Johnny to return the pistol. He found Johnny at his current girlfriend's house.

"I thought you and Gina were together tonight," Johnny's girl Jennifer said, after Bob was seated.

"We were, but Sam was getting ready to act a fool, so I left her there to tell him to get lost if she wants to be my girl," Bob said, feeling proud of himself for what he'd done.

"I ran across Gina at the store today and she told me you said if Sam said anything to either one of you, you was going to kick his butt," Jennifer said perplexed.

"And what gave her that idea?" Bob asked with raised eyebrows.

"Whatever Gina Samson wants, Gina Samson gets," Jennifer stated matter of fact.

"Well, not this time. Either she plays by my rules or we don't play at all. I'm not a male chauvinist pig, but a man has to show a woman that he expects certain things of her. And one of them is he's the only man in her life at the moment."

"Man, I just knew you were going to have to whip or shoot Sam's ass tonight. That's why I didn't go to the club. I'm not scared of Sam and those crazy fools he run with, but getting into shootouts is not my thing. Besides, I know you can take care of yourself. So what happens now? What will you do if she never calls you again while you're home?" Johnny asked.

"So what? Life goes on. I'd rather she didn't call me than to have to put up with her bullshit like crazy ass Sam and the rest of the guys she have screwed over, not to put you down good buddy," Bob said apologetically.

"More power to you, Bob. She sure had my nose wide open," Johnny admitted.

"Watch and learn, my friend," Bob said, feeling in total control of the situation.

"Don't worry, she'll call eventually. Gina doesn't take no for an answer," Jennifer assured him.

The next day Bob heard several different accounts of what happened after he left Gina at the club. However, the ending was always the same. She had told Sam to go screw himself at the top of her lungs and stormed out of the club with Sam on her heel. She caught a ride with one of her girlfriends and left him standing in the middle of the street. They said Sam had sworn he was going to kill Bob the very next time he laid eyes on his army ass, but Bob never had any problems out of Sam the remainder of his stay.

Bob was serious about not caring whether Gina called during the remainder of his stay. But as Jennifer had predicted, she did call several nights later. He was mildly surprised because he had also heard she told everyone as far as she was concerned, he no longer existed. Because of how Bob had treated her at the club, Gina learned for the first time that not all boys cared how pretty she was. She also learned she had to be a person who cared about other people's feelings as well as her own. When the phone rang, Bob happened to be the nearest one to it.

"Hello, Bob, I've been waiting for you to give me a call," Gina said in a strained voice.

"I started to, but from what I heard I'm the last person in this world you wanted to talk to," he said.

"I was just pissed because you walked out on me. Whether you realize it or not, that was very embarrassing," Gina said, almost losing control of her anger.

"Sorry about that, baby. I can't see myself fighting over a woman that's already supposed to be mine. And God knows I don't want to have to kill anyone."

"Who said anything about killing anyone?" she asked, pretending she didn't know what he was talking about.

"Hey, baby, you knew damn well Sam carries a gun. You told me yourself he was armed. So I borrowed Johnny's daddy's 38 Smith & Wesson. Gun plus gun equals shoot-out, and shoot-out means someone gets killed or hurt very badly," Bob schooled her.

"I didn't know you had a gun."

"Why the hell do you think I didn't hesitate to go into the club? You thought I was willing to fight a .32 caliber pistol with my bare hands? Besides, Johnny had already told me Sam carried a gun," Bob explained.

"Sorry. Well, anyway, I told him I never wanted to see him again. That you're my one and only man from now on," Gina informed him.

"Sounds like I heard that somewhere before," Bob said sarcastically.

"Aw, come on, Bob. Don't be so cold to me. You did tell Momma we would stay together this time," she reminded him of the stupid lie he had told her momma. "And I did make the first move by calling you. Didn't I?" she asked.

"Yeah, you did. When can I come over to see you?"

"How about right now? Momma and Daddy went to see a movie and I'm all alone in this big, old house," she exaggerated.

"When we get together we have a bad habit of doing unusual things. If you know what I mean," Bob cautioned.

Gina laughed and said, "OK, just pick me up and we can go for a ride or something."

"I'll be over in about fifteen or twenty minutes."

Bob's daddy looked over at him with a smile on his face. "A chip off the old block," he gloated.

However, Bob's momma was not amused. "Everyone is talking about what you did to that girl. If you don't want her, why do you keep leading her on?" his momma asked.

"I guess in a way I still like her. I do know I want her to feel the same way I did when she wrote me that Dear John letter. She even had the nerve to tell everyone to watch how she would get my nose opened wide again now that I was no longer around that slant-eyed bitch in Korea," he said, cussing in front of his momma for the first time in his life.

"Revenge is mine saith the Lord," his momma quoted the bible.

"I get your drift, Momma," he said, patronizing her.

"After you've gotten your revenge, then what?" his momma asked with raised eyebrows.

"I don't know. I guess I'll have to cross that bridge when I come to it," Bob said.

"Be careful, son, is all I'm saying. You know Miss Kwak is waiting for you way over there in Korea," she reminded him.

"I haven't forgotten, and I never will. That's where my heart lies," Bob assured his momma.

"As long as you know what you are doing," his momma finished.

"Believe me, Momma, I do."

Bob got the car keys from his daddy and drove over to Gina's house. They drove up to Lover's levee to watch the river boats pass by as they had done before he left for the Army. He parked in what used to be their favorite spot. The moon was so bright it was almost like day. The stars looked so close he felt as if he could reach out and touch them. Gina had her head lying on his shoulder, her eyes glazed over as if she was seeing this sight for the first time. They sat there, not saying a word. It seemed if they said anything at all, it would break the magical spell that had them frozen in place. The sight was so beautiful they lost all tracks of time. It seemed as if they had been sitting there all their lives. Several riverboats passed by lit up and as beautiful as he remembered. Bob was thinking how Miss Kwak was going to react at seeing this lovely sight for the first

PATRIOTISM

time upon her arrival to his hometown. Finally, a small voice from somewhere within his subconscious awakened him to the fact that if they sat there much longer with the engine off, they would freeze to death.

Bob started the engine. "We'd better get going. I don't have enough gas to sit here all night with the engine running," he said, breaking the silence.

"I could stay right here with you; just like this, forever. You want to know something, Bob? Tonight I realized I still love you very much. Sitting here like this, as we did before you went to the army, rekindled that old flame I felt for you so long ago. I haven't felt this good with anyone since you left. Assure me it's going to work this time," she pleaded.

"I don't want to lie to you, Gina. So much shit is going through my mind right now I'm not sure of anything anymore," he said.

"Go ahead and tell me. I know you're in love with your cute little Korean woman. So I guess that means I'll have to settle for being with you whenever I can," she shook her head sadly. The tears started to flow.

Bob took her into his arms and kissed her. "Gina, Gina, it seems we were not meant for each other," he said, feeling sorry for her. "It seems I only make you unhappy every time we get something started."

"Don't be silly, these are tears of joy," she sniffed. "I'm so happy when I'm with you. You make me the happiest woman in the world when we're together."

"Shit, you sure know how to get under a person's skin. I can say that much about you," Bob said, seriously.

"In time, do you think I could make you forget Miss Kwak?"

she asked.

"I seriously doubt it. But you're a very special lady to me. If things don't work out between me and Miss Kwak, and you're not married by then, I'll be looking high and low for you."

"I hope you mean that. And I'm not ashamed to tell you I hope it doesn't. I'll wait for you this time if it takes a lifetime. Maybe I'm a selfish bitch, but I know I love you more than she does," Gina tried to convince him.

"We'll have to wait and see about that," Bob cautioned.

Bob drove her straight home even though she protested all the way. Gina wanted to spend the night with him. They could stay at her friend's house. All she had to do was call and ask her. But he stood firm, even though he cussed himself mentally. He told her as badly as he wanted to stay with her, he needed some time to think before seeing her again. She got out of the car and asked if she would see him tomorrow. He assured her she would and left her standing in her driveway sniffling.

Hell, I may as well go ahead and take advantage of the situation, he thought. *If the table was turned, she probably wouldn't hesitate to screw my brains out and then go on to whatever it was she had planned.*

So for the remainder of the time he had left, he spent it with her. They slept over at her friend's house every chance they got. Even though it was fun being with her, he never forgot his true love in the Land of the Morning Calm. He still wrote Miss Kwak almost every day. Although his momma didn't like him spending so much time with Gina, she was happy to see he was not forgetting about Miss Kwak. Time passed and before he was quite ready to leave home again, it was time to report to

PATRIOTISM

Fort Leavenworth, Kansas. The farewells this time, except for Gina, were not as emotional. The night before he left, he took Gina to a movie and later for pizza.

"Is this the last time we'll ever be together?" Gina asked in a small, weak voice.

"I'm afraid so. The next time you see me, I'll probably have Miss Kwak at my side," Bob said truthfully.

"I haven't told you this, but since we've been back together I've experienced true hate for the first time in my life. And who do I hate? A woman I've never even met or seen. I'm sure if she was here right now, I'd scratch her eyes out. If anyone had told me you would be able to make me do anything you wanted, I would've said they were crazy. Not me, the playgirl of the seventies. And now look at me, about to break down and bawl like a damn baby who needs its diaper changed. Bob, can I come to Kansas and visit you sometimes?" she asked on the verge of tears.

"I don't think that would be a good idea, simply because it would only make things hard on the both of us. As I've been telling you all along, I'm going to marry Miss Kwak. And there's nothing, or no one, that's going to make me change my mind. I truly hate to hurt you, but you insisted on starting this shit all over again," Bob said.

Tears began rolling down her cheeks and dropping onto her plate. He felt temporary guilt for what he had done to her, but as he had said a long time ago, life's a bitch that cares for no one or anything.

"So what do I do now? I've run every man in Helena away because I thought if you saw I could be a one-man woman, maybe you would change your mind about us. Boy was I wrong. Why is life so unfair?" she asked and started crying softly.

"Come on, let's get out of here," he said, taking her gently by the arm and leading her outside to the car. "I'll be right back. I have to pay for the pizza before they call the cops on me."

After Bob paid for the untouched pizza and returned to the car, she asked, "Could we go up on Lover's levee for one last time together before you leave?"

"If that's what you really want," he said.

"Yeah, that's what I want. If I can't have you physically for the rest of my life, at least I'll have very fond memories of you. And when those memories take hold of my mind, I can always go up on Lover's levee to our favorite spot and pretend you're there with me, holding me in your arms as you've done in the past." The whole time she was talking, she was staring off into space. Her voice sounded distant and lost as if she was losing her will to live.

Bob heart went out to her, but he didn't quite know what to say. Because of her he had experienced that same agonizing pain of losing a love that meant more to him than life itself, or so he had thought at the time. He survived and so would she. Revenge wasn't as sweet as people in the movies made it out to be. Neither one of them spoke again until they reached Lover's levee and parked in their favorite spot. The spot was easy to get this time of year because the Levee was mostly a summertime lover's rendezvous.

"Gina, I never meant to hurt you so bad. However, I must confess I did want you to experience the same agonizing pain I felt when you never wrote again. Now seeing what you're going through makes me realize it's wrong for one human being to play with the emotions of another. Forgive me for being such a dick," Bob said.

Bob thought she was about to start crying again, but she kept control of herself and said, "I knew what your intentions were all along. I just hope I could make you so happy you would let bygone, be bygones. That maybe, just maybe, you would realize how much I love you and it would make you forget about Miss Kwak. I love you more than I ever thought possible. It was never a question of guilt. So, as you can see, I'm not crying because of what you did to me but what I did to us. Can you ever find it in your heart to forgive me? I'm the blame for everything that has gone wrong in this relationship," she said.

Bob believed she was truly sorry for causing him so much pain, but it was too little too late. But he tried to let her down easy. "It takes two to tango."

"Yeah, but at least you were willing to wait for who you wanted to tango with, whereas I thought I was the queen on the throne and needed no man. Now I've lost you forever," she again burst into tears.

Bob held her until her sobs subsided. "Do you want to go home?" he asked, not wanting to see her torture herself anymore.

"No. I want to spend the night with you. I've already made arrangements for us to stay at my friend's house tonight. That's, if you want to," she said pleadingly.

"Sure, if that would make you happy," he agreed.

"Please don't say that, because we both know what would make me happy," she said sadly.

Because of the honesty they shared with each other that night, they were able to enjoy their last sexual encounter to its fullest. The next morning he kissed her good-bye for the last time. And again he left her crying over a relationship not meant to be.

"Maybe another place, another time, things would've worked out for us," Bob said to her disappearing figure in his rear view mirror.

Chapter 8
MASTER SERGEANT CHANDLER

Sergeant Wood arrived at the 205th Military Police Company Fort Leavenworth, Kansas early that following Monday morning. The unit clerk was a black Specialist Five whose nametag said his name was Jones.

"Good morning, Specialist Jones. I'm Sergeant Wood, reporting to the unit," Sergeant Wood said, handing him a copy of his orders.

Specialist Jones stood and shook his hand. "Man, I'm glad to see another brother around this place," he said, sounding as if they were the only blacks in the unit.

"You mean we're the only two black soldiers here?" Sergeant Wood asked, looking around involuntarily.

"Well, not exactly. There's a Sergeant First Class Hart, smooth talking brother from Los Angeles, California working in the unit operations office, but he's nothing but an Oreo. The white people around here say jump and he only asks how high," Specialist Jones informed him.

"From the way you talk, you're not too happy to be here," Sergeant Wood pointed out.

"This damn post is run by a bunch of red necks, and the town by a bunch of racists. Believe me, not one of them like brothers. Except for the White women. They love themselves some dark meat," Specialist Five Jones laughed.

"Is that a fact?" Sergeant Wood asked, uninterested.

"That's a fact. There's also a Black E-5, Sergeant Terrell, in charge of the first squad, probably yours as soon as you finish in-processing," Specialist Five Jones predicted. "And he has a black Private First Class McGarity working for him. The grand total of blacks in this unit is five counting you. That's it."

"Hell, that's better than none," Sergeant Wood said.

After in-processing in the orderly room, Sergeant Wood was told to see Sergeant First Class Hart, the Oreo, first thing after lunch. He never judged anyone by what other people said, but Sergeant Wood was to learn what Specialist Five Jones said was true.

"Good afternoon, Sergeant Hart. I was instructed to see you for my in-briefing," Sergeant Wood introduced himself.

"I've been expecting you. Have a seat. Coming from Korea are you?" Sergeant First Class Hart asked.

"Yes, sergeant," Sergeant Wood answered.

"I've reviewed your 201 file and I must confess I was very impressed with all of the 'attaboys' you got volunteering for special details while in Korea. My only question is, when did you find the time to be a real MP on the road?" Sergeant First Class Hart asked in a sarcastic tone.

"If I'm not mistaken, Sergeant Hart, my record shows I was a squad leader in a line platoon prior to being assigned here," Sergeant Wood said, defensively. He concluded that First Sergeant Green's phone call from Korea must have preceded him.

"Yeah, it does, but people have a tendency to cover up the truth when it comes to young soldiers they like. We'll see in the near future what type of MP you are," Sergeant First Class Hart said, as if he had something against him, although they had just met.

PATRIOTISM

"Sergeant Hart, may I ask you a question?" Sergeant Wood asked frowning.

"Sure, go ahead," he said.

"Why's it I detect a note of hostility in your voice? You've nothing to fear from me. I'm only an E-5. So what's it about me you don't like even though you just met me?" Sergeant Wood asked, truly perplexed.

"I have nothing against you, buck sergeant. I talk this way to everyone in the unit. You don't like the way I talk?" Sergeant First Class Hart asked, defensively.

"It's not that, sergeant. I just don't want to get off on the wrong foot with my superiors, that's all," Sergeant Wood confessed.

"I guess I can understand that. I'll be getting back with you within the next couple days in reference to your duty assignment. Right now you can go over to the supply room and pick up your road gear and linen," Sergeant First Class Hart instructed.

"Does the supply room also issue the TA-50 gear (field equipment)?" Sergeant Wood asked, remembering the combat gear they were issued in Korea.

"You'll be happy to know we have no TA-50 gear here," Sergeant First Class Hart said.

"Thanks, Sergeant Hart. I'll see you in a couple days." Sergeant Wood walked out of Sergeant First Class Hart's office wondering why he disliked him.

After leaving Sergeant Hart's office, Sergeant Wood went back to the orderly room to have a talk with Specialist Jones. Maybe he could shed some light on what was going on behind the scene, because he didn't think Sergeant First Class Hart had come across like he did for no reason.

"You finished talking to Sergeant Hart already?" Specialist Five Jones asked when Sergeant Wood entered the orderly room.

"Yeah, why?" Sergeant Wood asked.

"Well, most of the time he keeps new arrivals in his office half the afternoon trying to either impress or intimidate them. Which did he try with you?" Specialist Five Jones asked.

"Intimidation. Let me ask you a question. Why do I get the impression Sergeant Hart doesn't like me? Hell, I just arrived to this unit today and I've never met him before," Sergeant Wood said.

"After you left the orderly room for lunch this morning, First Sergeant Hill was looking through your 201 file when Sergeant Hart walked in. He called him into his office and they went through your records together. I don't know everything that was said, but I did hear First Sergeant Hill say you must have kissed a lot of ass to get promoted to sergeant E-5 and be awarded the number of certificates of achievement you have in your records in just 17 months of active duty. The First Sergeant also said something about your letters of appreciation you received while in Korea, but I didn't quite catch what he said. As Sergeant Hart was leaving the First Sergeant's office, he was told to keep a close eye on you because he doesn't trust super cops," Specialist Five Jones informed him.

"Why? I'm no threat to either one of their positions," Sergeant Wood said.

"I don't know, but I think you'd better watch yourself. Sergeant Terrell got busted, well got into trouble, not long after his arrival here," Specialist Five Jones cautioned Sergeant Wood.

"For what?" Sergeant Wood asked. The way Specialist Five Jones had cautioned him led him believe Sergeant Terrell might have been set up by someone in the PM shop.

"He got caught sleeping on the desk," Specialist Five Jones said.

"That's nothing unusual," Sergeant Wood said. "Hell, a couple of desk sergeants in Korea got busted for sleeping on the desk."

"It is when everyone else is doing the same thing and he's the only one who gets busted for it," Specialist Five Jones said.

"I see what you mean. Is that the E-5 in charge of the First Squad you mentioned earlier?"

"Yeah. You know something, Wood? You seem different from the other black E-5's I've met since I've been in the army," Specialist Five Jones said looking him up and down.

"In what way?" Sergeant Wood asked.

"I guess it's because you seem to have total confidence in yourself," Specialist Five Jones said.

"I do. Don't you?" Sergeant Wood asked.

"You'd better believe they won't like that attitude coming from a black soldier. Not around here," Specialist Five Jones said, ignoring the question.

"What they see is what they get. I'll talk to you later. I have to go over to the supply room and get some linen and road gear," Sergeant Wood said.

"Here's the key to your room. Hey, good luck, sarge. I'm glad to have another brother in the unit," Specialist Five Jones smiled.

"Thanks, but I don't think I'm going to need it. Not yet anyway," Sergeant Wood said.

From the supply room Sergeant Wood went to the barracks and unpacked. Sergeant First Class Hart had told him to relax until the next day and someone would take him around post to in-process. The barracks were well maintained, a far cry from the wooden barracks at Fort Bragg and the Quonset huts in Korea.

On the third day after completing his in-processing, he was assigned to the first squad as their squad leader, as Specialist Five Jones had predicted. According to a couple of the white NCOs he happened to meet while watching TV in the day room, the first squad was the pits. The sergeant, the Black E-5 who had recently been busted, didn't give a damn about the army anymore. And as a result his whole squad had a fuck-it attitude. The day Sergeant First Class Hart assigned him to the squad he had said pretty much the same thing. Sergeant Wood could hardly wait to get back on the road again. He would show them that a Black NCO could be just as good, or better, than any other NCO when it came to leadership.

The first thing Sergeant Wood did after taking charge of the squad was to have everyone report for duty an hour early so they could get acquainted. He had tried to call Sergeant Terrell at home that morning to find out what the problems were within the squad so as to have some idea of what he was going to be up against. He never caught up with him.

Sergeant Wood first official day on the road at Fort Leavenworth, Kansas was a swing shift, 1500-2300 hours. Everyone was on time for the early briefing except for Sergeant Terrell. His troops were sitting in the briefing room, humming like bees around a hive when he walked in.

"Good afternoon, troops." Maybe half of them responded.

PATRIOTISM

"I know you're all wondering what I'm going to be like and what I expect of you. I've been in the army for seventeen months. Took basic training at Fort Bragg, N.C., AIT at Fort Gordon, Georgia, a thirteen month tour in Korea, and now here I am at good old Fort Leavenworth, Kansas. I'm originally from Helena, Arkansas. I want you all to know I love the army. The people who run it, that's a different story." It sounded like a joke, but Sergeant Wood was serious. Still the remark brought a chuckle from the majority of the squad. "Now for the reason I had all of you to show up early. Almost every NCO in the unit said you guys are by far the worst squad on the road. I'll tell you what I told them. There's no way anyone can convince me that a whole squad could be a bunch of screw-ups and still get the mission accomplished, that with the right squad leader and attitude about yourselves, you'll be the best squad on the road. Notice, I didn't say one of the best, but the absolute best. If there's anyone sitting in this room who doesn't think he can be the best MP on the road speak up now, and I'll do my best to get you assigned to another squad or someplace else," Sergeant Wood said.

At that point Sergeant Terrell walked in. "I'm sorry I'm late, sarge. I got caught in traffic," he called himself explaining.

"Did you call the desk to inform them so they could pass it on to me?" Sergeant Wood asked, sternly.

"No, I didn't. There weren't any phones on the highway," Sergeant Terrell attempted humor.

"Fine, I'll deal with you after this meeting. Be seated," Sergeant Wood instructed, not at all amused.

Sergeant Terrell glared at him as he moved to the back of the room and sat down.

"Now, as I was saying, if there's anyone who doesn't think he's good enough to be, or is, the best damn military policeman on the road, speak now. You can be assured I won't bite you for being honest with me. Nor will I try to get you busted or anything like that," Sergeant Wood assured them. Sergeant Terrell raised his hand. "Yeah, Sergeant Terrell," Sergeant Wood recognized him.

"It ain't that we don't like being MPs. It's just that it seems they picked this particular squad to fuck with," Sergeant Terrell said. The remainder of the squad agreed.

"Why do you think that is, Sergeant Terrell?" Sergeant Wood asked, trying to get a foothold on the situation. Sergeant Wood put the ball back in Sergeant Terrell's court, hoping he would give him something to go on.

"I don't really know," Sergeant Terrell said.

"Maybe someone else knows why. Come on, you were all in agreement with Sergeant Terrell that you're getting screwed with. There has to be a reason. Someone tell me why?" Sergeant Wood encouraged someone to speak up. When no one answered, Sergeant Wood said, "OK, I'll make that my first mission. Find out why this particular squad was chosen to be screwed with."

Before he could continue, Master Sergeant Chandler, the Provost Marshal's Operation Sergeant, walked into the room.

"Yes, Sergeant, may I help you?" Sergeant Wood asked, thinking he wanted to address the squad.

"I need this briefing room right now. You can finish talking about whatever it is you're talking about in the rewrite room," Master Sergeant Chandler said.

Sergeant Wood looked at his nametag and said, "Excuse

me, Master Sergeant Chandler, but could I talk to you out in the hallway?" Sergeant Wood asked, not wanting to confront a senior NCO in front of the squad.

"No, if you have anything to say, say it here," Master Sergeant Chandler provoked a response.

"Okay, Sergeant Chandler. There was no notification on the door saying this room was to be used at," he looked at his watch, "1415 hours. Otherwise, I would've waited another day to have this meeting," Sergeant Wood said, getting annoyed at not being respected as an NCO.

"For your information, buck sergeant, this meeting was not planned. The First Sergeant from the United States Army Disciplinary Barracks (USDB) and a couple of his NCOs will be here at 1430 hours to talk to me and I don't have enough seats for everyone in my office," Master Sergeant Chandler explained weakly.

"Master Sergeant Chandler, you mean to tell me you're going to put 16 of your own troops in a room with four seats so you and several other NCOs can use a room with 20 seats? Wouldn't it be easier if you just borrowed a couple of chairs from one of the other offices?" Sergeant Wood suggested. He was sure he was going to get cussed out in front of his squad for being so bold, but he had to show his squad members he was not afraid to speak up on their behalf. At the same time he knew for Sergeant Chandler to disagree with his logic would make him appear not to care about his own troops.

"Go ahead and finish your meeting, Sergeant Wood, but I want to see you right after you finish," Master Sergeant Chandler instructed.

"Yes, Sergeant, I'll be right up after I finish the meeting,"

Sergeant Wood said.

As soon as Master Sergeant Chandler was out of sight, Sergeant Wood continued as if he hadn't been interrupted. "As I was saying, I'll find out why you guys were being screwed with. In the meantime I want you all to perform your duties to the best of your abilities. Do anyone have any questions for me?" Specialist Four Harper raised his hand. "Yes, Specialist Harper," Sergeant Wood acknowledged him.

"Sergeant Wood, I think the reason we've been getting screwed over is because we didn't have a good squad leader who would stand up for us," Specialist Harper said nervously. He then turned to Sergeant Terrell and said, "I don't mean to put you down, sarge, but you know it's the truth."

Sergeant Terrell was about to protest but Sergeant Wood said, "Let's cut it right there. I don't want a pissing contest right now. I know I asked you all to be honest, but I see I'll have to use a different approach. What can you guys tell me about Master Sergeant Chandler before I go up there and get my ass reamed?"

Sergeant Terrell said, "He doesn't like black E-5's trying to be NCOs. If he don't make all of your decisions for you, he's going to try and fuck you over."

"Damn," Sergeant Wood groaned. "I thought I left him in Korea. Anything else?"

Private First Class McGarity, the black private Specialist Five Jones had mentioned being in the squad spoke up, "He's mean as hell. Whatever you do, don't piss him off sarge. He eats E-5's for lunch."

"Oh yeah? Well, you guys just hang loose. Hopefully I'll be back down in time for guard mount. If I'm not, you know Mas-

PATRIOTISM

ter Sergeant Chandler had himself a damn good meal," Sergeant Wood joked.

Sergeant Wood went upstairs and knocked on Master Sergeant Chandler's office door. All the while he wondered why only the blacks in the squad had anything negative to say about Master Sergeant Chandler.

"Who is it?" Master Sergeant Chandler asked.

"It's Sergeant Wood. You said you wanted to see me after I finished with my meeting," Sergeant Wood reminded him.

"Well, I'm busy now. Come back after guard mount," Master Sergeant Chandler instructed through the closed door.

"Yes, Sergeant," Sergeant Wood said.

Sergeant Wood went back downstairs to the briefing room and found Sergeant Terrell and Specialist Harper going at it tooth and nail. "What the hell is going on here?" Sergeant Wood asked.

"Specialist Harper is the main reason I got busted. The little ass-kissing, brown-nosing son-of-a-bitch set me up for Sergeant Chandler to catch me sleeping in one of the detention cells. He was supposed to wake me up, as we always do for each other, when he saw the red neck bastard coming. Did he? No, he didn't. Why? Because Sergeant Chandler had already made plans with this little dip shit to set me up. Sergeant Chandler even laughed when he told me about it. And he said if I mess with Harper, he'd have my ass," Sergeant Terrell explained heatedly.

"Sergeant Terrell, I understand how you feel, but you had no reason in the world for sleeping on duty. Also, as long as I'm in charge of this squad, I never want to see you arguing with a subordinate. Come into the rewrite room. I want to talk to you man to man," Sergeant Wood said, leading the way to the rewrite room across the hall. When they entered the rewrite room, he turned to Sergeant Terrell and asked, "What the fuck is your problem, man?"

"I don't have a problem. Not anymore. You've taken all 15 of my problems away. And more power to you, brother," Sergeant Terrell said in a huff.

"That's a piss poor attitude for an NCO in the United States Army to have. Let me tell you something right here, right now. Sergeant First Class Hart said you'd be going on permanent CQ (Charge of quarters) within the next two weeks. But until that time arrives, I expect you to act like an NCO. Do you have any problems with that?" Sergeant Wood asked, staring him down.

"No, Wood, I don't. I'll do my thing to the max as long as you keep Mr. Charlie off my ass," Sergeant Terrell answered.

"You got it. Get the troops ready for guard mount," Sergeant Wood instructed.

"Yes, Sergeant," he said and turned to leave. But before he left he added, "You know something, brother? If things go the way you have them planned, I just might ask to stick around as your assistant. Oh, by the way, don't think Sergeant Chandler is going to roll over and play dead while you do your thing. You'll find that out after you finish talking to him," Sergeant Terrell informed him.

"Let's hope for the best," Sergeant Wood said. They returned to the guard mount area and he stood in the background while Sergeant Terrell prepared the squad for guard mount.

"Guard mount isn't for another twenty minutes," he heard someone whisper.

After Sergeant Terrell had them formed and ready for inspection, Sergeant Wood inspected his squad and was very disappointed in what he saw. He started with Sergeant Terrell.

"Sergeant Terrell, your boots are not shined to standard, and it's easy to tell you're wearing the same uniform you wore on duty yesterday. Not to mention you need a trim. How can you expect your troops to follow you if you don't set the example you want them to follow? We'll discuss this later." Sergeant Wood said this low enough so the rest of the squad couldn't hear the dissatisfaction he had expressed with Sergeant Terrell's appearance. Sergeant Wood would never embarrass a fellow NCO in public.

When he got to Private Brown he couldn't believe his eyes. Even a Private should've known better than to show up for guard mount as ragged and unkempt as he looked.

"Private Brown, please tell me this is the first time you've ever shown up for guard mount looking the way you look right now. Tell me the leadership in this unit hasn't been letting you walk around in public dressed as you are now?"

"Not always sergeant, but sometimes," Private Brown answered.

"Private Brown, let me ask you a couple of questions. Did you sleep in that uniform last night? Do you have more than one uniform? Do you send your uniforms to the laundry to be pressed, or do you iron them yourself? Do you know you're wearing combat boots that are supposed to be highly shined? Talk to me, private," Sergeant Wood said running out of questions.

"My other uniforms are pressed, and my display boots are shined if you want me to go and change Sergeant Wood," Private Brown said nervously.

"I think I'll allow you to do just that after I finish my inspection," Sergeant Wood said going on to the next soldier in line.

Several soldiers down the line Sergeant Wood stopped in front of Specialist Smith. "Specialist Smith, I know you're married and have a baby girl that keeps you busy when you're off duty. However, I refuse to believe your wife and daughter keep you so busy you don't have time to shave before reporting for duty. So my question is, do you have a skin condition that I don't know about that prevents you from shaving on a daily basis? Because you don't have a five o'clock shadow, you're working on a freaking beard. Talk to me Specialist Smith. I'm sure you're hoping to make sergeant E-5, in the near future. Am I right?" Sergeant Wood asked.

"Yes, sergeant. I go before the board in a couple of months. As far as not having shaved, it's my fault," Specialist Smith answered.

"Private Brown, do you have a razor and some blades Specialist Smith can use while you're changing your boots and uniform?" Sergeant Wood asked looking back down the line.

"Yes, sergeant, I do," Private Brown answered.

"See how much your fellow squad member likes you, Specialist Smith," Sergeant Wood said.

Upon completion of his inspection, Sergeant Wood let them know he was disappointed with their appearance as a whole. He called Specialist Smith and Private Brown aside. "As of now you're officially relieved of duty until you correct the deficiencies I pointed out to you. You have about 15 minutes to get to the barracks and have your asses back here before the duty officer holds guard mount. And if either of you ever come to my guard mount looking this way again you'll receive a counseling statement or some other form of disciplinary action. Do you understand me?" Sergeant Wood asked.

"Yes, sergeant," they answered simultaneously.

"Go, and you had better be back in time for guard mount," Sergeant Wood instructed.

Sergeant Terrell was pissed for being chastised in front of the troops, although they didn't hear what was said. He understood what Sergeant Wood was trying to accomplish, but his ego had been bruised. Through clenched teeth he assured Sergeant Wood he would do whatever he could to help him for the remainder of the time he was a member of the squad.

Fortunately for Specialist Smith and Private Brown, they made it back in time for guard mount because the duty officer was late himself. Sergeant Wood advised the whole squad they looked like shit, but in the future he expected them to look as good as he did or better. No one would ever come to his guard mount looking the way they did that day.

Second Lieutenant Hoover, the duty officer, after holding his guard mount, told Sergeant Wood his squad was the worst looking bunch of people he had ever inspected. Sergeant Wood didn't believe it was true, but played the game. He informed the good lieutenant that starting tomorrow, he'd see a hell of an improvement in their appearance. After the lieutenant finished giving his briefing on what they could expect during their tour of duty, Sergeant Wood went up to see Master Sergeant Chandler. This time when he knocked on the door he was told to enter.

"Sergeant Wood, the super trooper from Korea. Tell me something, Sergeant Wood. Do you think you'll be as successful here at Fort Leavenworth as you were in Korea?" Master

Sergeant Chandler asked smiling.

"If I'm allowed to do my job, there shouldn't be any problems," Sergeant Wood answered, showing he had confidence in his leadership ability.

"Well, you certainly started out on the wrong foot. The next time I tell you to do something I expect you to do it without questions or complaints. You understand?" Master Sergeant Chandler asked, more annoyed than angry.

"To be perfectly honest with you, Master Sergeant Chandler, I don't understand the logic behind something like that," Sergeant Wood wouldn't let it go that easily.

"Look, buck sergeant, there's nothing to understand. I tell you to do something, and you do it. I can't explain it any simpler than that," Master Sergeant Chandler said.

"Sergeant Chandler, can I ask you a question NCO to NCO?" Sergeant Wood asked.

"Yeah, go ahead," Master Sergeant Chandler said.

"Would I be asking too much to be treated like an NCO? What I mean is you could've come up to me, called me aside, and said get the fuck out of here, I need the briefing room right now. I still wouldn't have agreed with the logic, but it wouldn't have bothered me as much. But when you make it appear, in front of my troops that I'm nothing, I have no other choice as an NCO but to defend my position and my troops. Let's say the situation was reversed and you were the E-5, how would you have felt?" Sergeant Wood asked, hoping he hadn't stuck his foot too deep in his mouth.

"I guess the same as you did. A nobody with three stripes," Master Sergeant Chandler said sounding slightly upset.

"Right, sergeant, but what would upset me the most is for my troops to look at me the same way. I was told by senior NCOs in Korea that one NCO doesn't embarrass another NCO in front of their troops," Sergeant Wood said, letting Master Sergeant Chandler know that he knew how things in the military were supposed to work.

"You think you're pretty smart, don't you, buck sergeant?" Master Sergeant Chandler asked.

Sergeant Wood didn't like the tone of Sergeant Chandler's voice. He had to back peddle. "No, Sergeant Chandler, I don't think I'm smart, but I want to learn things the right way," Sergeant Wood said sounding humble.

"Ok, buck sergeant. You have two months to get that bunch of garbage to look, act, and perform like MPs or I'll have to show you how it's done," Master Sergeant Chandler said.

"You got it. And thanks. You won't be sorry, that I promise," Sergeant Wood assured Master Sergeant Chandler.

Sergeant Wood left Master Sergeant Chandler's office feeling that maybe Master Sergeant Chandler would leave him alone in the future and let him do his thing. He had no way of knowing Master Sergeant Chandler would eventually become one of his biggest enemies before he left Fort Leavenworth, Kansas. He attributed the differences he and Captain Hicks had while he was stationed in Korea to Captain Hicks obvious dislike for black people in general. After all, Mississippi was known for its racist acts and attitudes. Master Sergeant Chandler on the other hand would baffle him. Specialist Five Jones said Sergeant Chandler had grown up in the mist of black people because he was born and raised in Harlem, in New York. That he was always the first White NCO in the unit to speak up for the equality of black soldiers in the army when the subject of race raised its ugly head.

What Sergeant Wood failed to realize was after 27 years in the United States army, Master Sergeant Chandler had very little patience for cocky young non-commissioned officers who wouldn't back down from a confrontation, and would challenge authority figures when they felt they were right about an issue. And it didn't really matter if the soldier happened to be black or white. In the past no matter how long it took, he had always managed to bring them around to his way of thinking through diplomacy. With Sergeant Wood it would be do as I say or else. The strong arm tactics wouldn't work with Sergeant Wood because of the confidence he had in his ability to lead his troops, and because he was bullheaded. Sergeant Wood would be the first and only young soldier to ever cause Master Sergeant Chandler to lose his military bearing, "Totally." Therefore, more often than not, Master Sergeant Chandler would find himself in a position where he couldn't respond or correct Sergeant Wood as he wanted to during the many confrontations they would have prior to Bob's departure from Fort Leavenworth, Kansas.

During that first evening on the road, Sergeant Wood wanted to make sure he got a good idea of what was going on, so he rode with Sergeant Terrell. He found out one of the most important missions on the post was performed at the command and General Staff College (C&GSC) during retreat. That first afternoon he had Sergeant Terrell handle the lowering of the flag detail because he didn't know how. In Korea the Honor Guards had that mission. There were colonels, lieutenant colonels, majors, captains, and lieutenants from a dozen countries around the world who stood outside to watch the MP's lower the flag every

PATRIOTISM

day. Sergeant Wood had to admit, Sergeant Terrell was very impressive. It was hard to imagine him as a fuck up. Later on he showed Sergeant Wood the hiding places of all the patrols. Sergeant Wood wanted to ask Sergeant Terrell what or who had turned him against the army. He figured if Sergeant Terrell wanted him to know he would tell him sooner or later.

That night after getting off shift, Sergeant Terrell asked Sergeant Wood if it would be all right if he stopped by his room and talked to him for a while. Sergeant Wood was more than willing, because he was curious to hear Sergeant Terrell's story. He could hardly wait. Neither one of them said anything until they were in his room.

Sergeant Wood offered him a beer, which Sergeant Terrell accepted and said, "I hope you don't believe everything you've heard about me."

"I don't base my feelings on anything people have to say about anyone. I've been on the wrong side of the army brass ever since I've been in the army. I have to go on what I observed today. First you show up late for my meeting, and then I walk in the briefing room and there you are arguing with Specialist Harper as if you're of equal rank. What should I believe? I can say for a fact you really impressed me tonight with your knowledge of military police work. Why don't you tell me your side of the story," Sergeant Wood encouraged him.

"When I first got here from the Nam," Sergeant Terrell began, "I was full of piss and vinegar and ready to solve all the crimes of the world by myself. I was so proud of myself. I'd made E-5 in only 15 months, received an ARCOM, a silver star, a purple heart, and was told I was an outstanding young NCO who would probably make a lasting impression on the military for other black young

313

soldiers who would follow me.

Man, I relive how I won that silver-star every day of my life. My platoon, 32 men, was dropped off near the Cambodian border and we humped our way in the rest of the way to make our rendezvous with a Special Forces unit that briefed us on our mission. Man, those guys gave me the creeps. They had human ears and noses hanging from their web gear like souvenirs. You could see in their mannerisms they were born to kill. And they enjoyed their job. This mission was one of the first before those lying bastards in Washington admitted we were carrying on operations in Cambodia. The Special Forces team leader told us that all we had to do was a routine route reconnaissance of the area where the NVA had an encampment. It'd been reported by Military Intelligence (MI) that the North Vietnamese Army (NVA) was gathering just across the Vietnamese/Cambodia border and they needed to get an idea of their strength. The Special Forces leader said they'd do it, but they had been called back for a special assignment. All we had to do was get in, take some pictures, and get the hell out. It would be easy as that. And you know us MPs, always looking for a chance to see a little action. We couldn't let the grunts have all the fun. Yeah right.

As far as our Lieutenant could tell from the coordinates we had been given by the Special Forces leader, the enemy should've been no more than five clicks away from our position. I guess someone forgot to tell the NVA they were suppose to play by the rules and wait until we found them.

We hadn't humped no more'n two clicks when the hair on the back of my neck stood straight up. I couldn't see them, but I could actually feel the cold stares of the NVA soldiers waiting in the underbrush to kill us. We had wandered unaware into a well-planned ambush. I caught movement out of the corner of my eye to my right and yelled ambush, but before we could hit the ground all hell broke loose. Gunfire, grenades, explosions, yelling and screaming erupted all around me. I hit the dirt trying to figure out which direction I should be firing in. Enemy fire was coming from all directions, so the lieutenant ordered us to formed a circle and we lit up the jungle in all directions. You can't imagine what it sounds or feel like to be in the middle of a full fledge gun battle with all guns blazing and grenades exploding in all directions. It's so weird because in the middle of this chaos you can identify the sound of every weapon that is being fired. And you understand why it's the machine gun that you want to take out first. I remember hearing the sound of a weapon I couldn't identify, so I made a promise to myself that if I got out of this alive I was going to find out what kind it was.

We were being chopped to pieces by a machine gun off to my left. The lieutenant stood to get an appraisal of our situation and was blown in half by a RPG round. The platoon sergeant said someone had to take out the machine gun or we would all be wasted. Without thinking I stood and charged through the jungle, zigzagging, dodging bullets and grenades exploding around me and took out the machine gunners. I took over the position and with the machine gun now in my hands, I tore into those bastards. From my new position I could see that the majority of my platoon was either dead or wounded. I yelled for the remainder of the platoon to get behind my position as I laid down suppressive fire. Only eight guys made it to my position with Charlie on their tails. The machine gun barrel was red hot and I thought it would start to melt at any moment, but I didn't let up. Charlie was determined to kill us all. The last NVA soldier I shot fell on top of me. I guess he was out of ammo because he was trying to bayonet me. Being knocked away from the machine gun I thought I was done for because two other soldiers were right behind him. Fortunately for me the two remaining platoon members cut them down before they got to me, and everything fell silent. The silence was deafening. I pushed the dead soldier off of me and took up my position with the machine gun again, along with my two remaining platoon members. We kept waiting for Charlie to come and finish us off, but they never came. I don't know how long we held our position before anyone moved.

After we were convinced we were safe, we walked around looking for the radio to call the evacuation choppers that were supposed to pick us up if we ran into trouble. We were told they would be no more than ten minutes away from our position. The scene was unbelievable. The jungle floor was littered with the dead and dying, both American and NVA. Body parts were everywhere. The platoon sergeant, Sergeant First Class Barber, found the radio and called for an airlift chopper to get us out of there. While we waited for the choppers to arrive we helped the wounded as best we could, which ended up being only two. The wounded NVA soldiers we put out of their misery. I have to admit though, I didn't think it was right to shoot defenseless soldiers, enemy or not. But I thought, war is hell and if the role was reversed they probably wouldn't have had any problems with shooting my black ass without a second thought. The weapon I couldn't identify during the battle was a French caliber, semi-automatic rifle. I looked into the eyes of the dead NVA soldier as I pulled the weapon from his hands. I sold it to my commander when we got back to Saigon. I don't even remember what the brand name of the weapon was.

Of the 32 that humped into Cambodia, only five came out alive.

PATRIOTISM

The twenty-seven American soldiers that died in Cambodia were reported as being killed while on a mission in a remote area of Vietnam. Sergeant First Class Barber recommended me for the Congressional Medal of Honor, reporting that I had single handedly saved their lives when I charged and took out the machinegun. And during the course of the battle I reportedly killed 30 to 40 of the enemy. Of course they downgraded it to the Silver Star. And believe it or not, through all that shit, I didn't even get a damn scratch. Sergeant First Class Barber was shot four times and the other three soldiers with us were shot several times themselves. For a long time any loud noise caused me to go into panic mode, but things have gotten a little better. But I still hit the dirt sometimes whenever I hear a car backfire or someone shoots a gun that catches me by surprise. I was treated like a hero after that battle by my commander and fellow soldiers in the unit. When I got back here to the real world, I was made to feel by the draft dodgers my Silver Star medal didn't mean shit, but it didn't dampen my spirit.

I was gung-ho as hell until I got here. Master Sergeant Chandler gave me all of this shit about how he wouldn't get involved with how I ran the squad as long as I got the mission accomplished. Well that lasted about five months. He then started making little off-the-wall comments like, *'I sure would hate to be a White boy on your squad.'* He said this in front of the squad without giving an explanation as to why he said it. Every time I asked him why he made remarks like that he'd laugh and walk away. What I didn't realize at the time was he was telling my white troops they could get rid of me if they wanted to. At first only Specialist Harper picked up on what he was saying. But believe me, it didn't take long for him to hip the rest of the white boys to what was going on. They started giving me some back talk when I made them do things they felt they shouldn't have to do. And when I started writing them up for it, they ran to Master Sergeant Chandler complaining. The final blow for me came after I'd been here about six and a half months. They found a joint on the rear seat of the sedan I'd driven the night before. Since then I've been labeled a drug user by the overhead personnel," Sergeant Terrell finished.

"Who found the joint?" Sergeant Wood asked.

"Sergeant Chandler, who else? Man, I didn't even smoke that crap when I was in Nam. It didn't matter to them that a different person drives those damn cars every night. Hell, Sergeant Chandler probably planted the shit anyway. They had me where they wanted me, although the proof against me was weak and they couldn't prove anything. The damage was done because the squad and the other NCOs in the unit all lost respect for me. My squad was hard to control after that. And what would Sergeant Chandler do? Come down to guard mounts and jump knee deep in my shit for any little thing I'd done wrong. Needless to say, that's why I have a fuck-it attitude. Even Sergeant First Class Hart went along with them the whole time this shit was going down. That really blew my mind, especially after his telling me if I ever needed help with anything to let him know. The damn Oreo," Sergeant Terrell said bitterly.

Nothing he said surprised Sergeant Wood. "I see. I guess I would have a pretty bad attitude also. However, the only thing I can't understand is, you knew they were out to get you. And you still slept on the desk because everyone else did," Sergeant Wood pointed out to him.

"Dumb, I know," Sergeant Terrell admitted.

"So why didn't Captain Harris, the unit commander, take

PATRIOTISM

your stripes for sleeping on duty?" Sergeant Wood asked.

"Captain Harris said it would be too easy to prove discrimination because the white NCO's sleep on the desk or in the detention cells all the time. He said since I thought I was big shit because of my war record and medals they just wanted to show me if they wanted to get me they could. He fined me a couple hundred dollars and made me sleep in the barracks for a week for sleeping while on duty. I don't have to tell you how well that went over with the old lady. She hasn't let me live that stupidity down," Sergeant Terrell finished.

"The only thing I can ask of you is that you give me all the support you can. We'll show these white bastards that black soldiers aren't as dumb as they think we are. By the way, they never said anything about any drugs. Only that you got caught sleeping in the detention cell," Sergeant Wood said.

"Yeah. Watch yourself, man. They hate to see a black man excel at anything," Sergeant Terrell said, feeling stupid for allowing himself to fall into their trap.

Sergeant Terrell finally left for home at three o'clock that morning. Sergeant Wood asked himself for the two thousandth time, *Who's the real enemy, the North Vietnamese or the White Americans who wear the same uniform as himself?* He thought he'd left all that prejudice bullshit in Korea with Captain Hicks and First Sergeant Green.

The word spread quickly about him standing up to Master Sergeant Chandler. To him it was no big deal. It was just one NCO asking for respect from another NCO. However, from all the feedback the incident was receiving, there was more to it than that. A couple of weeks later after guard mount, Master Sergeant Chandler, the duty officer, asked if he could have a few words with the troops after finishing his inspection.

"Sure, Sergeant," Sergeant Wood said, not knowing what he had in mind.

Master Sergeant Chandler addressed the squad. "I wanted you all to know I'm very proud of you guys. In just a couple of weeks you've shown me you're all capable of being good MP's. And in the process you've also managed to make Sergeant Wood look good. Keep up the good work," he said, giving Sergeant Wood a sneering smile.

Sergeant Wood started to say something but let it pass.

"Do you have anything you'd like to say, Sergeant Wood?" Master Sergeant Chandler asked, expecting him to say something because in reality he had put his leadership capabilities down.

"No, Master Sergeant Chandler, I'm not looking for a pat on the back today. Maybe after I get the squad to perform their mission without me having to ride shot gun over them, then I'll have plenty to say," Sergeant Wood controlled his temper.

"Good luck," Master Sergeant Chandler said and walked out.

After Master Sergeant Chandler was gone, Specialist Harper asked, "Sergeant Wood, why did Sergeant Chandler say that when he knows without you we'd still be considered the misfit squad?"

"I'm sure he has his reasons. But I'm not going to worry about that right now. We still have a long way to go before we can even begin to think we're the best on the road. I know in time we'll be. Right?" Sergeant Wood shouted.

"Right!" they responded in unison.

Sergeant Wood had to admit to himself, their appearance had improved one hundred percent in that two weeks period of time.

PATRIOTISM

Sergeant Wood didn't care what Master Sergeant Chandler said because everyone else knew he was doing his job. Things were going so well, Sergeant Terrell asked Sergeant Wood to talk to Sergeant First Class Hart about letting him remain with the squad.

So one morning after getting off midnight shift, Sergeant Wood stopped by Sergeant First Class Hart's office to talk to him about Sergeant Terrell's request.

"Come on in, Sergeant Wood, and have a seat. I've been hearing some good things about you. What's on your mind?" Sergeant First Class Hart asked cheerfully.

"I'm here on behalf of Sergeant Terrell. He wants to remain in the squad as my assistant if he can," Sergeant Wood said.

"Are you serious? The last time I talked to Sergeant Terrell, the road was the last place he wanted to work. What changed his mind?" Sergeant First Class Hart asked, curious.

"I guess he likes the way I run things," Sergeant Wood said.

"I don't know if there's anything I can do for him. It seems the PM Shop wants to get rid of him pretty bad," Sergeant First Class Hart said.

"Have you tried to find out why?" Sergeant Wood asked.

"No, not really. But I would guess it's because he was suspected of possessing grass while on duty, and was busted for sleeping while on duty," Sergeant First Class Hart tried to worm his way out of the conversation. He felt guilty for not standing up for the only other black NCO in the unit.

"Didn't you try to find out if it was true or not? Especially the drug possession that he was never charged with," Sergeant Wood asked, not letting Sergeant First Class Hart off that easy.

"Sure, I asked him and he denied it," Sergeant First Class

Hart said matter of fact.

"Maybe I'm wrong Sergeant Hart, but it sounds as if you don't care when black troops get screwed in the unit," Sergeant Wood said.

"Look, buck sergeant, the man fucked up, ok? I'll tell you what. I'll talk to Master Sergeant Chandler today and let you know what he said in the morning when you come off shift. How about that?" Sergeant First Class Hart asked.

"Yes, sergeant. I'll see you first thing in the morning," Sergeant Wood let it drop because he knew Sergeant Terrell was as good as gone. That night he told Sergeant Terrell what Sergeant First Class Hart had said.

"Well, Sergeant Wood, if we have to depend on Sergeant Hart, I'm as good as gone," Sergeant Terrell said what Sergeant Wood had thought.

"Hey, come on. Let's give the man a chance. What do you say?" Sergeant Wood asked, trying to give Sergeant Terrell hope.

"What choice do I have? As you would say let's hope for the best," Sergeant Terrell said, knowing his days in the squad were numbered.

"Even if they say no, we'll still be able to talk to each other. Hell, we can still show these white people no matter where they put us, we have our shit together," Sergeant Wood assured him.

"You got it, man. I'm with you all the way," Sergeant Terrell smiled, trying to get Sergeant Wood to do the black handshake they called doing the 'dap' that was popular in Korea and Vietnam.

"Sorry, brother. I never learned any daps while I was in Korea," Sergeant Wood informed him.

"Hey, that's cool. I still dig you man," Sergeant Terrell said.

Sergeant Wood's belief that Sergeant Terrell was going on permanent CQ was confirmed the moment he walked into Sergeant First Class Hart's office the following morning.

Sergeant First Class Hart sat behind his desk looking like a whipped dog. "I did my best to convince them to let Sergeant Terrell stay in your squad, but they were determined to get rid of him. What am I supposed to do?" Sergeant First Class Hart asked apologetically.

"You know something, Sergeant Hart, you might as well save a place on the CQ roster for me. Because I'm not going to kiss these people's asses. I see it no longer bothers you to see a black soldier get screwed," Sergeant Wood said.

"Look, you smart ass bastard. Everything I've heard about you so far is good. Don't get too cocky and mess it up," Sergeant First Class Hart warned.

"Sure, sarge, I get your drift. They got Sergeant Terrell. They can get me. Right!" Sergeant Wood quipped and walked out of the office.

Sergeant Wood had everything down pat on the road, so it didn't bother him that Sergeant Terrell was no longer in the squad. The first night Sergeant Terrell was on CQ, he stopped by the orderly room and had a long talk with him. Afterward, somewhat of a bond was established between them.

Two months after becoming the squad leader of the First Squad, Sergeant Wood's squad was at the top of the list. And they all knew they were good. The Provost Marshal, Lieutenant Colonel Gray, must've heard what an outstanding job he was doing with the misfits because he wanted to see him one day before he went on break. Or so he thought.

Sergeant Wood went upstairs and told Master Sergeant Chandler the PM wanted to see him.

"I know. I'm the one who sent you the message. Wait here." Master Sergeant Chandler said and went into the PM's office. When he came out he said, "OK, you can go in now." Master Sergeant Chandler had a silly smile on his face.

Sergeant Wood knocked on the Provost Marshal's door and was told to enter.

"Good afternoon, Sergeant Wood. Go ahead and have a seat. I've been hearing a lot about you. Most of it unfavorable I'm afraid," Colonel Gray said.

"I beg your pardon, sir," Sergeant Wood said, totally surprised.

"Yes, Sergeant Chandler has been keeping an eye on you. And he says you're very disrespectful to your superiors, and that you're a hotdog who hates for anyone to tell you anything or give you advice. However, he did say you've straightened the first squad out. So I guess you deserve a pat on the back for that, but you have to learn to be a team player," Colonel Gray advised.

"To be honest with you, sir, I don't have the faintest idea what Sergeant Chandler is talking about. It's true we had a disagreement the first day I was on the road. But since then I haven't said anything that he should be upset with me about," Sergeant Wood presented his case.

"Look, Sergeant, if Sergeant Chandler says you're being a pain in the butt, I believe it. So you'd better get yourself together before you end up on permanent CQ along with Sergeant Terrell. You understand?" Colonel Gray threatened.

"No, sir, I don't. The only thing I've done since I've been

here is the best job possible. I've shown all my superiors the respect I would want if I were in their position. If this is the credit I get for being a good soldier, sir, please put me on CQ. Or better yet, help me to get assigned to Vietnam. That's where I've been trying to get since I was drafted," Sergeant Wood said without thinking.

"Who do you think you're talking to, Sergeant? I'll have your stripes for disrespect to an officer," Colonel Gray said, losing his composure.

"Sir, I've shown no disrespect toward you and you know it. I know when someone is trying to set me up for a fall. If you would, sir, I would like for you to call Sergeant Chandler in here so we can straighten this matter out. I hate to be accused of something I haven't done," Sergeant Wood wanted to plead his case.

"You get the hell out of my office before I say something I shouldn't," Colonel Gray said, but with some doubt that Master Sergeant Chandler was telling him the truth.

Sergeant Wood didn't say another word. He just got up and walked out.

Master Sergeant Chandler was waiting for him as he exited the Provost Marshal's office. "How did it go, Sergeant Wood?" he asked with a big smile on his face.

"Fine, Sergeant Chandler. What did you expect?" Sergeant Wood responded and continued down the stairs. He didn't dare stop or he knew he would have been in trouble because he would have cussed that bastard out.

The next day, Sergeant Wood's first day of break, he went to see the unit commander.

When Sergeant Wood entered the orderly room, Specialist Five Jones jumped from his chair and asked, "Man, what the hell did you did say to Colonel Gray? He called over here yesterday and told Captain Harris he had better do something about you before he busts your wise ass. Captain Harris is fit to be tied."

"I didn't do or say a damn thing that he should've jumped my ass for. Sergeant Chandler lied about me. I wasn't going to sit there and get my ass chewed because they thought it would be a fun thing to do," Sergeant Wood defended his actions.

"Well, it's a good thing you came in. I was about to come and get you anyway. The Captain wants to talk to you about yesterday. Wait here. I'll let him know you're here," Specialist Five Jones instructed.

While Specialist Five Jones was in the captain's office, Sergeant Wood debated with himself as to what course of action he should take in trying to get himself out of the situation. It was either be humble or stand up to Captain Harris. *I haven't done anything wrong. Why should I have to explain myself?"* Sergeant Wood asked himself. *I'll be damned if I'm going to let these bastards walk all over me. I don't even care if it means I'll be kicked out of the army.*

Specialist Five Jones came back in, interrupting his thoughts. "The commander will see you right away, Sergeant Wood," Specialist Jones announced, being formal.

Sergeant Wood knocked on the door and was told to enter. "Sergeant Wood reporting as requested, sir."

"Have a seat, Sergeant Wood. I hear you and Colonel Gray had a disagreement yesterday afternoon. Want to tell me what happened?" Captain Harris asked.

"Sure, sir. The Colonel called me into his office and said

PATRIOTISM

Sergeant Chandler had reported to him that I'm very disrespectful to my superiors. When I disagreed with what Sergeant Chandler said, Colonel Gray got upset," Sergeant Wood explained his side of the story.

"What's this I hear about you telling the colonel you didn't give a damn if you were put on permanent CQ?" the captain asked frowning.

"I didn't put it quite that way, sir. But after he said I'd better get my act together or that's where I would end up, I said fine with me. I also said I wanted to get transferred to Vietnam, and that's the truth. That's where I've been trying to go ever since I've been in the army. All the commanders I've had so far think I'm some kind of nut or something. Would you let me re-enlist for Vietnam when my re-enlistment time comes around? I want to do my part to help end the war over there," Sergeant Wood changed the subject.

"Are you serious? Do you really expect me to believe that patriotic crap? I don't know what kind of game you think you're playing, Sergeant Wood, but it's not going to work around here. So either you get your act together or you're in for a long tour of duty here at Fort Leavenworth, Kansas, if you don't end up in the USDB first," Captain Harris warned.

"For what, sir? For being an NCO and standing up for myself when I know I've done nothing wrong?" Sergeant Wood asked.

"What're we talking about, Sergeant wood?" Captain Harris asked.

"Sir, I've done nothing but the best job I can since I've been here. I've not had any run in with anyone of a higher rank, so I don't understand why Sergeant Chandler would tell Colonel

Gray something like that. I may speak my mind, but I'm not a troublemaker, sir. My records show I haven't had any problem working with other people," Sergeant Wood said, feeling he was always on the defensive.

"I'll give you credit for that. Your records are very impressive, but that was in Korea. Apparently, the commander or PM over there let you have your way. However, you're no longer in Korea. You're in Kansas. And when you're in Kansas, you do what we tell you to, or you won't last long. Understand?"

"Ok, sir. If I keep my nose clean, will you allow me to re-enlist for Vietnam?" Sergeant Wood figured he had to give a little if he was to get anything in return from Captain Harris.

"I'll have to think about that. You're the first black soldier I've ever had in this unit to request such an assignment without having already served a tour there. I'll see what I can do. I'll get back with you later," Captain Harris said, not knowing if Sergeant Wood was serious or just pulling his leg.

"Yes, sir," Sergeant Wood stood, saluted, and departed.

When Sergeant Wood came out of the commander's office, Specialist Five Jones asked, "What did he say?"

"He said he would see if he could get me assigned to Vietnam," Sergeant Wood quipped and walked out, leaving Specialist Five Jones with his mouth hanging open.

Sergeant Wood spent the rest of his three days off writing letters to his momma and Miss Kwak, and playing basketball. On his first day back at work, Sergeant First Class Hart wanted to see him right after guard mount. Specialist Harper had become his assistant since his loss of Sergeant Terrell and was made an "Acting Jack" NCO, so Harper was left in charge while Sergeant Wood went to talk to the Oreo.

Sergeant First Class Hart was waiting for him as he walked into the orderly room. "Come to my office young man. We have a lot to talk about," he said leading the way into the office. Once inside he said, "Have a seat. What's your problem, man? Don't you know these people will put you in jail if you don't do what you're told?" he asked.

"Not before I get my day in court, they won't. Besides, they don't scare me," Sergeant Wood said, finding himself on familiar ground.

"I'm not talking about whether you're afraid of them or not. I'm talking about them trumping up false charges against you and making them stick. You won't be the first one they've done that to, you know?" Sergeant First Class Hart warned.

"Maybe not, but I'll take my chances," Sergeant Wood said, more determined than ever.

"Don't be a damned fool boy. You'd better take my advice before you get yourself in trouble," Sergeant First Class Hart said.

"You know something, Sergeant Hart, you sound just like the people you're warning me about. I think you've been around them too long. But don't get me wrong. I appreciate what you're saying. I just don't agree with you," Sergeant Wood stuck by his guns.

"Well, at least I tried," Sergeant First Class Hart said giving up.

"That you did, Sergeant Hart, and if they ask me if you had that daddy-to-son talk with me, I'll tell them you did your best. It's just that I don't need anyone to stand up for me when I've done nothing wrong," Sergeant Wood said, frustrated that Sergeant Hart was not willing to take his side.

"You can leave. I've nothing more to say to you," Sergeant First Class Hart said, ending the conversation.

"Thanks a lot, Sergeant Hart," Sergeant Wood said.

Sergeant Wood left Sergeant First Class Hart's office and went back to work. It seemed his squad members worked twice as hard to insure no one would have anything to say to him about their job performance. The next few days passed without incident. However, as he had heard time and time again, every good thing must come to an end.

On the squad's third night of midnight shifts, Captain Moore, the duty officer, caught Private McGarity asleep at the front desk at the C&GSC and relieved him of duty. The duty officer came back to the station and had the radio operator call Sergeant Wood to the station. The moment he entered the station, Captain Moore motioned for Sergeant Wood to follow him upstairs.

"I caught Private McGarity asleep at the college and relieved him of duty. When was the last time you checked there?" Captain Moore asked.

"I would say about half an hour ago," Sergeant Wood answered.

"Was he asleep when you checked?" Captain Moore asked.

Sergeant Wood couldn't help from smiling at such a stupid question. "No sir. He wasn't asleep when I made my check."

"I want to see you and Private McGarity the first thing in the morning after you come off shift," Captain Moore instructed.

"Yes, sir. Is that all, sir?" Sergeant Wood asked.

"Yes, you can go." Captain Moore said.

After chewing McGarity out and sending him to the barracks, Sergeant Wood rode around the remainder of the night

PATRIOTISM

thinking of ways to explain to Captain Moore that sometimes privates screw up, without pissing him off. After gathering all the patrol reports at the end of his shift and releasing the squad, Sergeant Wood went to the barracks and got Private McGarity.

"Wake up, sleeping beauty. You have some explaining to do," Sergeant Wood informed him.

As they were going upstairs at the MP Station, Master Sergeant Chandler was coming down. "Well, I'll be damned. One of the super troopers got caught screwing up, one of your soul brothers no less. I want to see how you talk your way out of this one," he laughed.

Sergeant Wood didn't even reply. He kept right on up the stairs.

Captain Moore was the operations officer in the Provost Marshal's office, and as far as Sergeant Wood was concerned, the fairest of all the officers in the whole command. He knocked on his office door.

"Who is it?" Captain Moore asked.

"It's Sergeant Wood along with Private McGarity, sir." Sergeant Wood said.

"Come on in," Captain Moore said.

"You make sure you report when we get inside, McGarity," Sergeant Wood said in a stern voice. He went in first, followed by McGarity, who reported to the captain.

"Sergeant Wood, you may have a seat. Private McGarity, I'm going to ask you a question and you'd better give me a straight answer. If you don't, you're going to be in more trouble than you're in right now. Do you understand?" Captain Moore asked Private McGarity.

"Yassuh," Private McGarity answered nervously.

"When Sergeant Wood made his check at your post last night, were you asleep?" Captain Moore asked.

"No, sir. When Sergeant Wood made his check at my post last night I was making my security checks. Private Gordon was at the desk," Private McGarity answered truthfully.

"You wouldn't lie to protect Sergeant Wood would you, Private?" Captain Moore said in a firm voice, trying to scare Private McGarity.

"Nossuh, I wouldn't. But I'm sure whenever Sergeant Wood does mess up, everyone in the unit will know about it", Private McGarity was brave enough to point out.

Captain Moore smiled and said, "That's all. You can wait outside."

Private McGarity saluted and did an about face and exited the office.

Captain Moore then turned to Sergeant Wood. "Sergeant Wood, I'm going to let you handle this little problem. I'm sure you'll do what's right," Captain Moore said, showing confidence in his judgment.

"Yes, sir, I will," Sergeant Wood assured the captain.

"That's all. You can also leave," Captain Moore said dismissing him.

Sergeant Wood left the captain's office thinking, "There has to be more to it than this." To his surprise that was the end of it.

Sergeant Wood gave Private McGarity a counseling statement and five days extra duty cleaning up the station with the understanding that if he was ever caught sleeping again on duty, regardless of where it was, he would be seeing the commander for an Article 15. Sergeant Wood did not have any more problems from Private McGarity after that incident.

PATRIOTISM

A couple of days after the incident with Private McGarity, Private Gordon told Sergeant Wood he overheard Sergeant Chandler telling Acting Sergeant Harper to report to him if he ever saw Sergeant Wood asleep while on duty. Sergeant Chandler was assured by Acting Sergeant Harper that Sergeant Wood didn't play games when it came to anyone in his squad screwing up, himself included. Only Master Sergeant Chandler didn't believe a word Specialist Harper or anyone else on the squad had to say when it came to Sergeant Wood's dedication to duty.

The following day after this revelation, Sergeant Wood asked Acting Sergeant Harper about it.

"Yeah, sarge, I was instructed to report anything you do wrong. I told them the truth. It seemed they want to get something on you for some reason. Master Sergeant Chandler even said I was lying to protect you," Acting Sergeant Harper confessed.

"Trying to protect me from what?" Sergeant Wood asked.

"I don't know sarge," Acting Sergeant Harper answered.

"Thank you for telling me about this. I appreciate that," Sergeant Wood assured him.

"I'm sorry I didn't come and tell you what was going on. I was afraid you'd be pissed at me for them trying to use me. After all, I was the one who helped them set Sergeant Terrell up. And Master Sergeant Chandler said it'd be wise if I didn't say anything to you about it, but I've felt nothing but guilt and shame for what I did to Sergeant Terrell" Acting Sergeant Harper confessed.

"Can I trust you, Sergeant Harper? You went along with Sergeant Chandler and whomever else was involved once, how do I know you won't do it again?" Sergeant Wood asked.

"Believe me, Sergeant Wood, I like you too much to stab you in the back. You're the best NCO, black or white, I've ever worked for," Acting Sergeant Harper praised him.

"Yeah. Let's get to work," Sergeant Wood sighed.

Here he was again having to watch his every step, caught in the white man's web, trying his best not to make any waves lest he be gobbled up and devoured by a pile of shit in the outhouse of life. The pressure Sergeant Wood felt while stationed in Korea was nowhere near the pressure he felt at Fort Leavenworth. At least in Korea when he felt he needed to get away from his fellow Americans, all he had to do was leave the compound and mingle with the Korean people who had befriended him. They were shop owners, security guards, and bar owners. One even owned one a small hotel in downtown Seoul. There in Kansas everything was just like back home in Arkansas. All the businesses in Leavenworth, Kansas were run and owned by white people, who didn't give a shit about black people unless they were spending their hard-earned money in their establishment.

The black neighborhoods were nothing but ghettos. The people, as in all ghettos, were running around using drugs, fighting, and killing each other. The white politicians in America knew the problems plaguing the black community, not only in Leavenworth but throughout the nation, were caused primarily by white oppression. Still, Sergeant Wood could never understand how his fellow blacks could run around killing each other, or go through life believing no matter what they did, they would never get anywhere. Sergeant Wood felt he had to be just as careful when dealing with his own people as he did when dealing with his white counterparts, because many of them labeled him as trying to be white. As far as his White counterparts were concerned, they could kill him and eat him, but it didn't mean he had to taste good.

The only people Sergeant Wood felt comfortable with were Sergeant Terrell and his wife Tracy. They were both from North Carolina and had gotten married right after graduating from high school. Five months after they were married Sergeant Terrell received his draft notice, and after completing his training, was sent to Vietnam.

Being Tracy protested the war along with the majority of her generation, she found herself torn between supporting her husband's actions and condemning those of his fellow soldiers. Eventually she came to realize he couldn't be set aside as blameless for what he had to do. If she called one soldier a baby-killer, she had to call them all baby-killers and she would never call her man that. The final blow came when her best friend, a diehard believer that a man should go to jail rather than to Vietnam, told her it was immoral to love a man who was murdering innocent men, women and children, whether they were married to them or not. Tracy never joined another protest march after that, although her main protest was against the United States Army using minority soldiers to kill minority Vietnamese people who had never done anything to Black people in America.

Tracy constantly preached to anyone who would listen that the black man's true enemy was the unfair, evil white racist American Institutions here in America that kept their feet on the necks of black people to hold them down, not the Vietnamese people in Vietnam. She was so against the military establishment, the only time she would go on post was when it was absolutely necessary, which was to go to the hospital or to see her husband.

Sergeant Wood really enjoyed talking to her although they didn't have much in common. They didn't agree on very much, but they were able to discuss their different beliefs somewhat intelligently. The first night they met, they argued like hell about what it was going to take for the black man in America to get ahead. Tracy believed the only way black men in America were going to get ahead was to take up arms and blow whitey away; whereas Sergeant Wood believed it was going to take time. He didn't believe God would let such an evil race of people remain in power indefinitely. Tracy was a true believer that time was something the black man in America didn't have. Their time to act was fast approaching.

Sergeant Wood didn't let her know he was slightly upset to hear a black person say there's no place in America for the black man after all they'd done to help make this country what it is today. Sergeant Terrell sat back and listened while they gave their different views.

The second time he visited Sergeant Terrell and Tracy, she asked if he was married or engaged. "I'm engaged, but knowing how you feel, you'll probably disapprove," Sergeant Wood said.

"Not unless you tell me she's white," Tracy gave Sergeant Wood a warning look.

He laughed. "She happens to be Korean," Sergeant Wood said.

It was her turn to laugh. "Black nigger, yellow nigger, what's the difference? Whitey hates us all. Maybe you can get her people and their friends to join us in wiping these blond-haired, blue-eyed devils off the face of the earth," she said seriously.

PATRIOTISM

"You know something, Tracy? I hope to God you never become a one-day headline," Sergeant Wood said, remembering Black Panther members being set up and shot down like dogs by racists law enforcement policies directed by the FBI.

"Don't worry about me, Sergeant Wood. As long as I got this strong, handsome dude here beside me, I know how far to go. Believe it or not, this man sitting right here is supposed to be an American hero. Silver star, purple heart, the fucking works. And what happens when he gets back to the good ole U.S. of A.? These evil white people try to make everyone believe he's a black junky trying to get over on the system. They don't realize what they've put this man through. When he first got back home from Vietnam we went to visit my parents in Charlotte, N.C. Early one morning before we got out of bed my little brothers decided to see who could shoot the most soda cans out of the air with daddy's shotguns. I was in bed with Terrell but I wasn't asleep. So I watched Bobo, 13, and Scooter, 11, out of the bedroom window gathering soda cans. I also noticed that they had daddy's shotguns with them, and were probably planning on shooting them, but it never dawned on me to warn Terrell of their intentions.

Anyway, after they had about five cans apiece they flipped a coin to see who would shoot first. Since Bobo was the oldest and had been hunting the longest I figured he would be the better shot. Scooter won the toss and loaded his gun. Bobo stood off to the side so he wouldn't be in the line of fire when he tossed the can in the air. I watched with anticipation as Bobo threw the can into the air. Scooter aimed and followed its path as it sailed through the air. Up and up it went. When the can reached its height, Scooter cut loose. Boom!

The next thing I knew I was being thrown to the floor and

dragged under the bed. I must have screamed because Bobo and Scooter ran to the window and peered through the bedroom window to see what was going on. Momma and daddy came running into the bedroom to see what had happened to me. I must've been yelling for Terrell to let go of me because after everything was over my momma said they thought he was killing me under the bed. Terrell kept hollering "incoming, incoming, stay down, stay down." Realizing he was having a flash back from his experiences while in combat in Vietnam, my daddy got down on his knees and looked under the bed.

In a calm voice he said, "Sergeant Terrell, stand down, stand down. Everything okay, everything okay! The all clear signal has been given." While he was talking to Terrell, my daddy was slowly pulling me from under the bed.

When Terrell got his bearings and realized where he was and saw Bobo and Scooter outside the window rolling with laughter, he didn't want to come from under the bed. He was so ashamed he burst into tears and curled himself into a tight ball and refused to move. I never loved this man more in my life than at that moment. I couldn't say I understood what he was going through because I didn't, but I knew I had to do something to convince him he was no less of a man for being affected by the war. I crawled under the bed and held him. I asked everyone to leave us alone. He kept saying he'd become a coward afraid of his own shadow. It took a while but I coaxed him from under the bed and we sat down on it.

'I'm sorry for the way I acted. I guess I'm still in that survival mode. I've never been so embarrassed in my life. What must your daddy and momma be thinking of me right now?' he asked. 'I could see the look of fear in their eyes. They thought I was going to hurt you. God knows hurting you would be the last thing on this earth I'd do. I love you, Tracy. I love you more than anything in this world,' Terrell told me.

By this time I was a blubbering idiot. I told him I loved him and I'd always be here for him. My daddy understands what Terrell is going through because he was in the Korean War and had his share of nightmares when he got home. My momma told us about some of the episodes she went through with him, and she never wanted me to experience it from my husband. I convinced her I was just as strong as she was and everything was going to be all right. As for Bobo and Scooter, they were told not to do any shooting around the house whenever Terrell was there. Terrell tried to convince them that it'd be all right as long as he knew they were going to be shooting, but they never shot the guns when he was around. We got through the visit and here we are. No one is ever going to hurt my hero. He's paid too big of a price protecting this damn country for a bunch of rednecks to try and take away the honor he's earned. I swear I'll die before I sit by and watch them destroy him," Tracy spat. She lost control of her emotions and sounded as if she was about to cry, but continued. "Why's it that no matter how much of himself a black man gives to America, white people find a way to discredit him?" Tracy asked on the verge of tears.

"Tracy, don't," Sergeant Terrell said, putting his arms around her. "You know how upset you always get when talking about my situation. But we're going to be alright," Sergeant Terrell assured her.

"Maybe I should leave," Sergeant Wood said, getting up from his chair.

"No, man. You don't have to leave. She's ok," Sergeant Terrell said, holding up a hand.

"Yeah, I'm ok, Sergeant Wood. It just pisses me off the way these people have treated him since we've been here. They don't give a damn that he risked his life in defense of his country. How're you getting along with these prejudice-ass red necks?" Tracy asked Sergeant Wood.

"Not too well. Sergeant Chandler tried to set me up by telling the PM I'm very disrespectful to my superiors. And of course Colonel Gray didn't believe anything I had to say. I had my say anyway. Sergeant Chandler even tried to get Acting Sergeant Harper to lie on me by saying he has seen me asleep while on duty. The only thing I have to say about the whole matter is they may get me, but not without a fight," Sergeant Wood updated her on his situation in the unit. They talked a while longer about the problems facing the world before Sergeant Wood called it a night.

On Sergeant Wood's next day of break, Sergeant First Class Hart stopped by his room to update him on the feelings of his superiors. "Sergeant Wood, I need to have a serious talk with you," he said.

"Oh shit! This doesn't sound too promising," Sergeant Wood quipped.

"God dammit, Sergeant Wood, you're one of the sharpest E-5's I've ever known since I've been in the army. You don't run around saying 'Yo, my man', or calling your fellow black soldiers "nigger" the way the other young soldiers your age are doing. You're very mature for your age. And you have all the confidence in the world in yourself. I admire you for that. However, we're in one of the most racist states in the nation. Sometimes you have to give in to them even though you know you're right. I'd rather see you leave here with a rocker on your sleeve than a specialist-four eagle," Sergeant First Class Hart said. He was truly sincere in what he was saying.

"So would I, Sergeant Hart. But if it means I'll have to give up my manhood, I'd rather leave here a buck private. I've used all the tack I can muster since I've been here. What do they want from me, to say *'Yassuh boss, or nossuh boss'* every time they say something to me? I couldn't say that even if I tried. I was born and raised in the south, so I know what it means to sometimes give them their way. And I refuse to grovel at anyone's feet or kiss anyone's ass no matter what happens to me," Sergeant Wood said.

"I'm not asking you to kiss anyone's ass. The only thing I'm saying is try and be a little more tactful," Sergeant First Class Hart almost pleaded.

"Ok, Sergeant Hart. I will. I'll do my best not to piss anyone off," Sergeant Wood promised.

Chapter 9
MAXINE

Sergeant Wood wasn't a disco duck, so very seldom could he be found in a nightclub. The few times he had gone out it was to the NCO club where he sat at the bar and talked to the bartender most of the time he was there. Every once in a while a female patron of the club would ask him to dance, or a female patron would catch his eye and he would ask her to dance. It was nothing exciting enough to write home about. Besides, he knew other than the few civilian women who frequented the NCO club, the majority of the lovely ladies were dependent wives of his fellow service members. Sergeant Wood had never fooled around with a married woman and had no intention of doing so now. The civilian women he'd met at the club so far didn't appeal to him. It would take an extraordinary woman to make him even consider cheating on Miss Kwak again.

The incidents with Master Sergeant Chandler, Colonel Gray, Captain Harris, and Sergeant First Class Hart had set his nerves on edge. He needed to get away from the atmosphere of Fort Leavenworth to unwind. So he asked Sergeant Terrell where off post he could go to have a few beers and listen to some good music. It would be the first time he'd been to a bar off post since he'd been at Fort Leavenworth. Sergeant Terrell's house was the only place he'd been off post. Sergeant Terrell told him the 'Webb', where the brothers and sisters hung out, was the place to go. He also said it got pretty rough sometimes, and it wasn't the nicest place in the world. But the music was awesome. Not to mention the sisters were easy on the eyes.

Sergeant Wood arrived at the club around 9 p.m. and the place was already packed. Sergeant Terrell's assessment of the club was right on target. The club was not the most luxurious in the world, but since the club had the Temptations doing their thing when he walked in he could ignore its appearance. It had been a while since he'd seen so many beautiful black sisters in one place. He found an empty bar stool and ordered a beer. He settled back to enjoy the night. To Sergeant Wood's disappointment a fight broke out before he finished his first beer. There were no knives or guns used during the fight, but the incident had left so much tension in the air he knew there were going to be more fights before the night was over.

Sergeant Wood walked out of the club without a clue of where he was going to go from there. Sergeant Terrell hadn't told him of any other clubs in town where he could go to have a good time, so he decided to put his fate in the hands of a taxi driver. *The taxi driver should know where a man could go around here to have a fun time,* Sergeant Wood thought.

Sergeant Wood caught a cab and told the driver he was new in town and had no idea where to go to have a good time. The cabbie looked in his rearview mirror and asked, "What's wrong with the Webb? They got some hot chicks in there."

"Maybe so, but I don't feel like watching a wild-west show tonight," Sergeant Wood answered.

"Another fight, huh? So what kind of place are you looking for?" The cabbie asked, pulling away from the curb.

"Someplace nice and quiet with a dance floor and a view, if you know what I mean," Sergeant Wood laughed.

"The Webb is the hottest club in town for the black view.

The only other place I know is the Horse Shoe Lounge. There're always a couple of sisters there, but mostly white bread. I hope you know interracial unions don't go over too well in this part of the country," the cabbie said.

"All I want is a couple of brews and a view. I'm not trying to pick up anything tonight. So, I guess the Horse Shoe Lounge is where I want to go. What the hell, I may learn to square dance," Sergeant Wood laughed settling back for the ride.

Ten minutes later the cabbie pulled over and said, "Here you go, soldier boy. I hope you like country music, because that's about all you're going to hear in this joint."

The club had a big metal Horse Shoe nailed above the entrance door. *I guess that's why it's called The Horseshoe Lounge*, Sergeant Wood thought as he entered the club. The first two people he saw upon entering the club were Master Sergeant Chandler and Sergeant First Class Hart sitting at the bar drunk as skunks. The club was nice and spacious with a relaxing atmosphere. It also had a big dance floor. But the one thing that stood out more than anything else was he and Sergeant First Class Hart were the only two black faces there. Sergeant Wood headed toward the opposite end of the club intending to get as far away from where they were sitting as possible. He hadn't taken ten steps before Master Sergeant Chandler spotted him and called him over.

"Well, I'll be damned if it ain't the barracks rat. What brings you out this way?" Master Sergeant Chandler asked, his speech slurred.

"I thought I'd get out of the barracks for a while since this is my first weekend off since I've been here," Sergeant Wood answered.

"Well, why ain't you over at The Webb trying to pick up one of them little black gals? They're hot as hell. Will put out for anyone," Master Sergeant Chandler laughed.

"I'm not looking for a woman. I came out to have a couple a drinks that's all," Sergeant Wood informed him.

Sergeant First Class Hart said, "We're not talking about falling in love. Know what I mean?" he winked.

Master Sergeant Chandler and Sergeant First Class Hart laughed, so he pretended to laugh with them. Sergeant Wood could hardly wait to get away from them so he could be alone.

"Don't think you're going to pick up any white nooky in here," Master Sergeant Chandler choked out a phony laugh.

Sergeant Wood tried his best not to respond because he knew what he was going to say would piss Master Sergeant Chandler off, but try as he may he couldn't help asking, "Why not? Don't the white women around here have pussies too?" It was Sergeant Wood's turn to pretend to break into a big laugh.

Master Sergeant Chandler turned redder than the local fire engine and said, "I don't think that remark was funny worth a goddamn. It'd probably be better if you left here and went to The Webb and picked up one of those black whores down there," he spat.

"I told you. I didn't come out tonight to chase whores. And for your information, Master Sergeant, I don't like whores, regardless of their color. There must be a few whores in here, or you guys probably wouldn't be here," Sergeant Wood said.

"I don't like you, Sergeant Wood. You think you're too smart to go along with the program," Master Sergeant Chandler said.

"And what program is that Sergeant Chandler?" Sergeant

Wood asked, staring him eye to eye.

"Keep acting like you're king of the hill and you're going to find out you're not," Master Sergeant Chandler warned him.

"You know something I don't like, Sergeant Chandler, is people who stab you in the back. They should have the guts to deal with me man to man. If they can't, maybe should give their stripes to someone else," Sergeant Wood said, shooting off his mouth before thinking.

"You black sum-bitch. How dare you say something like that to a senior NCO? I hope you don't think you're going to get away with this," Master Sergeant Chandler fumed. He had been talking so loud everyone in the club had turned to stare at them.

Sergeant Wood picked this opportunity to make it seem as if Master Sergeant Chandler was a first-class ass hole. He said, "Sergeant Chandler, I know you can bust me anytime you get ready, but that's no reason for you to embarrass me in front of all these people. I just came here for a couple of drinks. Can I please find myself a seat now that you've embarrassed me in front of all these people?" Sergeant Wood asked, sounding pitiful. He had sounded like the perfect little black soldier who had been chewed out for no reason by the big bad, redneck bully sergeant.

Master Sergeant Chandler almost choked on the words he wanted to say, but didn't dare risk making himself appear even more bullish than he already had.

Sergeant First Class Hart saved the day by saying; "Yeah, Sergeant Wood. Why don't you go find yourself some place to sit before you get yourself in trouble."

Sergeant Wood walked off with a satisfied smile crossing

his lips. He heard Master Sergeant Chandler tell Sergeant First Class Hart, "Willie, you'd better talk to that boy, or he's going to end up in the USDB before he leaves here."

"Don't worry about it, Gary, I'll take care of it," Sergeant First Class Hart had assured him.

Sergeant Wood found an empty table and sat down and ordered a beer. To his surprise, the music was pretty good though it was mostly country, and everyone was having a good time, except his two favorite NCOs. They stared at him as though they were contemplating murder.

After a couple of hours he was debating whether to stay longer or go back to the barracks when a beautiful white girl came over to his table. She was one of the most beautiful women, of any color, he had ever seen. Her tan was so dark she could almost pass for a high yellow sister, if not for the shoulder length straw blonde hair that shimmered and shined under the club lights. She had the body of a playboy centerfold.

"Hello, soldier boy. You alone?" she asked.

"Yes, I am," Sergeant Wood answered.

"Want to dance?" she asked.

"Sure, why not?" Sergeant Wood accepted the offer. He didn't give it a second thought that the girl was white. He didn't see what harm one dance could do. Besides, it was one of only a few disco-type songs they had played all night.

To get to the dance floor, they had to pass where Master Sergeant Chandler and Sergeant First Class Hart was sitting. As they passed, Master Sergeant Chandler called the girl white trash under his breath loud enough for Sergeant Wood to hear. After the dance ended, Sergeant Wood started back to his table.

"Hey, don't run off so fast," she said, grabbing hold of his arm to keep him from leaving the floor. "Would you mind if I sat with you a while and talked?" she asked.

"No, I don't mind. Maybe you can tell me the best places Leavenworth has to offer," Sergeant Wood said.

"I doubt that. I've been here six months and this is the only place I've been to here in Leavenworth. I usually go to Kansas City when I go out. But most of the time I can be found at home because all I do is work, eat and sleep. My name is Maxine Griffin. What's yours?" Maxine asked, laying on the charm.

"Sergeant, aah, Bob Wood," Sergeant Wood stammered.

"Hi, Bob."

"Hi, Maxine."

They returned to his table, where they laughed and talked until it was time for the club to close at 2 o'clock that morning. Sergeant Wood had noticed all the stares they had received throughout the evening, especially from Master Sergeant Chandler, who was so drunk now he could hardly stand. Sergeant Wood had learned she was none other than the USDB commander's daughter. Lieutenant Colonel Ray M. Griffin, a native Kansasian, and an officer he would come to know very well in the near future. He also learned Maxine loved doing things that upset her parents, and went against the norms of society. Carrying on with a black man in an establishment where the majority of the patrons knew her was an example of it because she knew someone at the club would tell her parents what they had witnessed.

Sergeant Wood told Maxine he had no intention of playing her games because it was wrong to stress her parents our like that. He didn't care how much he enjoyed being with her. When Sergeant Wood told her it was time to leave, Maxine asked if he needed a ride back to the barracks.

"No, I'm going to catch a cab back," Sergeant Wood said. He knew why she asked.

Maxine wouldn't hear of it. Her dad bought her a brand new Trans-Am when she graduated from Kansas State University.

On their way to the barracks Maxine informed him she was twenty-four years old and had a degree in Criminal Justice. She worked with a small law firm in Kansas City, Missouri. When he told her he thought she was only about nineteen, she laughed and said she knew there was something very lovable about him. Upon reaching the barracks she wanted to sit in the car and talk a while. He begged off, saying it was not a good idea. Maxine asked if it was because she was white or a colonel's daughter.

"Neither, it's became I'm engaged to be married and I don't want to be tempted by a beautiful woman who may cause me to temporarily forget the girl I love.   Besides, I'm not the most popular buck sergeant here at Fort Leavenworth. I'd hate for you to catch hell from your parents because of me," Sergeant Wood said.

Maxine laughed. "Believe it or not, I heard about you after the little incident you had with your operations sergeant. What's his name?" she asked, trying to remember.

"Master Sergeant Chandler," Sergeant Wood said.

"Yeah, Sergeant Chandler. The same yo-yo at the club tonight, right? I believe it was your first day on duty or something like that," Maxine said.

"Yep, the one and only Sergeant Chandler. Who in the hell told you about that?" Sergeant Wood asked.

"First Sergeant Taylor told my dad about it, and he told us. I guess Sergeant Chandler told First Sergeant Taylor about it,"

Maxine said smiling.

"I see. Man, how rumors fly," Sergeant Wood said.

"When you first told me your name, I didn't realize you were that Sergeant Wood," she laughed.

"Yeah, that's me, that proud young, black man with too much pride. The one Sergeant Chandler has his mind set on putting behind bars at the USDB, especially after tonight," Sergeant Wood emphasized.

"Why after tonight?" Maxine asked, curious.

"Are you kidding? First I make him appear as an overbearing bully. And then I leave the club with the most beautiful white girl in the state of Kansas. You sure you want to be associated with a wanted man?" Sergeant Wood asked. It was his turn to laugh.

"More than that wanted man wants to be associated with," Maxine said, with sexual undertones.

"Well, lets' both sleep on it for a few days and see what develops," Sergeant Wood said, attempting to exit the car.

Maxine put her hand on his shoulder to stop him from getting out of the car. "You're not afraid of me are you, Sergeant Wood?" Maxine asked.

"Why should I be afraid of you? Is there something I should know about you that scare men away from you?" Sergeant Wood asked, settling back into the seat.

"No, nothing that I know of," Maxine answered. She continued. "So, I guess that means you're afraid of what Sergeant Chandler and the other rednecks are going to say or do to you for having the balls to date a white girl. Is that it?" Maxine asked.

"I told you. I'm engaged to be married, and don't want to

put myself in a position that may hurt the relationship between my fiancée and me," Sergeant Wood answered.

Maxine laughed and said, "So you think I may be too much woman for you, huh?"

"Girl please, I haven't met a girl yet who I couldn't handle, if I chose to go that route. You would be no exception. The issue isn't whether I'm afraid of you or the military machine, it is whether I want to cheat on Miss Kwak," Sergeant Wood said.

"This Miss Kwak, where is she?" Maxine asked.

"Korea," Sergeant Wood answered.

"Thousands of miles away and you're afraid she'll find out what you did while you were here in the United States? She has ESP or something?" Maxine asked.

"No, she has me," Sergeant Wood said.

"What about we just talk sometime? I won't try to force you to do anything you don't want to do," Maxine promised.

"I guess that'll be okay," Sergeant Wood agreed.

"Ok, but if you don't call me, I'm going to call you," Maxine said, giving him her phone number.

"All right, until we meet again," Sergeant Wood said with a sigh of relief.

Sergeant Wood gave her a peck on the cheek and went into the barracks thinking of the hell he was going to catch, not only from Master Sergeant Chandler, but from Sergeant First Class Hart as well Monday morning.

Monday morning at 9 a.m. there was a knock on Sergeant Wood's room door. "Who is it?" he asked, knowing it was either Sergeant First Class Hart or Master Sergeant Chandler.

"It's Sergeant Hart," he said. Sergeant Wood opened the door and Sergeant First Class Hart entered his room. Without

PATRIOTISM

giving him a chance to say anything he said, "Sergeant Wood, get your ass down to my office right now."

"Yes, Sergeant. I'm on my way", Sergeant Wood said, moving out at a brisk pace on Sergeant First Class Hart's heels after locking the door to his room.

On his way to Sergeant First Class Hart's office Sergeant Wood made up a plan. He would tell Sergeant First Class Hart the only reason he'd said those things to Master Sergeant Chandler was because he was drunk and didn't realize what he was saying. That he really had no intentions of pissing Sergeant Chandler off. After entering the office, Sergeant Wood was told to have a seat.

"Dammit, Sergeant Wood, I don't even know where the hell to begin. Never in my fifteen years of service have I had to contend with an individual like you. Not only did you manage to make Sergeant Chandler look like a red neck bully, you turned around and rubbed salt in the wound by leaving the club with Colonel Griffin's daughter," Sergeant Hart said pissed, beyond what Sergeant Wood was used to seeing.

"Oh, so you and Master Chandler know her," Sergeant Wood said.

"Shit man, everyone who patronizes that goddamn club knows her," Sergeant First Class Hart informed him.

"Hell, she asked me to dance and if she could sit at my table and talk for a while. What was I supposed to say? Tell her no there were too many white people in the club that would get upset if I danced or talked to her?" Sergeant Wood asked.

"Damn you, Sergeant Wood. Why do you persist in pissing Sergeant Chandler off? All he was trying to do was make a little small talk with you as a member of the unit. He had just

353

finished telling me that maybe he was being unfair to you because of how you turned the first squad around; and because of the leadership you're showing on the unit basketball team. And now this," Sergeant First Class Hart said exasperated.

"Sergeant Hart, whether you want to believe it or not, even if I go along with what Sergeant Chandler says, I doubt if he would like me any more than he does already. Besides, he was implying that the black women here in Leavenworth, KS are nothing but whores. And if he called them whores, he'd call my momma and sister whores. Maybe in time I'll be able to let those type of comments pass. But for now I'm going to let them know where I stand," Sergeant Wood concluded.

"Well, I've tried to tell you what it's going to take for you to make it around here. You're on your own from here on out," Sergeant First Class Hart said.

Sergeant Wood had to bite his bottom lip to keep from laughing. "Sergeant Hart, I've been on my own ever since I've been in the army. But I'm grateful for all the advice you've given me since I've been here. It's the same everywhere I've been since I've been in the Army." Sergeant Wood truly appreciated the little advice Sergeant First Class Hart had given him since his arrival at Fort Leavenworth, but they were from two entirely different eras.

"Meaning?" Sergeant First Class Hart asked, realizing there was more to the statement than Sergeant Wood had said.

"Well, it seems the black NCO's give up on me before anyone else does. Therefore I'm more afraid of you than I am of them," Sergeant Wood explained.

"Afraid of me?" Sergeant First Class Hart frowned in disbelief. "Why?"

"If they ever do set me up they'll need your help. If they can get a black E-7 to say a black E-5 is nothing but a troublemaker, what chance do you think I'd have against them?" Sergeant Wood pointed out the obvious.

"I see you're thinking ahead. That's good, because Sergeant Chandler did say he was going to need my help to get you. I don't know why in the hell I'm even considering this but I'll tell you what, show me you're trying to be diplomatic with the leadership and I won't help them set you up. I still suggest you knock that damn chip off your shoulder, and stop antagonizing the white leadership in the command. Another thing, are you planning on seeing Maxine again?" Sergeant First Class Hart asked, searching Sergeant Wood's face for a telltale sign if he lied.

"Not if I can help it. She's too damn wild and bold for me," Sergeant Wood admitted.

"Good, you can leave now, but don't forget what the hell I said about being more diplomatic with these people. Especially with Sergeant Chandler," Sergeant First Class Hart said, not wanting to appear as one of the bad guys.

Sergeant First Class Hart understood the phase Sergeant Wood was going through because he was a recreated version of himself during the sixties while he was stationed in Vietnam. He was in a command where he swore the white leadership was trying to get every brother in Vietnam killed. The blacks had caught hell in that command until his company commander was fragged. No one was ever convicted, so his death was reported as killed in action. Although he didn't do the fragging, Sergeant First Class Hart never got over the guilt of condoning the killing of his company commander.

"Yes, Sergeant, and thank you for understanding," Sergeant Wood said, honestly meaning it this time.

Sergeant Wood spent the remainder of the morning spit shinning his boots and preparing his uniform for duty. He knew Master Sergeant Chandler would be waiting for him when he reported for duty at the MP station. Sure enough Master Sergeant Chandler was waiting for Sergeant Wood when he walked into the briefing room.

"Come right on upstairs. I want to talk to you," Master Sergeant Chandler said leading the way upstairs. After closing the door to his office behind them, Master Sergeant Chandler asked, "You think you're one smart black son-of-a-bitch, don't you?"

"I don't know what you're talking about, Sergeant Chandler," Sergeant Wood lied.

"You had everyone in the goddamn club believing I was a big red neck bully picking on an innocent little black soldier. That was cute, and to top things off, you leave the club with the USDB commander's daughter. You have balls, boy. I've got to give you credit for that. Too bad I'm going to have to bust them. Colonel Griffin was very upset to hear his daughter was seen dancing and carrying on in public with a, how did he put it, black ass nigger. He wants your stripes, buck sergeant. He wants them bad. And I'm going to deliver them to him on a silver platter," Master Sergeant Chandler promised. When Sergeant Wood didn't respond to what he said, Master Sergeant Chandler added, "It won't do you any good to change your attitude now. Your ass is grass. Now get out of my office." As Sergeant Wood was leaving his office, Master Sergeant Chandler noticed the slight smile on his face. "Have I said something that you find amusing?" Master Sergeant Chandler asked angrily.

"No, Sergeant Chandler. You didn't say anything funny," Sergeant Wood answered, the smile now gone.

"By the way, Colonel Griffin said if he ever hears of you talking to his daughter again, he'll take care of you himself," Master Sergeant Chandler informed him.

"Is that all, Sergeant Chandler? My troops are waiting for me to conduct guard mount," Sergeant Wood said with a blank look on his face.

"You're a real pain in the ass, Sergeant Wood. Get the hell out of my office," Master Sergeant Chandler ordered for the second time.

On his way downstairs something in the back of Sergeant Wood's mind said, *Show these white crackers that you know how to screw people over also. You have damn near a whole squad of white boys working for you. Screw them over the way Sergeant Chandler is trying to screw you.* But Sergeant Wood knew no matter how tempting it sounded, it was not his style.

After guard mount Acting Sergeant Harper asked, "Is Maxine any good in bed?"

"How the hell should I know? And how did you find out about her anyway?" Sergeant Wood asked, surprised that anyone other than Master Sergeant Chandler and Sergeant First Class Hart knew about the encounter.

"Hell sarge, Sergeant Chandler stopped by the barracks yesterday and told the white NCO's in the barracks about it. He even told them about you making him look bad in front of everyone in the club. As you've probably guess by now, the only reason he told them is because he wanted them to get pissed off because you had the balls to talk to a white girl. He then asked if they'd help him set you up for a fall," Acting Sergeant Harper informed him.

"And what did they say when he asked for this favor?" Sergeant Wood asked.

"They told him you're the closest thing to a perfect NCO they've ever seen. That whether he wanted to believe it or not, you never do anything wrong when it comes to performing your duties. They said you go strictly by the book, and they all support you. Sergeant Chandler got pissed and said he would get you himself. And that was it," Acting Sergeant Harper finished.

"Thanks for letting me know what Sergeant Chandler has in mind for me. I hope they meant what they said, because I also know how to screw over people," Sergeant Wood said, letting Acting Sergeant Harper know he was not above screwing someone.

"I'm not shitting you, sarge. You can believe me," Acting Sergeant Harper assured him.

"Sure I can," Sergeant Wood said under his breath. He'd learned a long time ago as a young boy no matter how much a white person pretends to like you they wouldn't go against their own for an extended period of time. This included Specialist Harper who was about to make sergeant. So he knew it was not just Master Sergeant Chandler he had to keep his eye on.

It was business as usual until two days later. Sergeant Wood was told to see the Provost Marshall prior to going on duty. He knocked on Colonel Gray's office door and was told to come in and have a seat.

"What is this I hear about you and Colonel Griffin's daughter?" Colonel Gray asked nonchalantly.

"I don't know what you heard, sir," Sergeant Wood answered

truthfully.

"Well, let me tell you what the colonel told me. He said Maxine told him you two hit it off so well she's going to continue seeing you. What do you have to say about that?" Colonel Gray asked.

"Sir, believe me, I told Maxine there's no way a relationship between us could possibly work out. Not even a casual thing because of the waves it'd make," Sergeant Wood said, trying to be diplomatic.

"That's putting it mildly, but I hope for your sake you're telling the truth," the colonel warned.

"I am, sir. I have no intention of ever seeing her again," Sergeant Wood, said not even saying her name.

"That girl is going to be the death of that man," Colonel Gray said to himself. "You can go, sergeant. But remember, I'm holding you to your word," he said.

"Yes, sir," Sergeant Wood assured him as he was leaving his office.

Sergeant Wood was about to go downstairs when Sergeant Chandler stopped him and asked, "What did the colonel have to say about your little escapade with Maxine?"

"As it turns out, Sergeant Chandler, Maxine isn't white trash after all. And believe it or not, Colonel Gray wants me to insure her reputation as a good and decent little white girl remains intact," Sergeant Wood answered and bounded down the stairs. Sergeant Chandler didn't dare say anything lest everyone would know he'd called the colonel's daughter a tramp.

Sergeant Wood had told Colonel Gray the truth. He had no intention of calling or seeing Maxine, even after accepting her phone number. He'd thrown it in the garbage upon entering the barracks the night she gave it to him. Maxine, on the other hand, was true to her word.

A few days later, on the first day of his next break while watching television in the day room, Maxine called. At the time he was told he had a phone call, he thought it would be his momma because she was supposed to call that day. If he'd known it was Maxine he would have told the individual answering the phone to tell her he wasn't there.

"Hello, this is Sergeant Wood speaking," he answered the phone.

"Hello, wanted buck sergeant. I thought you were going to give me a call?" Maxine said.

"I would've, but I misplaced your number somehow," Sergeant Wood lied.

"I'm sure you did," Maxine said accusingly. "My father told me about the promise you made to Colonel Gray," she said.

"What promise are you talking about?" Sergeant Wood asked, knowing full well what she was talking about.

"Don't play dumb with me, Bob. I didn't think you would be scared off so easily. You know they can't bust you for having a girlfriend, even if she happens to be a colonel's daughter. Besides, I told my Dad if anyone messes with you because of me, they would be sorry," Maxine said, sounding proud of herself.

"Meaning?" Sergeant Wood asked, not liking the direction in which the conversation was going.

"Meaning, if they don't leave you alone we'll be seen together all over post," she explained.

"Wait just a minute, my beautiful little over-reacting friend. I do have a say so in this matter, you know," Sergeant Wood informed her.

"I know that, Bob. Don't you want to see me again?" Maxine asked in what she must have thought was her sexiest voice.

"I told you, Maxine. I have enough problems without messing around with the USDB commander's daughter. And believe me, it has nothing to do with you personally. Because not only are you beautiful, you're fun to be with. But you know as well as I do we'd be making tidal waves if we started seeing each other on a regular basis. Not only will it cause trouble for myself, but for you as well," Sergeant Wood tried to reason with her.

"To be honest with you, I don't really give a damn what people think or say. I like you, and want to see you again. If you don't meet me someplace, I'm going to stop by your barracks to see you," Maxine said, sounding serious.

Now how do I get myself out of this shit? he asked himself. To her he said, "I know I have charm and charisma, but I never had a woman fall head over heels for me after just one night of talking. Where do you want to meet?" Sergeant Wood asked, giving in. The last thing he wanted was for her to come to the barracks to see him.

"I'll pick you up in the parking lot behind the credit union at 1830 hours," Maxine used military time.

"1830 hours, huh? You're a military brat alright. How did you know I was off today anyway?" Sergeant Wood asked.

"Easy, I called the desk from the office and told them I worked for the Federal Credit Union here on post and needed to talk to you about your car loan application," Maxine laughed.

"Until then," Sergeant Wood said and hung up.

When Sergeant Wood returned to the day room, the guys

wanted to know who the girl on the phone was because she sounded white. He told them she was a loan officer at the credit union. He was talking to her about a loan because he was thinking about buying a car. Sergeant Wood used the same lie Maxine had used because it jived with what the desk sergeant would tell everyone about the inquiry of his where about at the MP desk. It didn't cross any of their minds that the white girl on the phone may have been Maxine.

Sergeant Wood showed up half an hour late, on purpose, hoping Maxine would get tired of waiting or get pissed and leave. That way he'd be able to say he was there, but she never showed up. To his dismay, she was sitting in her car waiting for him.

"Hi, sorry I'm late. I hope you haven't been waiting too long. I lost track of time," Sergeant Wood apologized.

"That's alright. I just got here a few minutes ago myself. I thought maybe you had gotten pissed and left. I was about to call your barracks again," Maxine said.

"So where do we go from here?" Sergeant Wood asked.

"Some place where no one will see us. Would you mind going to a hotel if I paid for it?" Maxine asked.

"I don't think that would be a good idea. If you just want to talk, we can go to a park or someplace like that," Sergeant Wood said, not trusting himself nor her motives.

"I didn't say I just wanted talk, now did I?" Maxine teased.

"No, you didn't, but that's all I have in mind," Sergeant Wood said.

"Well, if that's all you want to do we can talk in a hotel room. Beside, the chance of anyone accidentally running across us in a hotel room is less likely to happen," she reasoned.

Sergeant Wood couldn't argue the point, but he knew her motives for wanting to go to a hotel was not to talk. He knew she would try everything within her power to seduce him. But he couldn't risk her coming to his barracks for the world to see as she had threatened to do. So he was caught up in a situation where Maxine called the shots. The million-dollar question was, would he be able to resist her womanly charms? And if he were able to resist, what would her next move be?

"I can't argue that point, but you had better behave yourself. Otherwise, I'll be catching a cab back to the barracks," Sergeant Wood warned her.

"I'm not going to promise I won't try anything, but I'll do my best," Maxine said in a low, sexy voice.

"I'm not getting in the car until you promise not to try anything once we get to the hotel," Sergeant Wood said, standing back with his arms folded.

"Oh, alright, I promise. Party pooper," Maxine sounded disappointed.

"Shit, lets go you conniving little heifer," Sergeant Wood said getting in the car.

Maxine laughed and burned rubber leaving the parking lot. Sergeant Wood was still telling himself he was making a big mistake by going to a hotel with Maxine when she pulled into the parking lot of the Kansas City International Airport Holiday Inn Hotel. They registered under the name of Mr. and Mrs. Kasaam Ali, from Los Angeles, California. Their luggage hadn't been on the same flight. Mr. Ali would pick the bags up later. They requested a bottle of champagne be sent up to their room right away. Maxine had given him the money to pay for everything prior to their arrival at the hotel. She said it wouldn't look right for the woman to be the one paying for the room. Sergeant Wood agreed with her while accepting the hundred dollar bill she handed him. After entering the room and the champagne was delivered, the battle of wits and bullshit began.

"Ooh this is so cozy. I'm just tingling all over," Maxine swooned. "Do you mind if I take a quick shower?" she asked.

"You don't need to take a shower to talk," Sergeant Wood said.

"I know, but since I'm here and the room is paid for I may as well use the facilities," Maxine said matter of fact.

"I guess you're right," Sergeant Wood conceded.

"You sure you don't mind me taking a shower before we talk?" Maxine asked heading for the bathroom.

"No, take your time. I'll just sip my champagne and watch T.V. until you finish," Sergeant Wood said, flipping on the television set.

"Why don't you join me? We could scrub each other's backs," Maxine offered.

"No, thanks. I for one just came here to talk, remember?" Sergeant Wood reminded her.

"Yeah, you came here to talk," Maxine said flippantly as she swayed her way into the bathroom.

Sergeant Wood tried to mask the effect Maxine's flirting was having on him, but he could tell by the look on her face he hadn't succeeded. He knew if he did end up in bed with her, it would be hard to get rid of her after that. And if he didn't take her to bed, he didn't know what she would do or say once they returned to the fort. Sergeant Wood's mind was racing at a breakneck speed trying to figure out which way was best to get out of the predicament he was in without getting his butt in a sling. He never imagined himself getting caught up in a situation such as this. Here he was in a hotel room with one of the most beautiful and horniest women he'd ever been associated with. And he was trying to figure out how he could get out of the hotel room without screwing her. Although he had tried to keep his mind occupied so as not to think about sex, it kept drifting back to the sound of the shower running, and who was in there. His mind flashed visions of a soft, tan body with firm breasts. Breasts with pink tipped nipples hard as nails. His mind also pictured her thin luscious lips begging to be kissed, soft slender thighs waiting to be caressed and nibbled on. And a love canal hot and steamy, waiting for his hard throbbing manhood to plunge deeper and deeper with each stroke until it quivered and creamed over and over again.

The vision was still running through his mind when Maxine walked back into the room wearing the sheerest nightgown he had ever seen. And underneath she wore only the briefest of bikini panties. Her breasts and nipples showing through the nightgown were just as he had imagined. He nearly choked on the champagne as she walked toward him.

"Where the hell did you get that?" Sergeant Wood asked, his voice quivering.

"I had it in my purse, do you like?" she asked, twirling seductively.

"Yeah, but that's not what I came here for," he insisted.

"Don't be a drag. Why don't you take your clothes off and relax. Where's the champagne?" Maxine asked, sounding disappointed she hadn't been able to excite Sergeant Wood as she thought she would.

Sergeant Wood handed her a glass and refilled his own. "I

know things aren't working out the way you'd planned, but you should've taken my feelings into consideration before you started this little charade. It's not that you don't appeal to me," he stood so she could get a good look at the bulge straining against the front of his pants, "because you do. Right now I want you more than I've wanted a woman in a long time, but what I'm concerned about is what happens after you've had your way with me. Do you threaten to tell your daddy I screwed you every time I refuse to do your bidding? You're spoiled as hell, and are used to getting your way. And with a mentality like that you probably don't care if someone is hurt in the process. Well, I don't intend to be your next victim. It would probably be best if I go ahead and let you lie on me. At least I'll be telling the truth when I say I didn't screw the colonel's daughter," Sergeant Wood pretended to be angry but caught himself babbling.

"It's true. I'm used to getting whatever I want, but with you I feel differently. I can't explain it. I guess it's because you're the first man I've thrown myself at and was rejected. After I went home the other night after dropping you off at the barracks, I realized that my beauty alone ain't going to get everyone to grovel at my feet. And now here I am sitting in front of you, almost totally naked, and instead of tearing my nightgown off and screwing my brains out, you sit there trying to get me to assure you I won't try to control you once I've satisfied my lust. Damn, that turns me on. I'll be your sex slave. You make all the rules and I'll obey them. Do something, please. Anything to show me I'm a desirable woman." She sat on the bed beside him and started stroking his hard erect member and making soft, moaning sounds. "Oh my god, it feels so big. Can I take it out and see it?" Maxine asked.

PATRIOTISM

Sergeant Wood felt he was in total control. He also knew people would say anything to get what they wanted. "I wish I could believe that Maxine," he said pulling himself from her groping hands. "You say that now, but how can I be sure you won't get back at me in the future?" he asked, trembling.

"Believe me, Bob. I've never begged a man in my life. Let alone tell him he can use me as he pleases," Maxine said.

"Why me?" Sergeant Wood asked, weakening.

"I told you. I don't know," she insisted.

"Hell, life itself is nothing but a risk," Sergeant Wood said to no one in particular. "Come here," he said, holding out his arms.

Maxine flew into his arms and offered her lips. Sergeant Wood kissed her gently but deeply, thrusting his tongue into her mouth. At the same time he was rolling a hardened nipple between the thumb and index finger of his right hand. She was moaning and squirming like nothing he ever had a hold of. He laid Maxine on the bed and removed her nightgown and panties. He placed a blazing trail of hot kisses from her sweet lips to her beautiful, tan thighs. Since oral sex was taboo and frowned upon in the black community in Arkansas, he went no further than kissing her thighs. When he finally touched her starving love button with his index finger, her body stiffened and she let out a loud gurgle as if she was being strangled.

After several spasms passed and her body relaxed Maxine said, "Damn, I've never experienced anything like that in my life. If that big thing is as good as I think it is, I may not be able to take it. But lets' get it ready," she said, tugging at his belt. Upon releasing his member she said, "Oh my God, so big, so beautiful."

Sergeant Wood had never experienced oral sex before, therefore he knew he was in for one hell of a time as her hot lips came closer and closer to his hard throbbing manhood. When her lips closed around him, it was the greatest sensation he'd ever experienced in his life. He tried to hold back, but after a few deep throat movements he felt as if his insides were leaving his body through his organ. To his amazement she wasn't even fazed by what was happening. During the whole episode she never attempted to pull away.

When he relaxed, Maxine started to deep throat him again, but Sergeant Wood was ready for some serious action. He rolled her on to her back and sank his big, black love tool deep into her hot steaming tunnel of love. She moaned so loud he thought he had hurt her.

Sergeant Wood started to withdraw from her but Maxine said, "No, no, please don't take it out." To insure he didn't, she wrapped her legs tightly around his waist with an iron grip.

Sergeant Wood pumped for all he was worth until he again exploded like he had never done before.

"Oh, I'm going to die. This is too good, too good," Maxine said over and over again.

After their passion subsided he asked, "Was it worth the wait?"

"If you make me get off like that a couple of more times, I think I'll have to move into the barracks with you. I don't think I could live without it," Maxine breathed.

"I don't know about you moving into the barracks, but you'll definitely get off like that every time," he bragged, his ego giving him a big head.

"Lets' take a shower first, and we'll see if you can live up to your promise," Maxine said.

"What is it with you and taking showers? Am I funky or something?" Sergeant Wood asked sniffing his armpits.

Maxine laughed and said, "No, you're not funky. I just have this thing about cleanliness. Do you mind?"

"Not since I'll be in the shower with you," Sergeant Wood said.

When they got in the shower Maxine used the washcloth to soap him and wash him, until his ebony skin gleamed. Sergeant Wood threw the washcloth aside and used his hands to soap and cleanse her excited body. As he caressed the soap from her body, he toyed with her straining nipples, and when he stroked the subs from between her thighs she jumped into his arms and held on when he penetrated her and took her to new heights as he lifted and lowered her onto himself.

It seemed they couldn't get enough of each other. When they reached their peak his knees buckled and they fell to the floor as if he'd been shot.

When the spasms passed and he could speak, Sergeant Wood asked, "Are you ok?"

Maxine laid there not moving with the water splashing on her exhausted body. She was panting as if she could hardly catch her breath. Sergeant Wood stood and reached down and helped her to her feet. Again, he asked her if she was alright.

"I have never gotten off this much in my life. I think I'd better take you back to your barracks before you screw me to death," Maxine panted.

"I'd never do a thing like that to you," Sergeant Wood laughed.

"Sure you wouldn't. What time do you want to go back to

the barracks?" she asked after they had dried off and were lying on the bed watching television.

"I have all night. Why? Do you have to go home to mommy and daddy?" he asked teasingly.

"No. I'll call them and say I'm staying overnight in Kansas City with a friend," Maxine said, excited by the idea of spending the night with him.

"Hey, you don't have to lie to your parents on my behalf. I'd just as soon go back to the barracks. Besides, they may be able to put two and two together, which would equal both Sergeant Wood and Maxine deciding to spend the same night in Kansas City. I sure in hell can't say I spent the night in downtown Leavenworth without giving a name because there ain't nothing to do there. And everyone knows I don't have a girl. Coincidence, maybe," he said.

"I don't care. I may never get another chance to be with you like this," Maxine said pouting.

"That's true, but what about your job?" Sergeant Wood asked, remembering she was a working woman.

"No problem. I'll change after I drop you off in the morning. My boss won't mind if I'm a little late for work," Maxine assured him.

"How often do you bring men to this hotel and seduce them? Then call your parents and tell them you have decided to spend the night with a friend. Especially on a weeknight when they know you have to be up early to go to work."

"Believe it or not this is the first time, but I'm sure my mom and dad won't make a big deal out of it this one time," Maxine said.

"No, it's best that we both go home tonight. It's already

eleven o'clock and you have to get up in the morning for work. You know you won't get any sleep if we stay here," Sergeant Wood said.

"Alright, but hold me for a little while longer," Maxine snuggled up to him.

Sergeant Wood held her close for a while and then said, "We'd better get going, Maxine. It's getting late."

After getting dressed Maxine pulled him down on the bed beside her and said, "Bob, please tell me this isn't the end for us. Assure me you'll continue calling me sometimes."

"I'll call you at work from time to time to see how you're doing. As far as these hotel rendezvous are concerned, we'll have to play them by ear," Sergeant Wood advised her.

"Why? Don't you like being with me?" Maxine asked.

"That's the problem. I don't want to end up enjoying being with you too much. After a couple of encounters like this one, I would be hooked on you like a junkie on dope. I can't allow that to happen. I'm already engaged to be married," Sergeant Wood said sincerely.

"Well, I'm already hooked on you. You're the type of man I've been looking for all my life. And now that I've found you, I'm not willing to let you walk out of my life this easily. One encounter, as you call it, ain't enough," Maxine said, trying to sound as if she was threatening him.

"So what're you saying?" Sergeant Wood asked, thinking his fear about allowing her to seduce him was coming to the light.

"Don't worry. There's no way I'm going to get you into any trouble. That would be the sure way of not getting to be with you again. And believe me, I'll do anything to be with you again," Maxine relieved his fears.

"Even if you have to wait until I choose the time and place?" Sergeant Wood asked.

"As long as you don't try to string me along until you get the hell out of Fort Leavenworth. I never thought I could get hooked on a guy after a couple of encounters. Live and learn my dad always says," Maxine quoted her dad.

Sergeant Wood and Maxine left the hotel room key on the night stand and locked the door behind them. He had her drop him off where she had picked him up. Sergeant Wood kissed Maxine good night and departed.

"Please call me tomorrow," Maxine called after him.

Sergeant Wood waved and continued on his way. He avoided the CQ by going through the back door of the barracks. He called her that following day at her job, but didn't talk too long. Maxine said she couldn't do anything right, because all she could think of was him.

"You'll survive," Sergeant Wood assured her.

No one said anything to him about Maxine over the next few days, so he figured she had kept her word.

When Sergeant Wood arrived at the 205th MP Company the unit basketball team had played three games and stood at two wins, one loss. After the first team practice Sergeant Wood made a prediction. 'I'm your savior. We won't lose another game this season,' Sergeant Wood told them. Although he said it in a joking manner, they took what he said to heart. They had never played with anyone as good as Sergeant Wood was.

At the end of Sergeant Wood's first basketball game with the 205th MP Company, there was no doubt in anyone's mind, he was the most dominant player at Fort Leavenworth. And because of that talent on the basketball court, everyone gave him nothing but praise. Also because of that talent on the basketball court, it would earn Sergeant Wood the envy of most every player in the intramural unit basketball league on post. His teammates included. His talent would eventually carry over into the civilian basketball world, via the Leavenworth Police Department (LPD), courtesy of none other than Lieutenant Colonel Ray N. Griffin.

Colonel Griffin was the coach of the USDB basketball team, the 205th MPs biggest rivals, so he'd heard of Sergeant Wood's basketball exploits but had never watched him play until the two teams met around mid-season. Colonel Gray and Captain Harris said the games between the USDB and the 205th MPs were the most important games of the season to them. It amounted to the jail guards against the cops. So they were ecstatic when Sergeant Wood led the team to victory over their rivals. As Colonel Gray and Captain Harris shook his hand he kept thinking, *man they're happier than pigs in shit.* Colonel Gray could hardly wait to rub their victory in Colonel Griffin's face.

"I told you we were going to whip your ass this year," Colonel Gray crowed.

"Yeah, but it took a renegade to do it. Isn't that black player Sergeant Wood? The one who gets under you guys skin because he's confrontational and danced with my daughter at the Horse Shoe Lounge club down town?" Colonel Griffin asked.

"It sure is, but I have to admit, Sergeant Wood doesn't make waves unless he feels he's being unfairly accused of misconduct on his part. Otherwise, he's one of the best damn troopers I've ever had in my command. As far as your daughter is concerned, I advised him to stay away from her because we don't allow race mixing here in Kansas. I believed him when he said he has no intention of seeing her again," Colonel Gray said.

"I hope he's serious because if I know my daughter, she's going to go after him just to spite me and her mother for getting involved in her personal affairs. She pitched a bitch when I told her not to embarrass us again by acting like white trash dancing with niggers, Colonel Griffin said shaking his head.

"I'll let you know if I hear anything. Say hello to Betty for me, will ya?" Colonel Gray said.

"Sure will Gaylord. You mind if I ask that boy to play for me with the LPD [Leavenworth Police department] team?" Colonel Griffin asked.

"Why not? That way you can keep an eye on him and Maxine yourself," Colonel Gray said.

Sergeant Wood was sitting in the bleachers cooling off before leaving the gym when Colonel Griffin walked over and said, "So you're the young, black buck sergeant who had the balls to mess with my daughter."

"Sir?" Sergeant Wood asked, confused because he'd never seen him before and didn't know who Colonel Griffin was.

"I'm Colonel Griffin," he introduced himself.

"It's a pleasure to meet you, sir. And as far as your daughter is concerned, the encounter was blown way out of proportion," Sergeant Wood said nervously.

"I believe you, Sergeant. That was a while ago, so let's drop it. Now that the small talk is out of the way, let me get to why I really wanted to talk to you. How would you like to play basketball for me downtown? I coach the Leavenworth Police Department's basketball team and we could use someone with your talent. And you're a cop, so there shouldn't be a problem with you being on the team. What do you say?" the colonel asked, putting his arms around his shoulder.

"It would be a pleasure, sir, that's if the games downtown don't interfere with my unit's games," Sergeant Wood said.

"I assure you, they won't. However, you may end up playing two games in one night. Besides, I'll be coaching the USDB when we kick the 205th ass the next time we meet," Colonel Griffin smiled.

"Wishful thinking, sir," Sergeant Wood responded and they both laughed.

That was how he met Lieutenant Colonel Griffin. Maxine was ecstatic to learn he was playing for her dad since she accompanied him to some of the police department's games. He rode to and from the games with Colonel Griffin. Sometimes Maxine and her mother accompanied them to the games. On the evening of the sixth game, the colonel called and said he was going to be a little late for the game that night. Maxine would be picking him up.

"I wouldn't be letting you two be alone if I didn't trust you," Colonel Griffin said before hanging up.

Yeah, I get your drift, sir, Sergeant Wood said after the line went dead. *The only thing you don't know is you're letting a reluctant fox into your hen house.*

Sergeant Wood was nervous as he waited for Maxine to pick him up in front of the barracks. He knew rumors would be started because she picked him up. He also knew her dad had provided her with the perfect opportunity she'd been longing for--to be alone with him. However, he was more worried about how he would react than what she would say or do because he hadn't been with a woman since their last encounter at the Holiday Inn. She called him constantly asking him to meet her someplace, but he always refused to meet her. Several of the guys in the unit were milling around outside of the barracks when Maxine stopped by to pick him up for the game.

When Maxine got out of the car, their eyes got big as silver dollars and their mouths dropped open as if they couldn't believe what they were seeing. Although they'd heard that Maxine was beautiful, it was the first time they'd gotten a close up look at her. She looked like a playmate centerfold; tall, tan, with the body to match, her curves swayed to the rhythm of her steps as she approached the barracks.

"Hello guys. I'm looking for Sergeant Wood," Maxine said in a sweet southern voice.

"Uh, uh, I think he's in the dayroom. I'll go check for you," Staff Sergeant Boone said looking her up and down.

Sergeant Wood had watched her arrival through the dayroom window. So he was coming out of the barrack as Staff Sergeant Boone was coming in. Sergeant Woods said, "Hi Maxine. You're a little early aren't you?"

"I can never be too early to pick up a hunk like you," Maxine said enjoying the wide-eyed expression on the faces of Sergeant Wood's fellow white soldiers.

"Uh, yeah. Let's go," Sergeant Wood said.

"You can't wait to get me alone, uh? This man's a real stud," Maxine winked at Staff Sergeant Greenway. She laughed when the look of lust turned to a look of hostility on his face. This was the sort of scenario that excited her.

The looks of hostility he and Maxine were getting from Staff Sergeant Boone and his cohorts weren't lost on Sergeant Wood. When they got in the car he asked her why she did shit like that.

"Maxine, you know Staff Sergeant Boone and those other

guys are going to make a big deal out of what you said, huh?" Sergeant Wood asked.

"That's why I did it. They're going to lie on me anyway, so I thought I would give them something to talk about. Anyway, by the time what I said gets to my dad it will be too outrageous to believe. My dad knows I like busting his balls, but I've never done anything stupid in public that embarrassed him too bad, except when I danced with you at the club. Did I ever tell you how pissed he was when Colonel Gray told him Sergeant Chandler said he saw me dancing with you?" Maxine asked.

"No, you never did. I wish you'd give me some type of warning when you're going to say something that makes rednecks want to whip my butt. At least that way I can play it off," Sergeant Wood said.

"There's nothing to play off. I meant what I said. You're a stud and I want you again," Maxine said reaching over and placing her hand in his lap. What she discovered there pleased her.

"Come on Maxine, I want to keep my mind on the game," Sergeant Wood protested. But basketball was the farthest thing from his mind at that moment.

"And I want to keep my hands on what has been on my mind for the last month or so. It's driving me crazy, being in the same car with you but not being able to touch you. And don't think I haven't noticed the bulge in your warm-ups whenever Mom goes to the games and we end up in the back seat together. You want me just as bad as I want you. Don't you?" Maxine asked giving him a gentle squeeze.

"You know I do. But we have to be even more careful than before. I'd really hate to get caught screwing up now that I know your Momma and Daddy so well. They're really nice people," Sergeant Wood said.

"Hey, you dumb shit. Don't you know anything? Now that my parents trust you they won't suspect a thing. They're always talking about how they wish you were white so they could get me married off to you. They just don't know. I'd marry you in a heartbeat if you asked me, just the way you are," Maxine said still holding on to him.

"Back off, lady. I'm already engaged. You know that. That day we shared at the hotel was for mutual satisfaction, nothing more," Sergeant Wood reminded her.

"I know that, mister. I may not marry you, but you won't leave Fort Leavenworth before we get together again," Maxine promised as if he had no say so in the matter.

"I know I'm going to regret this for the rest of my life, but I'll be off Wednesday, Thursday and Friday of next week. How about we get together Friday night?" Sergeant Wood asked.

"Promise?" Maxine asked.

"I'm a man of my word, most of the time anyway," Sergeant Wood said, remembering his conversation with Colonel Gray. "Just make sure you have a good alibi for spending the night in Kansas City. I still have three months left here and I don't want to get caught screwing up. The last month and a half have been the best since I have been here. Sergeant Chandler hasn't been riding my ass, and the PM has nothing but praise for me, thanks to basketball and your dad. Not to mention my squad is officially the best on the road. What more ...." but he didn't finish what he was going to say.

"What more could you ask for?" Maxine finished the sentence for him. She took his hand and placed it between her

PATRIOTISM

thighs so he could feel the dampness there. She shuddered and moaned as he inserted a finger into her wet love tunnel. The sensation was so intense she ran off onto the shoulder of the road. They both laughed as she regained control of the car.

Sergeant Wood had one of his most memorable games that night. He scored 45 points, had 12 rebounds, and ten blocked shots. Colonel Griffin was so pleased he said he was going to let Maxine pick him up for the remainder of the games they had left. He thought the colonel was kidding him, but to Sergeant Wood's surprise Maxine called the next day to confirm what the colonel had said was true. She was happier than a fly sucking on a fresh dropped turd. Colonel Griffin told her whatever it was she had said to him, to keep up the good work.

The following day at the station Staff Sergeant Greenway asked where he and Maxine had gone the previous day, and didn't believe Sergeant Wood when he told him she had picked him up for a basketball game.

"Sure," he said, and walked away with what he thought was a knowing smile.

Upon reporting for duty, he was told Master Sergeant Chandler wanted to see him. So up the stairs he went wondering what he had done this time to piss off his favorite sergeant. Master Sergeant Chandler waved him into his office before he even had a chance to knock on his office door.

"Have a seat, Sergeant Wood. What's this I hear about the colonel's daughter picking you up at the barracks yesterday?"

"Colonel Griffin was going to be late for the LPD game, so he told Maxine to pick me up. That's all there is to it," Sergeant Wood explained.

"I guess if I was to call the colonel he would confirm that?"

Master Sergeant Chandler asked.

"Yeah, he would," Sergeant Wood answered knowing Sergeant Chandler wouldn't dare call the colonel about something like that. Besides, he probably already knew and was screwing with him.

"You'd better hope this basketball shit lasts for the remainder of the time you have left here. Because if it doesn't, I'll still get my chance to bust your ass," Master Sergeant Chandler said.

"Sergeant Chandler, why are you so obsessed with the idea of busting me? I haven't done you any wrong." Sergeant Wood said.

"I just don't like you young, smart, black men who think they're somebody. And now this basketball crap is starting to make the troops think you're something special too. But I'm sure when Colonel Griffin hears you're telling everyone you're screwing his daughter, things will change," Master Sergeant Chandler said looking serious.

"I haven't told anyone anything like that and you know it," Sergeant Wood protested.

"Sure you have. I overheard you tell your whole squad that just the other day," Master Sergeant Chandler lied to get his point across.

"Do you really think my whole squad is going to lie on me knowing they'll have to face me every day they come to work?" Sergeant Wood asked, knowing they wouldn't.

"Those are minor details. I'm sure I can get Colonel Gray to assign you to another squad or section," Master Sergeant Chandler smiled.

When Sergeant Wood didn't respond, he was dismissed. He had to prevent this lie from circulating somehow. Sergeant

Wood knew by the time Colonel Griffin heard about it, it would be blown out of proportion. He also knew it would do no good to talk to Colonel Gray because he wouldn't believe anything he had to say once Master Sergeant Chandler put his two cents in. While he was checking his squad's patrol reports prior to going off swing shift a couple of nights later, he was told he had a phone call.

"Who would be calling me this time of night?" Sergeant Wood asked himself. He hoped nothing was wrong at home. He'd talked to his momma a couple of days ago and everything was fine.

"Sergeant Wood speaking, sir," he answered hesitantly.

"Sergeant Wood, this is Colonel Griffin. I'm having the police department team over to my quarters tomorrow night at 1900 hours and I wanted to know if you could make it," he said.

"Yes, sir, I can be there. I don't have to be on duty until 2300 hours tomorrow evening," Sergeant Wood answered.

"Good, I'll see you at 1900 hours here at my quarters. Do you know my address?" the colonel asked forgetting Sergeant Wood patrolled the post on a daily basis while on duty.

"Yes, sir, I've passed your quarters a number of times," Sergeant Wood said.

"Alright, I'll see you tomorrow night," Colonel Griffin said.

As soon as the colonel hung up, Sergeant Wood asked himself, *Is this the break I need to head Sergeant Chandler's little scheme off at the pass?* He knew if he waited until after the rumor had started, it would be twice as hard to convince the colonel it was a lie. It was a lot easier for a white officer to believe a white senior NCO, than a black buck sergeant. And then again, the colonel had seen that he treated Maxine with the utmost of respect. He never gave any indication he was interested in her sexually. Still, he wondered how the colonel would react upon hearing his daughter's name was about to be slandered throughout the MP company, possibly the whole post, and by a senior NCO at that. Sergeant Wood smiled to himself because he knew everything was going to be just fine.

Sergeant Wood arrived at the colonel's house as several of his LPD teammates pulled into the driveway. They all greeted him warmly and shook his hand. Although most of them were pure rednecks, Sergeant Wood thought they were a pretty good bunch of guys. What he didn't know was he was lucky as hell they never got wind that he may be sleeping with Maxine. Otherwise, he would have had hell to pay. Two of the cops were card carrying klan members. The first chance he got, he told Maxine what Master Sergeant Chandler had planned. She was irate.

"I'm going tell Daddy right now what the no good son of a bitch is up to," Maxine said, looking around the room for her dad.

"I think it'd be better if I told him what's about to happen. I don't want him thinking I'm using you to protect myself," Sergeant Wood said. Convincing her this was probably the best approach, he waited for an opportunity to get the colonel alone.

Although Sergeant Wood didn't want to admit it, Maxine was starting to grow on him a little. During the times her momma had accompanied them to and from the games she had attended, he and Maxine had snuck some intimate moments; which under normal circumstances would have easily resulted in sexual encounters had they been alone. However, she hadn't pushed the issue because she was abiding by his wishes that they wait until he was ready. They also shared plenty of heart-felt laughs. She turned out to be more than just a spoiled little girl who was out for her on satisfaction. Still he knew a relationship between them wouldn't work.

The whole team got ripped, that is everyone except Sergeant Wood, because he had to go on duty at 2300 hours. He didn't get a chance to talk to Colonel Griffin until just before he left the party.

"Sir, could I talk to you alone before I leave?" Sergeant Wood asked.

"Sure, son, come into the kitchen," the colonel said. Sergeant Wood followed him into the kitchen. Before Sergeant Wood could say anything, Colonel Griffin said, " If it's about that rumor that is supposed to get started about you and Maxi, forget it. Colonel Gray has already taken care of it. But I did wonder if you'd mention it before you left tonight."

"I didn't know you knew about it. When Sergeant Chandler talked to me yesterday he made it sound as if he had just thought of the idea. Do you know why he hate me so much, sir?" Sergeant Wood asked.

"When you get to be our age you'll understand what we're going through having to deal with you educated, determined young men. And by you being a young, black man, it's hard for you to realize the threat you present to Master Sergeant Chandler's position, as well as my own. Once you black, intelligent NCO's and officers reach our ranks in numbers, we'll be faced with the fact that not only can you deal with your own people, you'll be able to deal with white soldiers as well. And we feel that'll give you an advantage over us," Colonel Griffin explained.

"I have a long way to go before I can even think about being in his position, or obtaining his rank," Sergeant Wood said, also reading between the lines. The KKK mentality was coming in loud and clear, so Sergeant Wood understood exactly what Colonel Griffin was saying.

"I know, but do me a favor and don't say anything to him about our conversation. I know there's nothing going on between you and Maxi, and that's all that matters. Right?", the colonel asked.

"Right, sir," Sergeant Wood answered, and went to work with a smile on his face.

Sergeant Wood wondered how much longer he would be able to duck and dodge that determined, angry white man. Master Sergeant Chandler said he was just like the Canadian Mounties. He always gets his man.

You may get me my friend, but it won't be a walk through the park, Sergeant Wood said to an imaginary Master Sergeant Chandler.

After getting off duty several days later, Master Sergeant Chandler was on the desk talking to the desk sergeant, Staff Sergeant Tillman. As he was walking by, Sergeant Wood overheard Master Sergeant Chandler tell Staff Sergeant Tillman, "I'm going to get that black son of a bitch if it's the last thing I do in this man's army."

Sergeant Wood ignored the remark and walked on. He wanted to say, *Hey, Master Sergeant Chandler, Maxine sure has some good stuff.* He suppressed the remark because of Colonel Griffin's request not to antagonize him about his failed plan. It must have been taken care of because he hadn't heard anything more about the rumor that was supposed to have gotten started.

PATRIOTISM

Maxine called on Thursday to insure their date was still on for that coming Friday. Sergeant Wood assured her it was. On his first day off, he was sitting in the day room writing a letter to Miss Kwak when Specialist Five Jones came in and told him the commander wanted to talk to him.

"Am I in any kind of trouble?" Sergeant Wood asked.

"No, it's about your request to re-enlist for Vietnam," Specialist Five Jones said.

"Oh, good," Sergeant Wood said with a sigh of relief. He was off and running. Upon entering the commander's office and being told to have a seat, he could tell by the look on Captain Harris' face he probably wouldn't be able to re-enlist for Vietnam.

"Sergeant Wood, I know I told you earlier I'd take into consideration your request to re-enlist for Vietnam. However, I received this message," Captain Harris handed it to Sergeant Wood, "from the Department of the Army today saying they're cutting back on non-infantry personnel they're sending over there. I guess they're getting ready to wind down. Is there any place else you'd like to go? I hear your fiancée is waiting for you in Korea," Captain Harris said.

"Yes, sir, that's true. But as you know, I had my heart set on going to Vietnam upon completing my tour here. Is there a possibility at all that I may be allowed to re-enlist for Vietnam? If I miss this war and history repeats itself, I'll retire with twenty years in the service without seeing combat," Sergeant Wood said, ignoring the message in his hand.

"I'm afraid not. May I suggest you go back to Korea and get your fiancée before she finds someone who won't leave her behind when he leaves," the captain advised.

Sergeant Wood wanted to tell him his personal life was none of his business. What he said was, "I'll take your suggestion into consideration, sir." And that was the end of that conversation.

Sergeant Wood knew his only other choice for re-enlistment was Korea. The commander also knew that. He just didn't want to give Captain Harris the satisfaction of saying he knew what he was going to decide all along. Sergeant Wood went back to the day room and finished his letter to Miss Kwak. He omitted the part about the possibility of not going to Vietnam in hope the message from DA was premature. Also, he didn't want to get her hopes too high because if circumstances changed and he was allowed to re-enlist for Vietnam, he would.

That night he paid a visit to Sergeant Terrell's house. Sergeant Terrell had become a new person since he'd been taken off the road. He went from permanent CQ to unit training NCO. He'd built himself a reputation as being the best training NCO the unit ever had because he made the training realistic. Sergeant Terrell and Tracy were especially happy this night having learned Tracy was four months pregnant with their first child.

"What're you going to name him?" Sergeant Wood asked.

"You mean her," Tracy interjected. "Her name's going to be Shantey," Tracy said.

"And if it happens to be a boy?" Sergeant Wood asked.

"Sergeant Terrell, Jr., of course," she answered.

They all laughed.

The expression on Tracy's face changed and took on a serious one as she asked, "Bob, what's this I hear about you and that white girl, Maxine?"

"Hey, don't look at me. I didn't tell her anything. She heard that from Sergeant Hart," Sergeant Terrell said, defending himself because Sergeant Wood had shot a glance in his direction.

"What did you hear?" Sergeant Wood asked, turning his attention back to Tracy.

"That she's really hung up on you and is trying her best to get you into bed. Is that true?" Tracy asked suspiciously.

"From what everyone's been telling me it is, but she hasn't said anything to me about it," Sergeant Wood lied. "Besides, a white piece of ass ain't worth getting busted over. All these rumors started because she picks me up for the basketball games I play downtown. I guess they're jealous because they want to get in her pants and can't," he carried the lie further.

"Why don't you get a car of your own? Then she wouldn't have to pick you up," Tracy offered a solution.

"Because I'm saving as much money as I can so when Miss Kwak and myself get married, we won't start out in the hole. I'm not going to be here much longer anyway. I'm on my way back across the pond," Sergeant Wood said.

"I figured it had to be something like that. They hate it because you're one black brother, unmarried, who has his stuff together. They think every black man's mission in life is to screw a nasty white ass bitch. Still, you had better be careful. If she doesn't get what she wants, she might lie and say you did anyway, if you know what I mean. By the way, who are you seeing?" Tracy asked.

"Miss Kwak, every night in my dreams. I found out today I'll be seeing her sooner than I thought," Sergeant Wood said.

"Meaning?" Tracy asked when he paused a little too long to satisfy her curiosity.

"As you know, I intended to re-enlist for Vietnam so I could catch up with your old man in the medal department. Well, Captain Harris received a message from DA supposedly, instructing him not to let anyone in the unit re-enlist for Vietnam. It seems the only personnel they are allowing to re-enlist for Nam is infantry. So Korea is my only option as far as I'm concerned," Sergeant Wood explained.

"Good for you, or should I say for Miss Kwak?" Tracy laughed.

"Either way, I'm on my way out of here in the near future," Sergeant Wood said.

Maxine's name was not mentioned any more that evening. Sergeant Wood and Sergeant Terrell sat around shooting the bull and drinking until 2:00 a.m. before he bade him good night.

The next day Sergeant Wood called his parents to inform them of the possibility of his going back to Korea earlier than he had planned. They were happy for him, his momma more than anyone because her eldest son wouldn't be going to Vietnam. He wasn't as disappointed about not going to Vietnam as he had been in the past, even though he felt Captain Harris could've over rode the message from DA if he had wanted to. He said, *what the hell, if I can't go win medals I may as well be with the woman I love.*

The night he was to go out with Maxine he kept thinking to himself, if anyone found out about his little upcoming escapade with Maxine, his credibility would be shot to hell. And no one would enjoy that moment more than Master Sergeant Chandler. But Sergeant Wood had given his word that he would go out with her on Friday; therefore, he'd see it through. He just had to be extra careful.

PATRIOTISM

Sergeant Wood and Maxine made arrangements to meet outside of Kemper Arena after the Kansas City Kings/Golden State Warriors basketball game. He caught a ride with one of the guys from the USDB. He told him he wouldn't need a ride back because he was going to spend the night in Kansas City, seeing the sights.

During the game Sergeant Wood recognized at least twenty people from the fort, including Colonel Griffin and Maxine. During half time, he went to the snack stand to get a hot dog and a coke. Maxine must've been watching because she showed up at the snack stand before he was finished being served. A girl Sergeant Wood didn't recognize was with her.

"Hi, Bob. I would like for you to meet my friend Glenda Sue Evans. She's my alibi for tonight," Maxine introduced her.

"Hello, Glenda," he smiled, extending his hand.

"My, my. Maxi told me you were gorgeous, but I never thought ...." Glenda didn't get a chance to finish what she was going to say.

Maxine said, "You can stop creaming in your pants Glenda, he's all mine."

"He looks as if he could take care of the both of us with no problem," Glenda crooned, still holding his hand.

Sergeant Wood managed to grab his coke and hot dog with his free hand and said, "Hey, I'll see you foxy ladies in the parking lot after the game. You're driving your car, aren't you?" he asked Maxine.

"Of course I am. I'm parked in the west parking lot," Maxine answered.

"And your daddy?" Sergeant Wood asked, not forgetting the colonel was also at the game.

389

"Oh, you don't have to worry about him. He drove his own car to the game, and is going straight home after the game is over," Maxine smiled.

"Alright, until then," Sergeant Wood said, pulling his hand away from Glenda who was still holding on.

"I'll see you too," Glenda flirted as he walked off.

Sergeant Wood waved and kept going. The game turned out to be boring because the Kings blew the Warriors out, winning by 40 points.

After what seemed an eternity, the clock showed the Warriors some mercy by expiring. Sergeant Wood watched Maxine and Colonel Griffin disappear into the crowd. He waited until the arena was almost completely empty before leaving. He wanted to make sure he gave Colonel Griffin enough time to leave the parking lot before he made contact with Maxine. When he reached the parking lot he made sure Maxine's daddy was nowhere in sight. After making sure the coast was clear he made a beeline to where Maxine was parked. She and Glenda were sitting on the hood of her car giggling like crazy. He wondered if he was the cause of their laughter.

"Hey, can I catch a ride with you lovely ladies?" Sergeant Wood asked as he approached the car.

"My Daddy told me never to pick up tall, dark handsome strangers. There's no telling what they may do to me. He worries so much about me," Maxine said, pretending to be frightened.

"I wouldn't do anything you wouldn't approve of," Sergeant Wood said with a wink.

They oohed and aahed upon hearing that. "You could ride with me anytime, big guy," Glenda said, giving Maxine a girlish push.

"So, where do we go from here?" Sergeant Wood asked.

From the arena they stopped by Glenda's boyfriend's house and picked him up. His name was Sam Goddard, but to Sergeant Wood, it was asshole. They must've stopped at half the clubs in Kansas City. It would've been a very enjoyable evening if not for Sam.

As soon as Sam got in the car, he said, "I've never been on a double date with a big black buck before."

"Stick around, you may learn something," Sergeant Wood responded.

All night he made snide remarks about what he'd heard about black guys. They all had rhythm. They all could sing and dance; they all could play sports, etc., etc., etc.

Sergeant Wood played the remarks off until several bars later when Sam asked Maxine, "Maxi, how can you take all that big, black dick in your tight little white twat?"

"Sam, you're out of line," Maxine protested.

Sergeant Wood said, "Why, Sam, I didn't know you were into watching dicks. However, I've noticed whenever I go to the bathroom, you follow me. Have you seen anything you like? Are you sure you're not jealous because you want to get your hands on it, but you know you can't? I've heard about you white boys sucking each other off, and other weird shit like that."

Sam didn't respond. He grabbed Glenda and dragged her onto the dance floor.

"I guess that'll shut that stupid bastard up," Maxine said after they had left the table.

"Yeah. But what if he's pissed off enough to tell your daddy we were together tonight. Then what?" Sergeant Wood asked, knowing jealous people will do anything for revenge, especially to a black man messing around with a white woman.

"You don't have to worry about him. Glenda and I'll see to that," Maxine said in a tone of voice he'd never heard her use before.

"Damn, you sound as if you're planning on killing good ole Sam or something," Sergeant Wood said.

"We may not kill him, but he'd wish he was dead after we got through telling everything we know about him," Maxine said.

"That bad, is it?" Sergeant Wood asked.

"Yeah, so you see, you don't have anything to worry about. Believe me," Maxine assured him.

"Let's hope not. I've had my fill of good old Sam anyway. What do you say we split this scene so we can be alone?" Sergeant Wood asked.

"Best suggestion I've heard all night. As soon as they finish dancing we'll drop them off and go to my hotel room," Maxine smiled at him.

"You have a room already?" Sergeant Wood asked, surprised.

"Yes, I got it before we went to the game. I don't half-step when it comes to something I want," Maxine said with a wicked smile.

"So I've noticed," Sergeant Wood said.

When Sam and Glenda returned to the table, Maxine told them she was ready to call it a night. They all agreed it was a good idea that they go their separate ways. Glenda was clearly upset at Sam's behavior. Maxine dropped them off at Sam's house and she and Sergeant Wood went to the hotel. Sergeant Wood never thought it was possible, but the sex between them this time was even better than their first encounter because this time it was not just having sex. They gave themselves to each other completely, body, soul and being. He found himself wishing the encounter could last for the remainder of the time he had remaining at Fort Leavenworth, but he knew it'd never work.

That morning after getting dressed to return to the fort, Sergeant Wood took her into his arms and said, "Maxine, as much as I hate to tell you this, I feel I owe it to you. This is the last time I'm going to see you like this. We're becoming too deeply involved in a relationship that has no chance of working out. You turned out to be a lot sweeter than I thought you were. I caught myself secretly wishing last night would never end. I can no longer control myself when we're together. And as I said before, I can't allow that to happen." Sergeant Wood cussed himself mentally the whole time he was talking.

"I know deep down what you're saying is true. But dammit, I can't help it if you're everything I ever wanted in a man. When I'm with you, I feel like a woman should be made to feel. You're courteous, kind, and you still manage to get your message across that you're very much a man. It's as if you are saying, I'm the greatest and if you don't believe it, try me. That's a real turn on. All I ask is don't shut me completely out of your life. Lets continue playing the little games we always play going to and from the basketball games," Maxine begged.

"That's something else I wanted to talk to you about. After last night I don't think it's a good idea for me to continue riding with you to and from the games. So, I've decided to make arrangements with someone on the team to pick me up for the remainder of the games we have left," Sergeant Wood said sadly.

"Bob, please don't do this. I promise I won't try anything. I won't even touch your hand if you don't want me to, but please don't shut me out. My mom is always saying how my face glows whenever you're around. I would hate for her to notice the glow is gone," Maxine said.

"And your daddy? What does he have to say about this glow I put on your face?" Sergeant Wood asked, already knowing the answer.

"He's just like you. He keeps reminding me I would only get hurt to fall for a black man," she answered.

"I suggest you listen to your daddy because he's right," Sergeant Wood agreed with her daddy's logic. To get himself out of the situation without hurting her any further, he said, "I'll tell you what I'm willing to do. I'll continue riding to the games with you to keep everything normal, but no hanky-panky. If you so much as look like you're horny, I'll never set foot in your car again. Agreed?" he asked, knowing he had no intention of keeping his promise.

"Agreed," Maxine grinned and gave him a big kiss. She dropped him off near the gym. But before pulling off she said, "I love you, you know."

"Yeah, I know," Sergeant Wood responded and walked away with mixed emotions.

Sergeant Wood wanted nothing more at the moment than to tell her they would spend every chance they got together. But wise men piss with the wind and not against it because the piss would blow back in your face. Also, for the first time since he'd been back in the United States, he felt he was doing Miss Kwak wrong by banging every woman who would put out to him, even though the "all" he referred to was Gina and Maxine. It had to end. No one cared where he spent the night upon his arrival back to the barracks, so all went well.

When Sergeant Wood went on duty that afternoon it was business as usual. The only difference in his routine was he kept thinking of how he was slowly losing control of his emotions where women were concerned. He felt the head in his pants was starting to take control of his senses. Maxine was sweet, but he had to let her go. Quit cold turkey. Sergeant Harper, newly promoted, noticed something other than the normal day-to-day bullshit was bothering him this day.

"What's wrong, Sergeant Wood? You look as if something is bugging the hell out you. Want to talk about it?" Sergeant Harper asked.

"I appreciate the concern buddy, but it's something I have to work out on my own. Besides, it's not that serious anyway. Thanks just the same," Sergeant Wood put him off.

Upon completion of his shift that night, Sergeant Wood sat in his room with the lights out drinking a beer. His daddy had told him that his granddaddy often used this type of semi-solitude to do some serious soul searching whenever he had a tough decision to make. While sitting there in the dark, he weighed the pros and cons of being around Maxine. Needless to say, the cons outweighed the pros by a wide margin. There was only one answer. If he was serious about getting Maxine out of his system, he had to break all ties with her. If she showed up at his games fine, but he wouldn't associate with her in any form or fashion. He would continue being sociable toward her when her momma and daddy were around, but nothing more. If she showed up at the barracks, the conversation wouldn't leave the barracks area. Therefore, his conclusion was hands off.

After his deep soul searching, he had no doubt that Maxine was a fling of the past. Nothing, or no one, was going to come between him and Miss Kwak. Sergeant Wood made up a lie to tell Colonel Griffin as to why he arranged to ride to the games with someone other than Maxine. Colonel Griffin didn't even question him because he had a gut feeling that he knew the real reason the arrangements had been made. Sergeant Wood had no idea of the hell he would catch in the near future because of his decision.

Chapter 10
ON THE RUN AGAIN

    Sergeant Wood stood by his decision not to associate with Maxine on a personal level. He continued to be cordial with her and her mother when they attended the Leavenworth Police Department games.

    Whenever Maxine made covert moves to get close to him he would draw away from her. It was so subtle the average person would never pick up on it. Colonel Griffin had an idea of what was going on, but his internal racist feelings wouldn't let him admit to himself that his one and only daughter had fallen for a black man. So with Colonel Griffin's denial to himself and Sergeant Wood's ability on the basketball court, it brought him time to prepare mentally for the coming storm. The beginning of that storm arrived after the post championship game at Fort Leavenworth, Kansas.

    The unit intramural basketball tournament on post started on a Monday and Sergeant Wood entered it without a care in the world. He hadn't talked to Maxine personally since he had banned her from his life three weeks earlier. She had called the barracks several times, but he would always tell whoever answered the phone to tell her he wasn't in. He told them she was a nutty, white sounding broad he had met at the Web Night Club one weekend. The guys who answered the phone never realized it was Maxine they were telling Sergeant Wood wasn't in, otherwise his troubles would have started a lot sooner than it did. A part of the reason Maxine didn't go by Sergeant Wood's barracks since he had arranged transportation with a teammate was because it would have removed any doubt that she considered them an item, which would have caused a major scandal and embarrassment for her parents. However, the main reason she stayed away form his barracks was because she held out hope that by not pressuring him he would eventually see her again.

Sergeant Wood told Colonel Griffin and the rest of his Leavenworth Police Department teammates that during the tournament on post he would have to miss their games because they conflicted with his games with his unit, which they understood. Especially Colonel Griffin since he was the coach of the USDB unit basketball team.

As expected, the championship game came down to the 205th MP Company and the United States Army Disciplinary Barracks (USDB). It seemed everyone on post was at the game, including Maxine. She was waiting for Sergeant Wood out in the lobby of the gym when he arrived.

"What gives, Bob?" she asked, looking sad and pissed off at the same time. "I've been calling you off and on since I dropped you off three weeks ago. And they say you're never in. Have you been avoiding me?"

"Look Maxine, you know why I never answered your calls. Just standing here talking to you right now is making all kinds of weird thoughts go through my head. You know as well as I do what we started was doomed from the beginning. So I'm no longer willing to pretend we can somehow make it work. Now if you'll excuse me, I have a championship to win." He left Maxine standing in the gym lobby with tears in her eyes.

Prior to their warm-up drills he went over to wish Colonel Griffin luck. "I hope you know we're going to kick your ass tonight," Colonel Griffin said with a laugh.

"I hate to tell you this coach, but as good as I feel tonight, your boys are in big trouble," Sergeant Wood said as he shook the colonel's hand.

And so they were. Sergeant Wood scored 46 points, grabbed 17 rebounds, and had 9 blocked shots. He was voted most valuable player of the tournament. Everyone in the gym, including the USDB fans, cheered his every basket, rebound, and blocked shot. The USDB was never in the game, losing by 27 points. Captain Harris was happier than a crooked politician accepting a bribe as he accepted the championship trophy.

"Sergeant Wood thinks he's PCSing in the near future. He doesn't know he was just flagged for a couple of more basketball seasons," Captain Harris said.

Everyone cheered and applauded. After all the hoopla was over, everyone congratulated him on an outstanding game and season. When Maxine got her turn to congratulate him, she whispered, "I'm not going to let you go this easy. Sorry, I love you."

At that moment Sergeant Wood knew life for him for the remainder of the time he had left at Fort Leavenworth was not going to be a very pleasant situation or experience. Still, his mind was made up. He would not see Maxine again regardless of how much hell he caught. When Master Sergeant Chandler shook his hand, Sergeant Wood couldn't help but think how happy that white man was going to be after Maxine let the cat out of the bag.

Sergeant First Class Hart said, "I guess I was wrong about you, Sergeant Wood. This should keep you in high standing for a while."

"Yeah, a very short while," Sergeant Wood said louder than he had intended.

"What?" Sergeant First Class Hart asked, not sure of what Sergeant Wood had said.

"Oh, nothing. I was just thinking about the game," Sergeant Wood lied.

Captain Harris had promised them a party after they won the championship, and a party they had. Being they were pretty much in the same line of work, the USDB team was invited to join them. There was very little jealousy among them because guys on both teams played with and against each other on a daily basis at the post gym. They had an alcoholic blast of a time. Just before the party ended, everyone agreed the MVP should propose the final toast of the night.

Since he was feeling no pain and had watched pro athletes accept their accolades, Sergeant Wood stood up on unsteady legs and said, "What the hell. I propose this toast to my teammates who helped to make this moment possible. And to Captain Harris who never had any doubt in our ability to win it all, after we won it. To the USDB team who motivated us, because we knew if anyone could beat us it was you guys, because you guys have an excellent team. And last, but no way least, I would like to personally thank Colonel Griffin for all he has taught me about the game since I've been playing for him."

Everyone cheered and clapped. They then proceeded to half drown Sergeant Wood with cans of beer. He was given a four-day pass, Thursday to Sunday, for being selected MVP of the post intramural tournament by the commander of the 205th MP Company. The way they carried on you would think the government actually paid them for winning the championship.

Sergeant Wood caught the first bus leaving the following morning and went home to show off his new trophies. Little Harvey was so proud of him as he sat the two new trophies on the shelf along side of the others. Bob voided Gina the whole time he was home because he didn't want to give her any hope he was still interested in her. The day before he was due to return to Fort Leavenworth, he and his daddy went to Jim's Cafe for a few drinks.

After getting a couple under his belt, Bob said, "Daddy, I think I may have a problem when I get back to Fort Leavenworth. I need your advice on how to handle the situation."

"Women problems again?" his daddy asked, eyebrows raised.

"Yeah. This time it's a real lulu," Bob said.

"Go ahead and ask, but I can't promise you it'll be what you want to hear," his daddy warned.

"I've been screwing this white colonel's daughter. Her name is Maxine. She's twenty-four years old. Anyway, three weeks ago I told her we were finished because if we got caught together, I could kiss my stripes and reputation good-bye. She agreed with me then, but after Wednesday's game she said she loved me and wasn't going to let me go that easy. It wouldn't be all that bad if I didn't know her parents so well," he said.

"How well do you know them?" his daddy asked.

"As I told y'all in the letters, her father coaches the police team I play with. Her momma went to the games with us sometimes. Hell, they've had me over to their house a couple of times. Once for a party he gave for the Leavenworth Police basketball team, which I'm a member of, and again for a Bar-B-Q. I know if she tells them we're lovers, they're going to feel

I stabbed them in the back. Colonel Griffin told me he doesn't trust soldiers, regardless of color, when it comes to his daughter. However, he trusted me because he thought I was a man of my word. And my word was I would under no circumstances screw his daughter, no matter what she said or did to tempt me," Bob said.

His daddy suppressed a laugh and said, "If those people are stupid enough to think you can throw two horny young people together and don't think they're going to screw each other's brain out, they're crazy. Hell, she's older than you are. Why is she still living at home anyway?"

"She's so spoiled I guess she's afraid to strike out on her own," Bob said. He then filled his daddy in on everything that had occurred between them, including how good she was in bed. He also told him his belief that Colonel Griffin was a racist at heart when it came to his daughter and black men.

This time his daddy did laugh. He laughed long and hard. When he finally regained his composure, his daddy asked, "How much time you have left there?"

"Just a month or so. As soon as I can re-enlist, I'm on my way back to Korea," Bob said.

"So what's wrong with screwing her until you leave?" his daddy asked.

"I'm afraid if I continue on the present trend, I may mess around and get pussy whupped. I can't let that happen," Bob said seriously.

"Well, I see three options open to you: 1.) you can keep screwing her until you leave; 2.) you can try and lead her on to believe you two will get together again before you leave. She waited once maybe she would be willing to wait again; or 3.)

don't mess with her at all and take your chances. What do you think is going to happen if you don't mess with her again?" his daddy asked.

"She'll probably tell her daddy what has been going on between us," Bob said, concerned about losing his stripes.

"That shouldn't be too much of a problem. If he does threaten to do anything to you, tell him you'll let everyone in the state of Kansas know his daughter been screwing a black man. If he feels as you believe he does, that's the last thing he wants to get out. I'm afraid that's all of the advice I can give you," his daddy concluded.

"Hmm. I don't want to mess with her anymore in any form or fashion. I guess I'll have to deal with her old man. Thanks, daddy," Bob said.

"You make sure you keep in touch so we'll know you're ok," his daddy said.

Upon returning to Fort Leavenworth, his squad had only one day of work left before they were to go on break.

"I see you got back in time to go on break," Master Sergeant Chandler commented the following day. When Sergeant Wood didn't respond, he continued. "Sergeant Harper showed a lot of potential. If I were you, I wouldn't leave him in charge too often. You may return one day and no longer have a squad," he warned.

"That may be so, Sergeant Chandler, but it would still make me proud to say I was the one who trained him," Sergeant Wood said.

"You think you have an answer for everything don't you?" Master Sergeant Chandler snarled, becoming angry.

"No, I don't Sergeant Chandler," Sergeant Wood said.

Sergeant Wood turned and walked away. He felt he had to confide in someone there at Fort Leavenworth about the predicament he was facing. So that afternoon after getting off shift, he stopped by the training office and asked Sergeant Terrell if he would like to go to the Webb with him that night. He wanted to talk to him about something that had been bothering him lately. Sergeant Terrell agreed to pick him up at eight.

"Man, you wouldn't believe how cranky Tracy's become since she found out she's pregnant. She was pissed when I told her I was going out with you tonight. She finally gave in because she knows you don't go around chasing these loose-assed women," Sergeant Terrell said after picking him that evening.

After a couple of stiff drinks, Sergeant Wood and Sergeant Terrell started to feel pretty good. Every time Sergeant Wood attempted to tell Sergeant Terrell about Maxine, some woman would catch his eye and he was off and running asking her to dance. Thanks to Sergeant Terrell, they were dancing with every woman in the club that would dance with them. They were having so much fun they didn't bother to notice the time.

When last call for alcohol was given, Sergeant Terrell remembered he had a pregnant wife at home. "Holy shit, man. What time is it?" he asked, knowing he should've been home at least a couple of hours ago.

"It's one forty-five a.m., my friend. Are you in trouble with the little lady when you get home?" Sergeant Wood asked, already knowing the answer before he asked the question.

"Yeah, but don't worry. I can handle Tracy. I just remembered you wanted to get something off your chest," Sergeant Terrell said.

Sergeant Wood was about to tell Sergeant Terrell what he

wanted to talk to him about when two of the ladies they had danced with on several occasions throughout the night came over to their table.

"How'd you guys like to come over to my house for a night cap?" the woman who had introduced herself as Cathy asked.

"I appreciate the offer, Cathy, but we have to get up early in the morning. We have to be going," Sergeant Wood said, declining the offer.

"I told you these guys are married," her friend Maggie said as if she'd confirmed the answer to a million-dollar question.

"It's not that. We're military policeman and we have to be at work in three hours," Sergeant Wood lied. "We wouldn't be able to do you ladies justice in such a short span of time. When we do something, it has to be right. And that includes when we're satisfying the ladies. What do you ladies say about tomorrow night? The same time same station? Just the four of us," Sergeant Wood said.

Maggie was still unconvinced. "Come on, Cathy. He's lying through his teeth."

"Hey, wait a minute, lady. We're trying to be straight with you ladies. And you start talking a lot of smack. If you don't believe what we're saying, you bring your ass up on post tomorrow and run one of my damn red lights," Sergeant Terrell interjected.

This brought Maggie around to their way of thinking. "Alright, but if you guys stand us up tomorrow night, you'd better hope you never run across me again." She sounded serious as hell.

"Come on, lady, lighten up. If we wanted to fight, we'd have volunteered for Vietnam," Sergeant Wood said, taking Cathy by the arm and escorting her out to her car.

Sergeant Wood heard Maggie tell Sergeant Terrell she could walk just fine without his help. After seeing the ladies off, they laughed long and hard.

"We make a good team," Sergeant Terrell beamed.

"Yeah, but it's time you went home to your wife. I'm sure she's worried about you," Sergeant Wood reminded him.

"You know something, Sergeant Wood. I really like you. You always know where your priorities lie," Sergeant Terrell said seriously.

"You may change your mind when you find out what I wanted to talk to you about. But it's too late tonight. So let's get our late asses home before we get into trouble for real. I'll call tomorrow to see if it's safe for me to come over to your crib," Sergeant Wood kidded.

"Hey, brother, a man's home is his castle. And he does whatever he pleases," Sergeant Terrell said.

"Not when there's a pregnant queen in it," Sergeant Wood reminded him. They both laughed and left the club. *I guess I'll have to wait until tomorrow to get this crap off my chest,* Sergeant Wood said to himself as he staggered into the barracks.

The following day Sergeant Wood called Sergeant Terrell's house and Tracy answered the phone. "Hello, Tracy. This is Sergeant Wood. I called to see if it's safe to come over and visit you good folks."

"Yeah, you can come over. I wanted to talk to you anyway," Tracy said.

"I'll see you guys in a few," Sergeant Wood said, hanging up. He could tell by the tone of her voice she blamed him for Sergeant Terrell's lateness.

PATRIOTISM

Sergeant Wood wondered what their reaction was going to be when he told them he was screwing Maxine. Sergeant Terrell would probably say a man gotta do what a man gotta do. His image as a strong, young black man who couldn't be tempted by white flesh would be blown all to hell as far as Tracy was concerned. Especially after all the shit he'd talked about how stupid black men were to mess with white women, and how unjust white men are when black men mess with their women. He wished he could tell Sergeant Terrell without Tracy knowing, but he knew there was no way he could tell one without the other finding out. So he decided to hell with it. He'd tell no one. They would find out when everyone else did.

As soon as Sergeant Wood walked through the door Tracy was all over him, wanting to know everything they'd done that night. After listening to Sergeant Wood repeat what her husband had told her about their escapade the previous night, Tracy seemed satisfied to know her husband had not lied to her. Sergeant Wood lied to Sergeant Terrell and said what he wanted to talk to him about worked itself out. They spent a pleasant evening together.

Sergeant Wood's first evening of duty after his break, he was checking the post park/picnic area, which was off limits during the hours of darkness because of its isolated location. Several years before Sergeant Wood's arrival at Fort Leavenworth a couple of dependent wives were raped in the area on separate occasions. They were looking for a quiet place to think about what was happening in their lives, and what they could do to make things better. Instead their lives were ruined by a couple of deviates of society. So he personally checked this area every swing shift and midnight shift before getting off duty. Being this was a swing shift he normally checked it between 2100-2200 hours. This evening he found a young woman there in the area pondering the unfairness of life, and wondering why she was chosen to desire a man she knew she could never have.

Sergeant Wood had told her of this routine when they were still on speaking terms. She parked in the woods across from the park and watched the regular patrol make his security check at 2045 hours. When the taillights of the patrol car disappeared she pulled her Trans-AM into position and waited. She was so deep in thought, Sergeant Wood's patrol car was upon her before she realized the lights illuminating the darkness was no longer that of the full shimmering moon. She looked in her rearview mirror and watched as the patrol car approached. She braced herself for the confrontation she was about to have with the only man in the world who'd ever rejected her, and it didn't matter that he was right about the relationship being doomed from the start.

Sergeant Wood recognized the car as soon as it came into view of his patrol car headlights. The standard operating procedure was he was supposed to notify the MP station that he had a privately owned vehicle (POV) parked in an unauthorized area during the hours of darkness. But he wouldn't notify anyone about this car or this woman. The last thing he needed was to have it reported to Master Sergeant Chandler or Colonel Gray he was seen talking to Maxine in an unauthorized area on post and hadn't reported it, but it was a chance he felt he had to take. Because it would've been worse if he reported the car and his back-up arrived in time to see him and Maxine arguing, and it was reported she was highly upset about something he had said or done to her. Sergeant Wood knew Maxine would skip try-

PATRIOTISM

ing to entice him sexually. Instead she would remove the kid gloves and make demands and threats if he didn't give in to her wonton desire. *Well, let get this crap over with,* he said exiting his patrol car.

"Good evening, Miss Griffin. Do you realize that you're parked in an off limits area during the hours of darkness? I'm going to have to ask you to move on," Sergeant Wood said.

"Why the hell are you being so damn formal with me, Bob? I'm the same white girl you tried to screw to death a couple of weeks ago, or have you forgotten?" Maxine asked.

"This has nothing to do with you or me. You're parked in an off limits area during the hours of darkness, so I have to ask you to leave," Sergeant Wood explained seriously.

"Fuck you, Sergeant Wood. What're you going to do? Call for backup? And let everyone in your company find out I accused you of screwing me, and then throwing me aside like a used up whore? Huh? So what you gonna do, asshole?" Maxine asked getting out of her car.

"Look Maxine, I know you're upset because I won't see you anymore, but do you really want to hurt your parents with the knowledge you've been messing around with a black man? You know as well as I do if it gets out the USDB commander's daughter has been screwing around with a black man, they're going to be humiliated. You know how they feel about interracial affairs," Sergeant Wood tried to reason with her.

"Remember when you said I seemed like a spoil little bitch that would do anything to get my way, regardless of who gets hurt? Well guess what Mr. Smart-ass, you were right. If you don't see me again I'm going to tell my parents what happened between us, and I'm going to enjoy the look of horror on their faces when they hear their darling sweet daughter has been violated by a big, black brute. My dad, the colonel, will fuss and cuss for a while but afterward he's going to be after your ass. So what is it going to be? My way or yours?" Maxine finished her hands on her hips.

"You wanna know something, Maxine? I've been threatened about something I've supposedly done from day one since I've been in the damn army. One more threat doesn't mean shit to me. Look, I like you okay, but you know as well as I do black men and white women don't mix in Kansas. Besides, I told you I was engaged to be married upon my return to Korea," Sergeant Wood said.

"You just don't like me enough to be with me, right? Is that it, black boy? You sure as hell weren't thinking about your little fiancée when you were screwing me," Maxine spat the words at him.

"As I told you before Maxine, no one can intimidate me, and that goes for you too. If you want to make your momma and daddy the butt of the jokes that'll be told at the officer's club and around post because of this union, you go right ahead and tell them. Tell the world, but I'm going to deny it to my dying day. Unless you have pictures, it's your word against mines," Sergeant Wood informed her.

"My daddy is no fool. He suspected something was going on between us and you got spooked, and that was why you stopped letting me pick you up for the remainder of your basketball games downtown. He asked me if we were messing around after you made that decision, and of course I said no. But I think because of the disappointment he could hear in my voice, he didn't really believe me. And my poor Mom has this woman's intuition thing going for her. She knows we had something going on, but the poor dear is deathly afraid to say anything or ask me about it. Pictures or no pictures, you know everyone's going to believe me," Maxine gloated.

"I'm not stupid, Maxine. I know everyone's going to believe you, especially since you have Glenda and that asshole Sam in your corner. But you know what? They didn't see us do anything," Sergeant Wood said.

"I don't need Glenda's or that asshole's help. I'm going to help my dad burn your smart black ass," Maxine said.

"Unless I do what? Start sleeping with you again? If I did that I'd have no say so in the running of my life. No deal, Maxine, I couldn't live like that. Do what you have to do," Sergeant Wood said.

"Bob, you know I would rather not do this but I'll be goddamned if I'm going to let you treat me like a piece of meat you can use and then throw away at your whim. Because I do love you, I'll give you one more chance to change your mind," she said.

"You're parked in an off limit area, Miss Griffin. I have to ask you to leave. Go find yourself a nice white junior officer and make everyone happy," Sergeant Wood said.

"You black, son-of-a-bitch. Fuck you and your junior white officer. They're nothing but a bunch of suck ass wimps. You're going to regret the day you crossed me. The next time I see you it'll probably be in your jail cell at that USDB," Maxine said as she was getting into her car. When she pulled off, she spun her tires shooting dirt and gravel over Sergeant Wood and his patrol car.

"Oh well," Sergeant Wood said brushing the dirt off of his

uniform. He only had a little over a week before his re-enlistment date, and he would be on his way out of Fort Leavenworth and en-route to Korea.

Two days later Sergeant Terrell stopped by Sergeant Wood's room prior to him going on duty. "Hey, what's up, lady killer? You look like you saw a ghost," Sergeant Wood commented when Sergeant Terrell walked into his room.

"I just heard something in Sergeant Hart's office that blew me away," Sergeant Terrell said wide-eyed.

"Oh yeah. What?" Sergeant Wood asked, not ready for the bomb about to be laid on him.

"Sergeant Chandler stopped by Sergeant Hart's office and I overheard him say Colonel Griffin called Colonel Gray and said you've been screwing his daughter. And if that's true, they're going to set you up for a fall. Have you been screwing that white broad?" Sergeant Terrell asked, as if what Master Sergeant Chandler had said was the biggest lie he'd ever heard a white man tell.

Sergeant Wood tried his best to look surprised that anyone would accuse him of such a thing. "Where did they get such a bald faced lie?" he asked, avoiding Sergeant Terrell's question.

"I don't know. Sergeant Chandler must've realized that I was in the adjoining office, or Sergeant Hart told him, anyway they left the office to finish their conversation. That's what you wanted to talk to me about the other night, wasn't it?" Sergeant Terrell dared Sergeant Wood to admit it.

"Thanks for the inside info, but I haven't done anything wrong. I guess they're getting desperate to land something on me. But to tell an outright lie like this is bullshit," Sergeant Wood said.

"I guess you're right. Watch yourself, man. I'd hate for them to get you the way they got me. Tracy told you you'd better keep an eye on her," Sergeant Terrell reminded him.

"Yeah," Sergeant Wood said, surprised it had taken Maxine two days to spill her guts.

Upon reporting for duty Sergeant Wood was told by Sergeant Harper Colonel Gray wanted to see him after guard-mount.

"Do you know what it's about?" Sergeant Wood asked.

"Nope, just passing on the message," Sergeant Harper answered.

After getting his squad on the road, Sergeant Wood made his way upstairs. He could feel the palms of his hands sweating. A knot of fear was tightening his stomach muscles. For the first time in his life he felt he was in a situation he may not be able to get himself out of, because he was saddled with the belief that any black man stupid enough to mess with a white woman in a racist state was doomed in the long run, and got what he deserved if he was caught. The stairs seemed twice as high as usual as he mounted them one by agonizing one. As he was passing Master Sergeant Chandler's office, he was called in.

"I thought it was Colonel Gray who wanted to see me?" Sergeant Wood asked, trying to show the same level of confidence he'd always shown in the past.

"He does. I wanted to let you know what it's about. It seems word somehow got out you've been screwing the lieutenant colonel's daughter," Master Sergeant Chandler informed him.

"And who started a stupid rumor like that?" Sergeant Wood asked trying to sound upset.

"From what I heard it was Maxine herself who started that

stupid rumor," Master Sergeant Chandler said with a smile. "I do believe we have your smart ass now. Why, because you lied to the colonel. And he doesn't like liars," Master Sergeant Chandler said.

The muscles in Sergeant Wood's stomach tightened another notch as the realization set in that he'd finally given the establishment something they could possibly use against him. Although everything Maxine told them was true, like he told her, he'd deny it to the bitter end.

"I don't know why she'd say something like that when she knows it's a lie," Sergeant Wood said, hoping he sounded convincing. "I have enough problems of my own, I don't need anyone else's help."

Master Sergeant Chandler was somewhat surprised by Sergeant Wood's reaction. It was the first time he'd heard him so emotional when defending himself. Master Sergeant Chandler knew right away it was a defensive move on Sergeant Wood's part.

"You sound upset about this, Sergeant Wood. Not your usual cocky self, huh? What's wrong, buck sergeant, hit a nerve?" Master Sergeant Chandler asked.

"If you don't mind, I'd like to get this over with so I can get back on the road," Sergeant Wood said, ignoring his question.

"Sure", Master Sergeant Chandler smiled and went to tell the colonel Sergeant Wood was there to see him. "Sergeant Wood is here to see you, sir," Master Sergeant Chandler announced through the colonel's open door.

"Good, send him in," Sergeant Wood heard the colonel say.

Sergeant Wood knocked on the colonel's door and was told to come in.

PATRIOTISM

"Have a seat, Sergeant Wood. Do you know why you're here?" the colonel asked.

"Yes, sir. Master Sergeant Chandler briefed me before I came into your office," Sergeant Wood answered. *With pleasure*, he wanted to add, but didn't dare.

"So what do you have to say about it?" Colonel Gray asked.

"Well, sir, I may not be the smartest person in the world, but I do know where to hang my hat. I can't for the life of me figure out why she'd say a thing like that," Sergeant Wood lied.

"Not only did she tell her mom and dad you two have been sleeping together, she also said she's madly in love with you. Why do you suppose she'd tell her parents something like that?" the colonel asked, leaning forward in his chair.

"Sir, as I said before, I haven't the slightest idea. She knows as well as I do black and white don't mix here in Leavenworth, Kansas, hardly anywhere in America for that matter. And on top of that, she's a colonel's daughter and me a mere buck sergeant," Sergeant Wood said, trying to sound humble.

Colonel Gray had been soft spoken up until this point. Suddenly he became angry and harsh. "You tell me the goddamned truth sergeant, or so help me you have no future in this fucking man's army," he demanded.

What kind of future do you think I'd have if I confess to screwing a white colonel's daughter? Sergeant Wood wanted to ask. Instead he said, "I don't know what you expect me to say, sir. I do know I won't confess to something that ain't true."

"Colonel Griffin treated you like a son. And how do you repay his kindness? By screwing his daughter behind his back, making him the laughing stock of the officer's corps? You're one bold, black son of a bitch," Colonel Gray said angrily.

415

Sergeant Wood wanted to somehow get the colonel calmed down a little. He didn't like the present course the conversation was taking. So he asked, "Would it be out of line, sir, to ask you how all this mess got started?"

"Sure, why not?" the colonel said and continued. "Last night, after making a phone call to someone, you supposedly, Maxine hung up the phone and started crying, saying every time she calls that black bastard, they always tell her he's not in. She knew it was a lie. She ran upstairs to her room bawling like a baby. Being the caring mother Mrs. Griffin is, she went up to Maxine's room to console her daughter. While this consoling was taking place, the poor, heartbroken child spilled her guts. About the two hotel rooms she paid for. About using Glenda as an alibi so she could spend the night with you in Kansas City. And on and on the poor child babbled. And you have the nerve to sit here and deny everything," Colonel Gray scolded him.

"With all due respect, sir, it seems to me that nothing I say is going to change anyone's mind. I like Maxine, but not that way. Has it ever occurred to you, sir, she may be using me to protect the identity of the person she's involved with? After all, sir, I'm not the only black buck sergeant here at Fort Leavenworth," Sergeant Wood attempted to give the colonel something else to think about. From the look he was getting from the colonel, he knew the colonel wasn't buying it for one moment.

Colonel Gray lost his military bearing as an officer and a gentleman upon hearing that. "You goddamned, cocky bastard. Don't you ever try and use that fucking military police mentality bullshit on me again. However, since you brought up the possibility of another black buck sergeant being involved, I'm going to let you in on a secret. I'm assigning one of my Military Police Investigators [MPI] to find out if there is another black sergeant involved. If there isn't and he can prove you were anywhere close to the vicinity of these places at the times Maxine gave, I'm going to have you brought up on charges for disobeying a direct order. Do you understand me?" Colonel Gray asked.

"Yes, sir. However, you know as well as I do, you never gave such an order, sir. Furthermore, you know as well as I do that charge will not stand up in a court of law." Sergeant Wood had been around long enough to know it would be his word against Maxine's. He also knew when it came to the words of a white woman versus the words of a black man, his words didn't mean much unless they were backed up by an organization like the NAACP if he had to go that route.

"Whether you screwed that spoiled little wench or not, I'm going to put you in your place once and for all. Now get your ass out of my office before I do something very unprofessional to you," the colonel spat, dismissing him.

Sergeant Wood started to say, *A man is supposed to be innocent until proven guilty, sir. Or does the law still work that way?* Instead he left the colonel's office without any further comments.

Master Sergeant Chandler was waiting for him as he came out of the colonel's office. "How does it feel knowing your days are numbered?" he sneered.

"Probably like screwing your old lady. Not very good," Sergeant Wood growled and continued on down the stairs before Master Sergeant Chandler could reply.

After getting off duty at 2300 hours, Sergeant Wood grabbed himself a beer from his fridge and went to the day room to unwind. He was alone when the phone rang.

Sergeant Wood picked up the receiver and said, "Hello, Maxine. I figured you'd call sooner or later to see if they'd locked me up yet."

"How did you know it would be me calling at this time of night?" Maxine asked trying to sound cheerful.

"Why don't you cut the act, Maxine? You said you were going to bring this shit down on me and you did. So what the hell do you want?" Sergeant Wood asked.

"I'm sorry. It's just that when you wouldn't talk to me, I guess I went a little crazy. I love you," Maxine said.

"And this is how you show it. By putting me in a position to lose all the respect I've managed to gain since I've been in the goddamned army? Baby, with love like yours, who needs an enemy? Hey, I gotta go," Sergeant Wood said and started to hang up on her.

"Bob, please don't hang up. What can I do to make it up to you?" Maxine pleaded.

"For starters, you can tell your parents you lied about us. Tell them it was someone who's already left for Germany, Vietnam or Korea, I really don't care where to. Just get them off my back and then maybe we can talk," Sergeant Wood said.

"And if I do that, can I see you again?" Maxine had the nerve to ask.

"Maxine, you don't understand. What we had is dead. It was dead from jump-street. It wasn't meant to be. It doesn't really matter what you say now anyway. They smell blood and they're not going to give up that easily," Sergeant Wood explained the situation to her.

"But you just said...."

"Just a fleeting glimpse of hope there for a second, that's all," Sergeant Wood cut her off.

"I got you into this and I'm going to get you out of it." Maxine sounded as if she meant what she said.

"I would appreciate that very much. Gotta go. Bye," Sergeant Wood said. He heard her saying she still loved him as he was hanging up the phone. *Sergeant Wood, you knew you were screwing up when you got involved with that spoiled little bitch. So stand up and take your medicine like a man*, he admonished himself.

The next morning Sergeant Wood was in the supply room changing his linen when Sergeant First Class Hart came in. "Can I have a word with you, Sergeant Wood?" Sergeant Hart asked.

"Sure, Sergeant Hart. Everyone else has," Sergeant Wood said in a sarcastic tone.

"Dammit, Sergeant Wood. I just wanted to tell you Maxine retracted her story this morning. She said she had made everything up about you two because you wouldn't go to bed with her. That may get you off the hook," Sergeant First Class Hart informed Sergeant Wood.

"I truly wish I could believe that, Sergeant Hart. These people smell blood. My blood. And they have no intention of letting up until they at least make me bleed a little," Sergeant Wood said.

"If it's any consolation to you, they won't get any help from me. I've already told them I can't destroy the future of such an outstanding young NCO," Sergeant First Class Hart assured him.

"Thanks, Sergeant Hart. I guess I was wrong about you after

all. Is there any chance of my re-enlisting any time soon, so I can get the hell out of here?" Sergeant Wood asked hopefully.

"I'm afraid they've already covered that route. You can't re-enlist until after the investigation is complete," Sergeant First Class Hart informed Sergeant Wood.

"Don't worry about me, Sergeant Hart; I'm a survivor. I'll get through this somehow," Sergeant Wood assured him.

"Let's hope," Sergeant First Class Hart said, using Sergeant Wood's favorite saying when there is doubt in his mind. "If you survive until they allow you to re-enlist, you should be home free to continue your career," Sergeant Hart concluded.

"Yeah. Thanks again, Sergeant Hart," Sergeant Wood said.

After Sergeant Hart left the supply room, Sergeant Wood was thinking about doing the time he had left in the army and then getting out. But First Sergeant Tucker's question came rushing through his brain to the forefront of his thoughts. *Are you man enough to stick around and do whatever it takes to help change things for black soldiers even if you have to give up a mile to their inch?*

"I didn't think I would ever get myself into such a jam. Not hand them my ass on a silver platter," Sergeant Wood said to an invisible First Sergeant Tucker.

At that moment it was as if every slave, every black man, woman and child, who had died in America possessed his soul. His vision blurred, but his mind was crystal clear with the voices of those long dead souls saying, *Don't give in, don't give up, or things will never change if we can't believe in strong, black men like you. Whether you're in the army or civilian life, white people are going to try and destroy you for standing your ground. Be strong, be smart, be a man, but most of all be brave.*

PATRIOTISM

Represent those of us who fought to end slavery, those of us who fought to end Jim Crow, those of us who fought to get our children educated, those of us who had no voice, those of us who saw no justice during our lifetime, those who pray that through courageous young men like you we can rest assured our lives were not lived in vain. We know she seduced you, but that's not a crime. So lift your head, straighten your back, and show white America what type of young black men they're dealing with today. We believe in you. Please don't let us down. Please, please, please.

Sergeant Wood didn't know how long he stood there in the trance. The next thing he remembered was someone in the supply room asking him if he was ok. To this day he doesn't know who that individual was. The problem with Maxine was of minor consequences compared to the road of racism, prejudice, and hatred his ancestors had traveled. From that moment forward Sergeant Wood never doubted his ability to overcome any obstacle placed in his path by man. His path was being lit by a higher power than flesh and blood. He'd continue on that path knowing it made him an enemy of half the brass in the United States Army. But it was the path he had chosen and he'd continue to walk it come hell or high water.

Sergeant Wood called his parents and told them what was going on but told them not to worry because everything was going to be alright. They wished him well, and assured him that they supported him one hundred percent. If there was anything they could do to help him not to hesitate to give them a call. His daddy said if they harmed one hair on his head they'd have hell to pay.

Little Harvey said, "Just like them V.C.'s wasn't gonna get

you, the army folk can't get you either."

Maxine called Sergeant Wood a couple of nights later when he got off duty, which he knew she would. He picked up the phone on the second ring. "Hello, Sergeant Wood speaking."

"Hello, Bob, this is Maxine. I need to talk to you. Could you meet me behind the credit union tomorrow morning before it opens? I want to tell you how they're planning on busting you," she said, sounding nervous.

"Is that a fact?" Sergeant Wood asked.

"Yes, it is. I got you into this mess, and I'm going to get you out of it. Didn't they tell you I told my parents it wasn't you I was messing around with?" Maxine asked.

"Yeah, Sergeant Hart told me. So, why are they still out to bust me? Why don't you just tell me over the phone how they're planning on doing it?" Sergeant Wood asked.

Maxine hesitated as if she was conferring with someone who was telling her what to say. Finally she said, "Someone may be listening in on our conversation."

Sergeant Wood pretended to play along. "Sounds about right to me. They probably want to hear everything we say to each other now that I'm a fugitive from the law. I'll meet you over at the gym, not behind the credit union, around seven o'clock in the morning" Sergeant Wood said.

He picked the gym for the rendezvous spot because soldiers from other units would be going in and out of the gym during their morning exercise period, that way they wouldn't be completely alone. And there would be no doubt that he met her just to talk. If they managed to bust him after a public meeting like that, all he would be able to say is more power to them.

"Ok, lover....ok, Bob. I'll see you then," Maxine stammered.

PATRIOTISM

After hanging up Sergeant Wood said to himself, *If no one knew she was going to call, how could they be eavesdropping? He knew something was up. He could feel it deep in the pit of his stomach. Maxine, you're one stupid broad if you think I'm just going to waltz on over to the gym and fall into a trap. If it isn't a trap, fine, I'll apologize to you. However, I don't think an apology will be necessary,* he thought.

Sergeant Wood knew when push came to shove the average person will stick with their own. Playing on a hunch, he checked out Colonel Griffin's house around six o'clock that morning before going over to the gym. Sure enough, there sat Sergeant Belcher's blue Camaro in the driveway. The Military Police Investigator who was supposed to outsmart him.

"Damn, I'm smart," Sergeant Wood boasted to himself as he walked away whistling *What Kind of Fool Do You Think I Am?*

Sergeant Wood went to the gym and surveyed the areas that offered a good view of the gym parking lot. He knew if Colonel Gray and Sergeant Belcher hadn't already picked out a spot they would be there before he and Maxine met to pick one out soon. They would choose a location that would provide an unobstructed view where they could clearly be seen together. Sergeant Belcher would probably have a camera to take pictures so he wouldn't be able to lie if he denied meeting with her.

After finishing his survey of all possible camera angles Sergeant Wood sat back in his hiding place and waited for their arrival. He only had to wait twenty minutes before they arrived. Sergeant Wood stood behind a building and watched as Sergeant Belcher and Colonel Gray parked in one of the areas that provided an excellent view of the gym parking lot, and at the same time kept them hidden from the public's view. He suppressed a laugh as he waited for Maxine to show up.

Maxine arrived about ten minutes later. She didn't get out of her car. She sat waiting nervously. After half an hour passed, Sergeant Belcher was told to check inside the gym to see if Sergeant Wood was there. It was then that Sergeant Wood noticed that Sergeant Belcher had a camera hanging around his neck. Several minutes later Sergeant Belcher came back out and raised his hands, indicating Sergeant Wood wasn't inside the gym. They waited another fifteen minutes and left, at 0750 hours.

That's right super snoops go to work, Sergeant Wood said as they pulled out of the parking lot. He watched until they turned a corner out of sight. Maxine figured he was playing a game with them, so she stayed put for a while longer. With Colonel Gray and Sergeant Belcher gone, she thought she might be able to explain to him the set-up was planned by her dad. She wanted no part of it, but was forced to participate.

Sergeant Wood was beyond trusting any white person at Fort Leavenworth, Kansas. He came up on Maxine's car from the rear. "Like I said, with a friend like you, who needs an enemy?" he surprised her.

Maxine damn near jumped out of her skin. "Bob, you don't understand," she began.

But Sergeant Wood didn't let her say anything else. "You're right. I don't," he quipped and kept walking.

Later that morning Sergeant Wood stopped by the station to post his duty roster. Sergeant Belcher was talking to the Desk Sergeant.

"Sergeant Wood, I looked for you in your room this morning. I wanted to talk to you about that mess with Maxine. Where were you?" Sergeant Belcher asked.

"I know I took a hell of a chance, but I met Maxine at the gym this morning around 0750 hours. She told me she had straightened this so called mess out. I hope she's not bullshitting me," Sergeant Wood said. He walked out of the MP station, leaving Sergeant Belcher standing there with his mouth wide open.

"That son of a bitch knew all the time," Sergeant Wood heard Sergeant Belcher say before the door closed behind him.

Captain Harris had an open door policy that allowed any member of the unit to see him without having to make an appointment. So Sergeant Wood went to the orderly room and asked to see him.

Specialist Five Jones said, "Man, I don't know what you've done, but the captain and Colonel Gray have had some closed door discussions about you the last couple of days. What the hell is going on, Sergeant Wood?"

"It's nothing really. Is the captain in?" Sergeant Wood asked, ignoring Specialist Five Jones's question. He had no intentions of discussing his problems with anyone. Everyone in the unit had some idea of what was going on anyway. Specialist Five Jones was just being nosey. Sergeant Wood knew Specialist Five Jones couldn't be trusted because he had let Captain Harris talked him into re-enlisting for his present duty assignment there at Fort Leavenworth. Any black man wanting to stay in the 205th MP Company at Fort Leavenworth, Kansas needed his head examined.

"Yeah. Let me make sure he's not busy," Specialist Five Jones said.

As Sergeant Wood waited, he sat staring at the big championship trophy they'd recently won in the unit's trophy case. He'd damn near won the damn thing by himself. All for naught, he was thinking when Specialist Five Jones came back out and said the captain would see him. Sergeant Wood thanked Specialist Five Jones and knocked on the captain's door.

"Come on in, Sergeant Wood, and have a seat," Captain Harris offered. After Sergeant Wood was seated, the captain's voice took on a fatherly tone. "What can I do for you, Sergeant Wood?" he asked.

"I just wanted to know when I'll be allowed to re-enlist, sir," Sergeant Wood said.

"You're not ready to leave us already, are you?" the captain asked, pretending to be friendly.

"I'm afraid so, sir. Since I can't go to Vietnam, I thought it was about time I started thinking about going back to Korea to get my girl," Sergeant Wood said.

"I don't want to discourage you or anything, but those girls in Korea have been known to up and marry some other GI when you keep them waiting too long," the captain smiled.

"Yes, sir, I've heard that, but in the letter I received from her yesterday she assured me she's not only single, but is waiting for yours truly," Sergeant Wood informed the good captain.

"That's nice to hear. A true love story," Captain Harris said, still ignoring his question.

"Sir, if you don't mind, could we get back to why I'm here?" Sergeant Wood asked, showing his impatience.

"Sure, sure, I had a talk with Colonel Gray this morning and he said the investigation concerning you should be wrapped up in a day or so. After that you can be on your way," the captain assured him.

"Sir, I know the colonel thought he was going to wrap this thing up this morning. To be honest with you, sir, he's wasting all our time. We could be doing something more constructive," Sergeant Wood smiled.

"What do you mean the colonel thought he was going to wrap this thing up this morning?" Captain Harris asked, totally surprised Sergeant Wood knew about the stakeout.

"Nothing sir, just a wild guess. But from the look on your face, I must've guessed right," Sergeant Wood said.

"No, not really. I was thinking of something the colonel said yesterday," Captain Harris lied.

Sergeant Wood knew the captain wasn't going to ask him how he found out about the stakeout because in doing so, he would be admitting he had a part in it. And by the same token, the captain knew Sergeant Wood was not going to volunteer any information.

Captain Harris said, "Get back with me in a couple of days. We'll see how everything develops."

"Thank you, sir. I'll do that." Sergeant Wood saluted and walked out of the captain's office.

But he didn't leave the orderly room area. He stood in the hallway around the corner out of sight because he wanted to see how long it would be before the captain headed over to the Provost Marshal Office. Not five minutes passed before he told Specialist Five Jones if anyone needed him, he would be over at the PM's shop. *I may be black, but I'll be damned if I'm dumb,* Sergeant Wood smiled to himself on his way to his room. Sergeant Wood could imagine what the conversation between Colonel Gray and Captain Harris sounded like.

Captain Harris entered Lieutenant Colonel Gray's office

breathing hard. "Sir, Sergeant Wood just left my office. And he said something that led me to believe he knows you and Sergeant Belcher were trying to catch him with Colonel Griffin's daughter this morning."

"Yeah, Francis, I already know. That cocky bastard commented to Sergeant Belcher that he wasn't in his room this morning because he met Maxine at the gym. What I want to know is how the hell he found out. You, Sergeant Belcher, Colonel Griffin, Maxine and myself were the only ones who knew what was supposed to go down," Colonel Gray said, perplexed.

"You don't think Maxine tipped him off do you?" Captain Harris asked.

"I doubt that very seriously. Colonel Griffin called and told me Maxine said he showed up right after we left. Called her a few names and kept on walking. That son of a bitch was watching us the whole damn time we were there. Damn that pisses me off. What did he want to talk to you about?" Colonel Gray asked.

"He wanted to know when he'd be allowed to re-enlist. And when I told him you said this matter should be straightened out in a couple of days; he said, you thought it would be cleared up this morning. I didn't dare let him know I was in on that little fluke," Captain Harris sighed.

"You have to hand it to the black bastard. He definitely has his shit together," Colonel Gray commented.

"So what do we do now, sir?" the captain asked.

"I don't know, Francis. It's embarrassing as hell to be outsmarted by a fucking buck sergeant."

"Should I go ahead and let him re-enlist?" Captain Harris asked.

PATRIOTISM

"Why the hell not? If he stays around here and everyone finds out he outsmarted me, I'll be the butt of every joke told at the officers club here at Fort Leavenworth for the next six months. Send Sergeant Chandler in on your way out. Maybe he has something we can use in a last ditch effort to get that black bastard," the colonel said knowing better because he had already asked Master Sergeant Chandler not more than an hour ago.

"Yes, sir. Right away," Captain Harris responded and left.

Master Sergeant Chandler was just as anxious to be rid of Sergeant Wood as Colonel Gray and Colonel Griffin was. He'd told Sergeant Wood he was going to make sure he didn't miss his re-enlistment ceremony, because they all wanted him gone. Master Sergeant Chandler said his only regret was Captain Harris couldn't allow him to re-enlist for Vietnam. That it'd give him great pleasure to know a gook had blown his brains out.

Sergeant Wood re-enlisted for Korea the following day. And true to his word, Master Sergeant Chandler had a front row seat. Sergeant Wood's family was happy that everything had worked out for him. What he didn't tell his family was because of his attitude, this was just one of numerous encounters which he would have to face while serving with the Chandlers, Grays, Griffins, Greens, and Hicks, who wore the same uniform as himself. While walking around post clearing, he happened to run across Colonel Griffin.

"Don't think you got away with anything, Sergeant Wood. Everywhere you go for the rest of the time you're in the army, your commanders will know about the shit you got away with while you were stationed here. I'm going to see to that personally," Colonel Griffin said angrily.

"You know something, sir? Even though your prejudice came to the surface when you thought your daughter was fooling around with a black man, I still like you. And I also think you're one hell of a coach," Sergeant Wood said.

"What you think of me doesn't change a thing, black boy. If I ever run across you again, your ass is mine," Colonel Griffin threatened. He walked off with more hate in his heart than Sergeant Wood had ever seen in the eyes of a white person.

Sergeant Wood finished clearing Fort Leavenworth, Kansas, and hoped he never got assigned there again. He took fifteen days of leave and then it was off to Korea, 'The Land of the Morning Calm.' Calm until the arrival of Sergeant Bob Wood to his new unit anyway.

Sergeant Wood didn't see her, but when he climbed into the back seat of the taxicab that took him to the airport Maxine was parked across the street watching. A tear rolled down her cheek as she watched him get into the cab and depart. *Goddamn you, you black bastard. I'll always love you*, she said as the cab disappeared around the corner. Maxine knew her outlook on life would never be the same again. The best she could hope for was to meet a man, black or white, that would come close to exciting her as Sergeant Bob Wood had. She didn't try to fool herself because the whole world knows there's nothing like the real thing. Then again, the military community was not that big of a place and he had to return stateside sooner or later Maxine thought as she drove to work.

The End

EPILOGUE

After turning everything over in his mind that had occurred in just two short years, he asked himself, *Is this truly the democracy in which I'm willing to give my life to preserve?* He didn't answer his question because he already knew the answer. Even with all of Her faults, America is still the greatest country in the world. And he was going to do whatever he could to make it even greater.

Sergeant Wood thought about Sergeant Terrell and Tracy, but he knew they would be okay because they had good heads on their shoulders and they had each other. They hated to see him leave Fort Leavenworth but knew it was for the best that he did. Tracy said although he messed up by screwing that nasty white bitch, she forgave him because she was sure he had learned from his mistake As for Gina and Johnny, maybe they would find each other again, or the right person to make them happy.

Sergeant Wood had a lot to learn when it came to dealing with his white brothers and sisters in arms, but he was willing to learn. Sergeant Wood lay back in his seat and fell asleep thinking how good it was going to be to be with Miss Kwak again.

www.ingramcontent.com/pod-product-compliance
Lightning Source LLC
LaVergne TN
LVHW041606070426
835507LV00008B/151